In Good Company

In Good Company

Sixty Years with the Royal Ballet

Leslie Edwards

with
Graham Bowles

DANCE
BOOKS

First published in 2003 by Dance Books Ltd
The Old Bakery
4 Lenten Street
Alton
Hampshire GU34 1HG

Copyright © Graham Bowles
ISBN:1 85273 097 8

A CIP catalogue record for this book is available from the British Library

Printed and bound in Great Britain by Creative Print and Design Group,

Illustrations

Frontispiece: Leslie Edwards outside the Royal Opera House, Covent Garden (Roy Jones).

Between pages 86 and 87

1. *A Wedding Bouquet*, Leslie Edwards second from right (J W Debenham).
2. Archimago, *The Quest* (Gordon Anthony).
3. Benno, *Swan Lake* (Gordon Anthony).
4. The Beggar, *Miracle in the Gorbals* (Gordon Anthony).
5. Cattalabutte, *The Sleeping Beauty* (Gordon Anthony).
6. The Mime (Adam's spiritual adviser), *Adam Zero* (Gordon Anthony).
7. Hilarion, *Giselle* (Gordon Anthony).
8. 'Darling Leslie, All my love, Margot' (Richard Dormer)

Between pages 182 and 183

9. Bilby in *A Mirror for Witches* (Gordon Anthony).
10. With Nadia Nerina in *Noctambules* (Houston Rogers).
11. Thomas in *La Fille mal gardée*, with Alexander Grant (Houston Rogers).
12. *Marguerite and Armand*, with Margot Fonteyn (Anthony Crickmay).
13. HRH Princess Margaret at a Friends of Covent Garden Christmas party with, left to right, Anthony Dowson, Michael Batchelor, Stephen Beagley, Ross McGibbon (Anthony Crickmay).
14. The Tsar's Aide de Camp in *Anastasia* (Roy Round).
15. Dame Margot Fonteyn's Sixtieth Birthday Gala, Sir Robert Helpmann, Michael Somes, Fonteyn, Sir Frederick Ashton (Anthony Crickmay).
16. Celebrating the fiftieth anniversary of the re-opening of the Royal Opera House after World War II. Back row, left to right, Gerd Larsen, Oenene Talbot, Jean Bedells, Margaret Roseby, Julia Farron, Barbara Fewster, Leslie Edwards, Pamela May; front row, Dame Beryl Grey, Dame Ninette de Valois, Pauline Wadsworth.

All photographs except the frontispiece and numbers 8, 15, 16 courtesy V & A Picture Library.

Foreword

by Sir Peter Wright

In this book Leslie Edwards, with the help of his co-writer, Graham Bowles, takes us on an amazing journey through his life with the Royal Ballet. He first joined the company, then known as the Vic-Wells Ballet, in 1933 and recounts vividly the early days when Ninette de Valois, backed by Lilian Baylis, managing director of the Old Vic and Sadler's Wells theatres, created what was to become the well-known Sadler's Wells Ballet; this was the company that re-opened the Royal Opera House after the war with the famous production of *The Sleeping Beauty* designed by Oliver Messel. It took New York by storm in 1949 and made Margot Fonteyn into a great international star. Among the many memorable accounts is that of the time when the company escaped from Holland after the Nazi invasion and its eventual return to Europe in 1945 at the end of the war on a ten-week tour of Germany organised by E.N.S.A.

Leslie worked with many choreographers, including Ashton, Cranko and MacMillan, and he is witness to the way their ballets were shaped. He also reveals how his admiration for Fonteyn, whom he adored and with whom he often appeared on stage, blossomed into a lasting friendship. As the story unfolds, we read about the time when the company, having been granted a Royal Charter and become the Royal Ballet, undertook many world tours, to include Russia, the Far East, Australia and North and South America. Of considerable interest, too, is his work as ballet master to the Royal Opera – the singers loved working with him – and his directorship of the choreographic workshop at Covent Garden, which he founded to help and encourage young choreographers.

I knew Leslie for many years and we worked together on a number of occasions. I can honestly say that he was the most professional and selfless artist I have known and one who always put the interests of the company and the performance before anything else. What comes across so strongly in this book is Leslie's total dedication to the whole Royal Ballet organisation, his love and concern for his fellow artists and his amazing professionalism.

Introduction

by John Percival

No other dancer has matched, nor ever will, Leslie Edwards's amazing career with the Royal Ballet: more than sixty years of performances, starting in January 1933 and continuing even beyond his official, very reluctant retirement in November 1993. In addition, for the first six years he appeared frequently with Ballet Rambert, and later on he was involved with outside events often featuring Margot Fonteyn and Rudolf Nureyev. And something much more than simply the length and breadth of his career marked it out as special: there was also a great admiration and affection which he won from his audiences and fellow artists. One example will show what I mean. At the Royal Ballet's fiftieth anniversary performance, he played his familiar rôle of Cattalabutte, the master of ceremonies, in *The Sleeping Beauty* at the Royal Opera House. For whatever reason, audience response was surprisingly muted for most of the show. But at the beginning of the last scene, for the first time all evening, there was suddenly a tumultuous burst of applause when Edwards made his entry on an empty stage to lead the assembly for Princess Aurora's wedding. It began in the stalls, where many former dancers were sitting, but was at once taken up by members of the regular audience all over the house.

After reading his book, I suspect that Edwards would hardly have known whether to be touched and grateful for that spontaneous demonstration (which he is far too modest to mention), or to be embarrassed that his comparatively minor rôle was singled out above the night's official stars. But in a way it sums up the point of a most unusual career.

Over the years, he had a respectable share of leading rôles, among them the Lover in Antony Tudor's *Jardin aux lilas*, Frederick Ashton's own rôle of the Personage in *Les Masques*, the title part in Ninette de Valois' *The Rake's Progress*. Those three choreographers all created roles for him in other ballets and so did John Cranko, Robert Helpmann, Andrée Howard, Kenneth MacMillan and Léonide Massine. Dr Coppelius in *Coppélia* was his biggest rôle in the classics, but he was also a memorably sympathetic Hilarion in *Giselle*. However, he was seen far more often in smaller parts, and he showed again and again that these can make just as vital a contribution to the ballet's total effect. It is not by chance that both de Valois and Helpmann remarked to him that he knew how to 'make something' out of little material. Cattalabutte, already mentioned, was one example; others included the beggar in Helpmann's *Miracle in the Gorbals,* the Duke in Ashton's *Marguerite and Armand,* and the Prince's friend Benno in *Swan Lake.*

Apropos making something out of little, note how he invented and for many years led the Royal Ballet's Choreographic Group, to give ambitious young dancers the opportunity of creative work, and that's on top of his taking on the post of ballet master to the Royal Opera, teaching at the Royal Ballet School, instructing the children and extras taken on when the company toured, and organising, on a highly ambitious scale, the annual Christmas parties of the Friends of Covent Garden.

You can guess at his splendid bearing and appearance from the list of his parts; time and again choreographers chose him to create the rôle of an emperor, king, prince, duke or other dignitary. Yet perhaps his most valuable contribution to ballet was playing a simple vine grower in Ashton's *La Fille mal gardée.* Those who took this part in other versions of the ballet are, in my experience, entirely unmemorable. Yet the twinkling-eyed geniality Edwards gave this part, sauntering red-cheeked, red-nosed through the action, crucially benefited the humanity of the ballet, while his momentary fierce rage on being defied at the end put the happy-ever-after finale into perspective. His personality, his insight and his generosity played a part in shaping Ashton's *Fille* as the Royal Ballet's greatest creation and the twentieth century's best full-evening work. If he had done nothing else, that rôle would justify every ballet-goer's lasting gratitude to this delightful man.

Prologue

A short but ominous entry for Monday 20 November in my 1993 diary reads, 'Black Monday'. That was how I felt about the day chosen for my farewell performance as a long-time member of the Royal Ballet at the Royal Opera House, Covent Garden. I had dreaded the thought of retirement; life without being a dancer and ballet master to the Royal Opera Company in that splendid theatre would be insupportable.

The ballet scheduled for that night was a routine performance of Kenneth MacMillan's *Romeo and Juliet*. I appeared in my usual rôle as the Prince of Verona in the opening scene. I then waited offstage to cue in, for the last time, the young lads with their torches who usher the guests into the Capulets' magnificent ballroom and show them out after the ball is over. After that I returned to my dressing room to remove my make-up and costume; my dresser fetched me a cup of tea while I waited for the performance to end.

I had been told that morning to return after the final curtain call and to wear my dinner jacket, and, when I made my way back to the side of the stage, I saw Anthony Dowell and Jeremy Isaacs waiting to lead me on. We joined the assembled ballet company, who were acknowledging the final rounds of applause. A microphone had been placed on the stage, and both men made speeches thanking me for long years of service to the Royal Ballet and wishing me well in retirement. Their words were full of praise and I could not have wished for better.

I stood rigidly upright, staring straight ahead, but my thoughts were full of despair and misery, knowing that this was the end of everything I loved. I looked at that glorious, magical auditorium that I loved so dearly. I had first peered out at it in 1933 during a gala performance given in honour of the World Economic Conference then taking place in London. A cornerstone of that Conference was the distinguished economist, John Maynard Keynes, who from the very beginning had given support, help and advice to the valiant band of dancers called the Vic–Wells Ballet, founded with vision and foresight by Ninette de Valois and launched with courage and faith by Lilian Baylis at her two theatres, the Old Vic and Sadler's Wells. The programme for that gala long ago comprised the first and second acts of *Coppélia*, in which the rôle of Swanilda was danced by the former Diaghilev ballerina, Lydia Lopokova, and Act II of *Swan Lake*, with Alicia Markova and Anton Dolin. In the Royal Box that night was Her Majesty Queen Mary.

Suddenly my heart was lifted by the memories of the great artists who had been my dear colleagues, of all the special performances of both ballet and opera we had shared during those long years, and of the warmth and encouragement that I had received from audiences throughout my career. I wanted to express my appreciation for my great good fortune. Not wishing to be inhibited by a microphone, I stepped down to the front of the stage, hoping to be able to project my voice to the back of the gallery. I asked if I had succeeded, and a yell came back, 'Yes!'. With this, any sense of despondency or nervousness I might have had vanished.

I told the audience of that first gala, and at the mention of Queen Mary I detected a mixture of delight and incredulity that I had performed in the presence of that great lady. I spoke of my deep gratitude to Dame Ninette de Valois, who had made my long career possible. I ended with words written by Gertrude Stein, adding the appropriate gestures choreographed by Frederick Ashton for my rôle of Arthur in the ballet *A Wedding Bouquet*: 'Very well, I thank you, thank you, thank you,' and after the final and very assertive 'thank you', I made a deep bow.

Standing alone in front of the dancers of the Royal Ballet, sixty years on from that first gala, I listened to the thud of flowers landing around me on the stage. I felt I wanted to stand just there for all eternity. Then, to the delight of the audience, Pamela May and Beryl Grey, two ballerinas who had been my dear colleagues for so many years, came on bearing a large, framed picture of Margot Fonteyn and myself in the ballet *Marguerite and Armand*. On its white mount were affectionate messages from all the great figures of the Royal Ballet – most precious of all were words written by Dame Ninette herself.

The curtain fell. The company gathered around and there was much hugging and kissing. Friends who had been at the performance entered the stage through the wings, and cameras flashed. I was joined by a long-time friend, Wendy Toye; she, Pamela and I recalled that we had all, at one time or another, danced in *The Enchanted Grove*, the ballet in which I had made my début at Sadler's Wells Theatre. We remembered a rather unusual step in it, which we then demonstrated with much hilarity. Finally, we all trooped up to the Crush Bar and there, sitting at one of the tables, were Dame Ninette and Dame Alicia Markova. I was too excited to eat and went from table to table, greeting old friends and reminiscing. Sir Peter Wright had a letter that he had intended to leave for me at the stage door, but in the event he decided to read it to us all; it was a marvellous and affectionate tribute and it meant much to me that the words came from Peter himself.

Suddenly it was time to go home. Three young dancers, Gail Taphouse, Larissa Bamber and Iain Webb, helped me to gather up all my presents. There was a slight hiccup when we couldn't find the elegant and beautifully inscribed silver salver that had been given to me, but happily it was retrieved by another dancer, Peter Abegglen. As we left the theatre we took a last look at the display of photographs mounted in the glass cabinet in the foyer.

As we made our way to the car on this perishing cold night, members of the audience leaving nearby restaurants called out their goodnights and good wishes. It all reminded me of people leaving New Year's Eve parties in my salad days, exchanging greetings on their way to find a taxi home. We sped back to my house in Hammersmith, where Gail and Larissa helped to unload the car.

In a mood of surprising elation, I looked around my small hall packed with loot and thought, 'Black Monday, my foot!'

Chapter 1

The somewhat unusual circumstances of my birth and early child-hood led to the remarkable outcome that I ultimately arrived in the theatre, doing what I had always dreamed of doing, and following a single-minded ambition. How did all this come about?

My parents lived in Fulwell, Middlesex, in a small cottage attached to Fulwell Golf Club, of which my father was secretary. Before I arrived, two sons had been born to them, William Ernest and Frederick Joseph. When I was on the way, it seems that they felt it would be more convenient all round if I could be born in a somewhat larger house, called 'Melrose', belonging to close friends in nearby Teddington. This all happened in the middle of World War I, when it was usual to have your baby at home and not in hospital. So it was that I arrived in this world in the house of Mr and Mrs Young (whom I shall call Pat and Naggie), where in fact I was to spend the rest of my childhood. As that splendid character in the popular TV series, *Soap*, used to say, 'Confused?' Well, don't be. For me it all worked out very well.

My father left his Fulwell job about a year after I was born, and his career then seemed to take on a somewhat nomadic quality. He went into hotel management in London, first in Torrington Square and later in Soho Square, and then back to golf as secretary of Tirrell's Wood Club in Leatherhead. His last job was to manage three blocks of chambers in Petty France in Westminster, which he did for some years until he retired.

Throughout all this time, my life as a child at 'Melrose' was one of stability. In retrospect I think this is what my parents wanted for me, and they were happy for me to live physically apart from them in spite of our being very close as a family. Both with my parents and with the Youngs I felt no sense of alienation; on the contrary, I had as much love from them as would any child in more normal circumstances.

Of course, I don't remember the earliest days or the reasons why my parents felt it better for me to stay with the Youngs rather than to return to the cottage. I did in fact rejoin them when they later moved to a house in Teddington, although I was still too young to remember this; but the period was short-lived, and for me at this stage home was to be 'Melrose' and my foster-parents the mainstay of my life. All, as I said, worked out well. I would visit my parents and they in turn would come over to Pat,

Naggie and me, and we always managed to be together for Christmas Day and on my birthday.

'Melrose' was part of a small terrace of houses, and most of our neighbours had young children of my age who became friends. We played in one another's gardens and attended one another's parties; in the summer there were picnics by the river and in Bushy Park we invented scenes of derring-do, though my real delight was the winter's pantomime season, when I was immersed in a world of magic. We had no proper wireless, no '2LO calling', but my brothers had made a crystal set which they rigged up in a little room at 'Melrose' so that I could put on the earphones and listen to a broadcast, which they told me came from a theatre in London. As far as I remember it was called the Winter Garden, which was on the site of what is now the New London Theatre in Drury Lane.

My particular summer joy, when we went for a walk by the river, was the sound of the many wind-up gramophones coming from the punts in Teddington Lock playing the popular tunes of the day. It was a jingle-jangle of music; when the lock was up, so was the sound, and when the lock went down the sound diminished, to fade gradually as the punters began to pole their way gently along the river.

As a prelude to the life that I was to lead in the theatre, my early childhood could not have been more appropriate and happy. When I reached the age of five I was ready to go to the nearby church school, run by Miss Collis, a much-revered figure in Teddington and an excellent teacher of young children. I loved her school, particularly so at the end of term when we took part in a little concert for the parents. Naggie was delighted when I had a *succès fou* in one such concert as Little Jack Horner; perhaps this didn't come as a total surprise to her, because she had noticed that on our various visits to the pantomime I had loved every moment of the show. Even then I had begun to dream of being on the stage; when at home I played with my toy theatre, I saw not only the cardboard figures but also myself on stage with them.

Naggie also noticed that I seemed to be fascinated by music and particularly susceptible to the rhythm. She had seen the famous musical comedies at the Gaiety Theatre in London, and it had seemed to her that an important feature of these shows was the excellent dancing of the men in the company, as well as that of the famous Gaiety Girls. She was reminded of this when she heard from her neighbours that they were sending their small daughters to a Mrs Hepworth Taylor, who had just opened a dancing school in Teddington. Naggie saw no reason why little boys should not also join them, and nor did Mrs Hepworth Taylor. In no time at all I had been enrolled and was studying a rudimentary style known as 'fancy dancing', which involved much jumping and twirling about. This activity took place in her drawing room, which, unadorned, served as a studio. As we were later to discover, what I learned there added little to my knowledge of the technique of classical dancing; but what fun it was, and how we all enjoyed it.

My mother took me to see *The Queen of Hearts* – not a pantomime much performed nowadays – at the Lyceum Theatre in London. Although I was very young, I remember being thrilled by the beauty of this theatre, which had become famous with the productions of Henry Irving. The staging seemed incredible and I was delighted by the ballet dancing, as well I might have been, for, years later, I discovered from Ninette de Valois herself that she had been a ballerina there and had much admired the pantomimes, produced and directed by the Melville brothers, in which she had danced.

In addition to these visits to the theatre, Pat used to take me at weekends to the 'pictures' – silent films, of course. Even then, on returning home I went through an action replay, rescuing Lilian Gish from an icefloe in a D.W. Griffiths epic, or loosening the ropes that bound Pearl White to the railway track in the path of the oncoming express, my eyes every bit as terror-stricken as those of the hero. A film that made a deep impression on me was the silent version of *Ben Hur*; one moment we were on the edge of our seats at the excitement of the chariot races, spurred on by the pulsating rhythm of the pianist's accompaniment, while the next we were moved to a religious fervour at the appearance of Our Lord, when the pianist would lift her hands from the piano across to a harmonium, lent by the Baptist chapel, which wheezed out a suitably religious theme. To us, however, this equalled the sound that we were much later to hear from the Mighty Wurlitzer at the Odeon, Leicester Square.

I quickly grew to love Mrs Hepworth Taylor's classes, and loved even more appearing in the various performances in which she, like most suburban dancing teachers, willingly allowed her pupils to take part. These were held in the hall at St Alban's Church, Teddington, famous for the fact that Noël Coward's aunt sang in the choir there and became known as the Twickenham Nightingale. We would dance a number or two at the annual Teddington town fêtes which, although held in the middle of summer, were invariably accompanied by pouring rain. The music was provided by the Teddington Town Brass Band, and I well remember the excitement as we splashed our way through a spirited ensemble to the popular tune of that particular year, *Valencia*. One year the fête was opened by a West End star, Miss Peggy O'Neil, so famous that a song was written about her: '...sweet personality, full of rascality, that's Peggy

O'Neil'. With her smart cloche hat, her rouge and her lips painted in a cupid's bow, she walked through the mud with a roguish smile, in every way living up to the lyrics of the song.

Mrs Hepworth Taylor's school was a huge success; little girls flocked to it and suddenly the local church hall became far too small for the annual displays. Daringly, its begetter decided to hire the Kingston Empire itself. Appearing there was, for me, pure bliss and, being the only boy, I was naturally rather prominent; my sailor's hornpipe was popular and to the ballet music from *Faust* I performed a vigorous archer's dance, complete with bow and arrow. Later in the programme, as a male swan, I foreshadowed the award-winning production of *Swan Lake* with male swans of the late 1990s. Looking back on all this activity of my early years, I take great pleasure in the thought that, in the self-same Kingston Empire, I later saw so many great stars of the variety world, including 'Our Gracie' herself, Gracie Fields; it was while appearing at this theatre that she became the wife of the producer, Archie Pitt.

When she hired the Kingston Empire, Mrs Hepworth Taylor had to accommodate her show in whatever scenery was being used for the production of that particular week. It was not always a happy combination. On one occasion I remember we were pitchforked into *Alf's Button Afloat*, and it would have appeared that we had all landed up in the harem scene in the Sultan's palace in Morocco. The set included the most impressive staircase going from backcloth to footlights, which must have made it very difficult for the young dancers to find the all-important centre of the stage in the ensemble numbers. Not that it worried us overmuch; the main point was to get on stage at any cost, a view fortunately shared by Mrs Hepworth Taylor herself, who seemed unabashed at the fact that a Sultan's harem was not the best setting for her baby chicks' numbers.

One could say that my summer holidays gave me the best of all possible worlds. My mother, my brothers and I would go away to some pleasant coastal resort: Broadstairs, Eastbourne, the Isle of Wight on several occasions – these were firm favourites. Ensconced in a rather genteel boarding house, I always enjoyed myself enormously, and at the end of the seaside day I would sit on the esplanade with my mother, sizing up the holidaymakers and weaving imaginary stories about them. I realise that it was from my mother that I inherited this ability to be thus absorbed by observation. Meanwhile my big brothers had persuaded two of the young ladies staying at the boarding house to join them in a saunter along the promenade. We would all meet up later at the bandstand – unless it was raining, when, of course, it would be the 'pictures', my preference leaning heavily towards a musical with a number by the Goldwyn Girls choreographed by Busby Berkeley.

My father did not accompany us on these holiday jaunts. Why not? Heaven knows. I have an idea he found the whole thing rather tedious. However, he did once go off on a lone trip to Germany, and I received a picture postcard of a castle on the Rhine; cryptically written on the back were the words, 'A castle on the Rhine. Dad'.

Following my holiday with my family, I went away again with Naggie and Pat, who never changed their resort, Doctor Brighton every year, in rather simpler accommodation but with a very friendly and welcoming landlady. In spite of the differences between the two holidays, I always looked forward to both with equal pleasure, each having its own special appeal for me.

Brighton had an open-air theatre on the beach where a well-known local character, Jack Shepherd, performed with his pierrot troupe twice a day, the programmes changing every three days. We went each evening, well wrapped up in pullovers and macs and armed with umbrellas, as were the rest of the audience, seated in rows of deckchairs. The weather had to reach the state of being the worst 'since records began' before the faithful would give in and leave, missing the finale. Each week Jack Shepherd held a children's talent competition, and I took part in this on one occasion, performing a Hepworth Taylor dance, duly artistic. Most of the other competitors tap-danced away to such popular hits as 'Ain't She Sweet' or recited 'Come down to Kew in Lilac Time', doing their elocution teacher proud. I was sure that I had lost to a right little madam who belted out in fine Marie Lloyd music-hall style, 'My Old Man Said, "Follow the Van".' I won.

On Sunday evenings the pierrot troupe performed in the charming theatre at the end of the West Pier, when the winner in the talent competition gave a reprise of his or her prize number. The whole show was more theatrical, with the cast changing from their pierrot costumes with ruffles and pom-poms into dinner jackets and long evening frocks for the final numbers. Maybe I had had the casting vote on the sands from the rather refined soprano in the company who thought that my number, danced to *Poème* by Fibich, would be suitable later for the more select environment of Hove.

Years later I heard Ninette de Valois say many times that as a girl she had danced on every pier in England, so there was a good precedent. The importance of the performance of these seaside concert parties throughout the country cannot be overrated, since they provided wonderful entertainment and were also a showcase for so many well-known comedians and actors for the musical comedy stage, just as the repertory companies were for the 'legitimate' theatre. Clarkson Rose, Arthur Askey, Bud Flanagan and Max Bygraves were among the best known who started this way.

Naggie was, as usual, absolutely right about not budging from Brighton; like the Prince Regent before her, she knew there was much benefit to be had from this trip to the briny.

When, having reached the age of seven, the time came for me to leave Miss Collis, I went to the local council school in Teddington. Life there was tougher and a little earthier than it had been with Miss Collis. I felt rather ill at ease when I was marched down Broad Street to Bushy Park to play 'footer', and I lived with a certain apprehension of being seen by any of the mothers or pupils of the Mrs Hepworth Taylor brigade, rather like William Brown of the *William* books being spotted by Violet Elizabeth Bott. However, the teaching there was excellent, and I was given a good sense of discipline and introduced to an all-round education. Most of the all-male staff had recently seen service in World War I and, while disciplining us effectively, did not lack sensitivity. They were a great bunch.

After I had spent four years there, my father decided I should go to Hampton Grammar School. That I managed to pass the entrance examination was sound witness indeed to the quality of teaching at the council school.

When I arrived at Hampton I discovered that it was a great deal larger than the council school and had its own playing fields, so there was no more marching along Broad Street. To my surprise and pleasure I found that we had our own form master but separate masters for individual subjects, very different from the council school where one master taught his form everything. A special attraction for me was the assembly hall, used not only for assembly each morning but also as a stage for the traditional Christmas performances of Gilbert and Sullivan opera.

Away from the narrow confines of a concrete playground, Hampton offered a much broader canvas, ranging from the headmaster's study in the main building to the tuck shop, which was part of the caretaker's accommodation. At the sound of the mid-morning bell we would rush down there, where the caretaker's wife offered cream doughnuts to us on a first-come, first-served basis. I generally managed only to secure the jam ones provided for the also-rans. Further on were the stables, above which Mr Titterton, affectionately known as Tank, had his art room, with large windows and trestle tables at which we sat painting whilst Mr Titterton talked about his adventures in the far-flung Empire of that time. This divertissement we all studiously encouraged, regarding him with great affection and good humour.

When the time came to prepare for the Christmas opera, he would be seen painting away in the assembly hall, creating the scenery for it until, as the days passed, the headmaster might be intoning the school announcements, with the same reverence he displayed during prayers, upon the quarterdeck of HMS Pinafore. The year we did *The Mikado* he was, as if by magic, standing among the cherry blossom of the kingdom of Titipu. Another time, perhaps less impressively, he could be seen against the sepia backcloth for the court in *Trial by Jury*, where he might very well have passed for forty-three at the desk with the light behind him. The principal parts in these operas were almost always played by the masters and their wives, plus a few sixth-formers, whose voices had settled down to the appropriate level for pirates, peers or gentlemen of Japan; but I remember one popular and amply proportioned local contralto who was brought in to make the timbers shiver to the sound of dear little Buttercup or to admonish an ungrateful Iolanthe for failing to nestle in a dewdrop.

All these wonderful memories came back years later when I saw John Cranko's brilliant evocation of the Gilbert and Sullivan operas in his ballet, *Pineapple Poll*. At the time, however, I didn't feature at all in these school productions, although I longed to do so. I missed out because, being very shy, I never volunteered. I also had a sneaking feeling that, owing to my dancing expertise, my 'gaily skipping, lightly tripping' might appear slightly more proficient than that of the rest of the sisters, cousins and aunts. Then my cover would have been blown.

As far as theatrical activities were concerned, Hampton Grammar was really very well provided for. Besides the special Gilbert and Sullivan productions, the Dramatic Society put on such favourites as *The Monkey's Paw*, *A Maker of Dreams* and *The Knight of the Burning Pestle*, while Sir Philip Ben Greet visited us several times to give matinée and evening performances of Shakespeare on the headmaster's lawn. Ben Greet was a great Shakespearean actor of the time and worked as a producer for Lilian Baylis in the early days at the Old Vic. This was my first brush with the Bard; when I look back, the productions that introduced him to me at Hampton were somewhat stereotyped, with the costumes doggedly Elizabethan, whether the scene was in an Athenian forest or on Caliban's island, and I assumed all ladies performing Shakespearean rôles wore gauntlet gloves with huge 'prop' rings over them. These impressions remained with me until I saw those imaginative productions directed by Tyrone Guthrie at the Old Vic when I was a member of the Vic–Wells Ballet.

Sport was a great feature of the school. There was a weekly compulsory lesson in Sports and Gymnastics given by the sports master, Captain Hyde, but apart from all this the school members were delighted to follow the sport appropriate to the season. In the spring term the emphasis was on athletics, and this was the time when I was most seen on the field, as I was a reasonably good runner and not too bad at high jump. I also played cricket in the summer, mostly dreaming away the time in the deep field until rudely awakened by a ball whizzing past on its way to the boundary and the shout of 'Missed it' when I had. In the winter we played football (soccer), and that, for me, was a penance. It was mitigated by the fact that on Wednesday afternoons each week there was an 'option': we were actually free to do as we wished. I seized this godsend of an opportunity to take the train up to Waterloo and attend tap-dancing classes at a well-known school in Wardour Street, run by a prominent and successful musical comedy choreographer called Max Rivers. His shows were all the rage during the thirties, the most famous being *The White Horse Inn*, then occupying the Coliseum. I was not the only sports defector, however; there was a group of boy motor-racing enthusiasts who made their way to the nearby racing track at Brooklands, Weybridge. These tearaways would pedal helter-skelter on their bicycles, taking the bends in the road tightly, in the manner of their hero, Kaye Don, who soared round the steeply banked track of this famous circuit in his latest racing car.

Looking back on these times at Hampton I have a high regard for the whole staff of teachers, each with his specialised subject, and I have since felt, and I think I am not altogether alone in this, that I failed to do justice to their efforts to teach me. My father never interfered in my school career or criticised my progress in any way; but when at sixteen I showed no real interest in anything other than a career in the theatre, it seemed pointless to him for me to stay on at Hampton. At the end of the Christmas term, 1931, I left.

He and my mother were worried, and understandably so, about my joining such an unreliable profession; an actor or singer, perhaps, but a dancer? That was too dreadful to contemplate in those days. Dear father – I do wish he could have had a peep into the future of my profession and seen the high acclaim in which it is now held, even knighthoods falling right and left among its practitioners. Most of all I would like him to have watched fathers escorting their young children to classes at the Royal Ballet School in London where, as junior associates, they began to prepare for their future in the theatre.

The weeks that followed my leaving school were very depressing. It was essential to get a job performing in the theatre to prove that I was capable of following a theatrical career, but I had no idea how to go about it. I was also missing the companionship of my fellow-pupils at Hampton; although we were not that close and had very little in common because of my overriding obsession with the theatre, I had felt part of a lively organisation there and was content to be surrounded by friendly faces.

To help matters at this juncture, my rather formidable Aunt May suggested to my mother that I might be suitable for some sort of position at Harrods. This was a last-ditch stand on the part of the family to find a 'proper' job for me. They wrote to Harrods and I was duly granted an interview. The man who saw me was very agreeable and gave me a résumé of the positions I could attain in the store. He looked somewhat nonplussed at the sight of this tall, thin, sullen youth, but tried to evoke some enthusiasm in me by telling me that I might, if I made sufficient progress, become a floor walker. At my look of complete indifference to that height of eminence he said, 'What is it you want to do?'. I replied simply 'I want to go on the stage'. Equally simply he answered, 'I think you'd better'. I rejoined my mother and Aunt May and to the question, 'What did he say?', I replied, 'He said I should go on the stage'. That was the end of Aunt May's initiative to find me a 'proper' job.

So now it was back to square one, and the awful reality of being out in the big, cold world came upon me very suddenly. You would have thought that, having trained to be a dancer, and having read in *The Dancing Times* about the pioneering efforts of Marie Rambert in forming a company and of Ninette de Valois' group of dancers at the Old Vic and Sadler's Wells Theatres, it would have occurred to me to try to join a ballet company. In all fairness, I had never seen such a one or a ballerina of international renown. Frederick Ashton had received the call to join the world of Terpsichore when, as a young boy, he saw Anna Pavlova dancing in Lima, Peru. Robert Helpmann experienced the tongue of fire when he saw her in Melbourne, Australia, and both had achieved their earliest goals with Madame Rambert and Miss de Valois in London. But I had not seen and so had not been enraptured by Madame Pavlova myself, not even at her local theatre, the Hippodrome, Golders Green. I was so besotted with the idea of becoming another Jack Buchanan or starring in a Noël Coward revue that I had never once pictured myself as a member of a ballet company.

However, I still kept up my weekly classes, begun during my school years, with Madam Bromova in Gunnersbury, and she occasionally passed on news of a coming audition. I attended one of these, in the company of a fellow class member, at the Scala Theatre – sadly no more – off Tottenham Court Road. A gipsy band were looking for a pair of dancers to augment their act, violins accompanied by mandolins bowing their way through an arrangement of Liszt's *Hungarian Rhapsody*, the jangle of brass curtain-rings in their ears giving a Romany touch to the csárdás so popular in the early thirties. In spite of all the spirit and passion we two could summon up, stamping away in our red Russian boots in a positive frenzy of anger with the floor, Gunnersbury was no substitute for Budapest and we were rejected.

The well-known theatre newspaper *The Stage* gave the times and places of auditions for new musical productions, and I would join the crowd of hopefuls pouring through the stage doors of various West End theatres. 'Tall boys on the right, short boys on the left,' the stage manager would command, and we would scramble into some sort of line to be scrutinised by the producer and his staff. Sitting in the darkened auditorium, they would indicate in a sort of racecourse tick-tack code the ones they wanted, and the rest were told to go. I was always among the first batch told to leave, and on my homeward-bound train from Waterloo Station I would tot up the names of the West End theatres in which I had stood in line. The list was impressive and included the London Palladium, where I attended an audition for look-alike dance-band leaders to take part in a Royal Command variety performance. As usual, no luck, until one of the Tiller Girls saw me leaving wearing my specs and thought I might do for Billy Cotton; but, of course, one look and the producers could see that I lacked Mr Cotton's impressive rotundity. I might have passed, though, for Henry Hall, that slim, immaculate BBC bandleader with his slight and endearing stammer, 'This is H-Henry H-Hall and tonight is my Guest Night...'.

It was after that that I went to my last audition, one that might have ended in success and, who knows, might have changed the whole direction of my career. My teacher at the Max Rivers' School, which I also continued to attend on the Wednesday afternoons of my earlier schooldays, told me about it. It was held at the Adelphi Theatre and was not, as it turned out, one of the stand-in-line variety; you were required to take your music and dance to it. At the stage door a number was allotted to each hopeful who waited in the wings to be called. When my turn came I gave my music to the pianist and walked onto a stage complete with lights, footlights and a cyclorama, which was being used in the current production of *Helen!*, starring Evelyn Laye. It was the real McCoy. I found it magical and totally unlike the bare stages of previous experiences. Forgetting my nerves, I really gave out. Afterwards I was asked to stay on stage. A gentleman came up from the stalls and said, 'Well, we liked your dance very much. Would you now sing us your song?'. 'But I haven't got a song', I replied. I hadn't realised, in fact, that a song was required. He gave me a long look, asked me my age and, when I told him, said in a very understanding way that, although they had liked my dance, perhaps I had better come back in a year or two. Later, I found out that the audition was for Noël Coward's new revue, *Words and Music*, directed and produced by the great Charles B. Cochran.

Time was passing without a sign of a job and I was haunted by the fear that my family were just about to utter the immortal refrain, 'You must forget about all this theatre business and get a proper job'. After my failure to become one of Mr Cochran's young men, I really slumped into the deepest despair. I felt I was never going to make it in show business; there must be no more dreams of being Jack Buchanan, or one of the Lancashire Lads, slapping their lederhosen in *The White Horse Inn*, or even of joining Jack Shepherd on the beach at Brighton. So, I must find a job, any job. After the episode with Harrods, that noble emporium was out. Perhaps I might succeed with Dales, the flourishing haberdashers situated in the Causeway, Teddington – a stone's throw from 'Melrose', so I could get home for lunch. But someone near and dear had other plans for me.

Chapter 2

When I came down to breakfast a day or two after my renunciation of any hope of pursuing a theatrical career, Naggie, in calm and unruffled tones, announced, 'I've had a letter from that Madame Rambert'. She went on to disclose the contents, which were to the effect that, if it was convenient, we could go up and see her the following Tuesday at four o'clock.

I was absolutely astounded. Unknown to me or to anyone else in the house, Naggie had written to the distinguished lady who had made possible the birth of ballet in England, forming her own company. I was horrified to think what claims for my talent Naggie must have made to prompt Madame Rambert's swift reply and offer of an interview. The thought of being confronted by this great lady was overwhelming. When I questioned Naggie as to what on earth had made her take this step, she replied, 'Well, Madam Bromova is always going on about that Bobby Stuart joining Madame Rambert, so why can't you?'

Thus it was that, in June 1932, we travelled on a number twenty-seven bus from Teddington to Notting Hill Gate. There, next to a large and imposing church on the corner of Ladbroke Grove, was a small grey stone building with 'Ballet Club' written on a side wall in huge, black letters. By the entrance were pictures of the Rambert dancers in a large, glass-covered frame.

This company had first come to the notice of the public and critics in 1926 by giving performances at the Lyric Theatre, Hammersmith. It was small in number but bursting with talent, and destined to make its mark in the annals of British ballet; a young choreographer called Frederick Ashton was among its ranks. Following this early success at the Lyric, Ashley Dukes, Marie Rambert's husband and an extremely successful playwright, financed the acquisition of the halls in Notting Hill Gate. One was turned into a theatre, while the other served as a studio for a school and a rehearsal room for the company, which then gave performances there on Sunday nights. Works created by Ashton and later by Antony Tudor were augmented by a repertoire from the classical ballets. The theatre housed what became known as the Ballet Club and attracted a discerning membership. When plays were later produced there, it was renamed 'The Mercury', and became famous among other things for its association with T.S. Eliot's *Murder in the Cathedral*.

But back to that day in June 1932. On ringing the bell we were admitted by a lady whom we supposed to be Madame's secretary. In fact it was her sister-in-law, Renée Dukes, a charming person of whom I grew very fond and who always seemed to me to exert a calming influence on the establishment. As Madame was a little late in finishing her afternoon class, we were shown into a room and asked to wait. Gazing at the walls, I was very impressed by the pictures, which I later came to realise were part of Ashley Dukes' famous collection of romantic ballet prints. After a while we were told that Madame Rambert could see us, and we were ushered through double doors to find ourselves at the back of the smallest theatre I had ever seen; about 120 seats, covered with red plush, sloped down to a tiny stage measuring 18 feet by 18. Above each corner of the proscenium arch was a plaster figure of an angel. Incredibly, it was on this tiny, though not unworthy 'scaffold' that the greatest British choreographers, Ashton, Tudor, de Valois and Andrée Howard, created works of magic and genius. We proceeded through another set of double doors that led to the class and rehearsal studio – and there was Madame Rambert, a small but elegant lady wearing what was then an essential part of every smart woman's wardrobe, a 'little black dress'. Her jet-black hair, pulled tightly back into a bun, seemed to gleam, and her bright eyes shone with a penetrating and searching look.

Our interview was very short. After acknowledging that I was a pupil of Madam Bromova, she just said, 'Show foot'. I took off my shoe and pointed my toes, did a *plié* or two and then I was asked to do an *arabesque*. This was long before legs shot up to beyond your ears, so my leg, at a simple forty-five degrees to the floor, was considered adequate. In next to no time Madame said that she was willing to accept me as a pupil. Those alert eyes could see that we were not exactly affluent, so she made me an offer then and there, a contract guaranteeing to train me in classical ballet to the value of one hundred pounds. I would repay this amount in instalments by giving her fifteen per cent of any salary I happened to earn until the debt was discharged. There was no arguing or bargaining. We both thanked Madame, who seemed quiet, firm and matter-of-fact about the whole business. Goodness! Looking back, it was the only time I remember her being quiet or matter-of-fact; but firm certainly, then and always. If this brief audition seems, by today's standards, more than minimal, in those early thirties which directors could turn down the chance of training an extra male dancer for their company? There weren't many of us around.

As the door closed behind us, after we had said goodbye and began to walk down Ladbroke Grove, Naggie said, 'I think we could do with a nice cup of tea'. So we popped into the United Dairies for one before getting on the number twenty-seven bus back to Teddington.

My contract duly arrived, sealed and signed with two signatures – Marie Rambert's large, artistic and finely penned, and Naggie's simple and unequivocal, 'Florence Annie Young'. I could start classes immediately. Thus on the following Monday morning at ten o'clock, I was ready for my class in my practise clothes of black swimming trunks, white shirt and socks and black ballet shoes. This was not at all an unusual garb for male dancers of the day, for very few aspired to tights.

The class was taken by Antony Tudor. He was very sharp with his pupils, and in my case with good reason. Poor Antony, I must have been a trial to him. A short time after I had started, he told me in his characteristically unadorned way that I was a big disappointment to them all; they had expected someone more proficient and talented. Heavens! What could Naggie have put in her letter? And what could I do, with the almost certain knowledge that I would never earn fifteen per cent of anything with which to pay back the hundred pounds? This weighed heavily upon me. I thought that it would be best to remain very quiet and, if possible, not be a trouble to anyone. I didn't let on to Naggie and tried to look bright and content with my new life, but the awful thing was that I knew I was terrible. Dear Mim – the nickname for Marie Rambert that, years later, I was allowed to use – did not show the disappointment she must have felt when she saw my appalling lack of technique. This was an act of kindness for which I shall always be grateful.

Antony Tudor's class was followed at eleven o'clock by Madame's. She took part in it herself, wearing either a grey or a black tunic and black tights, and on her head a black bandeau, rather low over her eyes. She loved to dance. Before the class started she would take a small watering can and sprinkle the floor as depicted in the ballet studies by Degas. During the class there would be screeching and pungent directions to the dancers and, following the work at the *barre*, she would enter in with the rest of us, giving out a great deal of passion and fire. This was especially so if the pianist chose a glorious piece of Beethoven for the *adage* or, better still, a section of Tchaikovsky's Fifth Symphony, currently being used by Léonide Massine in *Les Présages*. If no pianist was available, Madame would supply music by whistling shrilly, whether to economise or not I never discovered.

Later, she found out that two of her pupils were up to playing suitable melodies for class; so when we had finished our exercises holding on to the *barre* for support and the time came to dance in the centre of the room, she divided us into two groups, always seeing to it that one dancer-cum-pianist was in each, to cover any musical emergency. This ingenious scheme worked out well. While the pianist in group A was playing, group B would perform; after a rapid changeover, pianist B would play for group A. However, as we repeated the exercises so many times and each group followed the other in rapid succession, the dancing pianists must have gained valuable tummy muscles from all that springing up and down from the piano stool. Although all this may sound bizarre, it was really very exhilarating and the classes gave us a wonderful feeling for the fluency of movement.

To reach the rehearsal room each day we made our own way from Ladbroke Grove down a small passage by the church. Once inside, we had to go through the studio to the changing rooms, which meant that the arrivals for the eleven o'clock session had to walk through Antony Tudor's ten o'clock class. This didn't seem to worry anybody; it was all part of the hugger-mugger way of things at the Ballet Club.

Then the moment would come when Madame herself arrived to change for class. Sometimes this would be a dramatic entrance, the banging of the double doors an accompaniment to her shouting back over her shoulder to someone who had displeased her on the way in. At other times she was quieter, perhaps discussing some special moment of the performance of the de Basil Company that she had seen the previous evening at the Royal Opera House, enthusing about Léonide Massine's magnetic presence on stage or the splendid qualities of the three young leading dancers, Baronova, Toumanova and Riabouchinska, known affectionately as the 'baby ballerinas'. Either way there was ample warning for us of what we would find in the forthcoming class. For our small group who did both the ten and eleven o'clock stints, there was no time in between to change our practise clothes or to clean up; Madame recommended that to meet this contingency we purchase large bottles of eau de cologne from Boots the Chemist, price one shilling.

On my very first day, in between the morning and afternoon classes, I made an exploratory tour of the district round Ladbroke Grove past the Coronet, once famous as a legitimate theatre but then, as now, a cinema. I was impressed by the streets and the lines of large, imposing houses redolent of a prosperous Victorian and Edwardian era. As if to match that scene, I noticed two figures walking along, both wearing straw boaters. I recognised them from their photographs in the front of the theatre as Frederick Ashton and Walter Gore. They were opting for the afternoon class, having been appearing in late-night cabaret produced by Charles B. Cochran at the Trocadero.

These ventures into midnight cabaret, revues, musical comedies and other commercial shows were the lot not only of these two but also of other talented artists. By these means they were able to earn some money to augment the pittance which, owing to the prevailing economic circumstances, was all the English ballet companies could afford to pay. Harold Turner, Maude Lloyd, Prudence Hyman and William Chappell were to be the future pillars of the ballet establishment, but they all had this earlier experience in the commercial theatre – and what better place to learn one's craft?

Although I was only a youngster at the time, I was well aware of the stringent economic conditions that obtained. After all, two of the most popular plays of the day in the West End were *Love on the Dole* and *The Wind and the Rain*, which centred on these hard facts. Later in life, when talking to many of my old colleagues, I realised that it had been the same story with most of us, and that we had all felt the shoe pinching. There were, of course, no grants from local authorities in those early days; we were subsidised by our families, while directors of companies, such as Marie Rambert or Lilian Baylis, had no public funding. The God-fearing Miss Baylis knew only too well that there were no pennies from heaven.

Classes continued for me at the Ballet Club until we broke up for the summer holidays. I was still very much a student and, having survived this first phase of my training, I looked forward to having a rest from the daily routine of tuition. It had, however, been an exhilarating experience working alongside professional dancers, and this had given me a degree of confidence in spite of my feeling of inadequacy in their presence. Little did I realise then that many of these artists would become my lifelong friends.

When the new term started in September, I resumed the routine of my training. Nothing out of the usual occurred until, at the beginning of December, Madame cancelled her afternoon class, announcing to our delight that she had seats for us all to attend the matinée performance of the Camargo Society at, of all places, the Adelphi Theatre, scene of my audition earlier in the year. This society had been created to keep alive the spirit of Diaghilev, who had recently died, and, in effect, to encourage English choreographers and composers; on this day, Monday 4 December, it was giving its last regular performance. The Ballet Club contingent was joined by Frederick Ashton, and we all sat together at the back of the dress circle. During the interval I noticed someone standing behind us leaning over the barrier and pummelling Fred's shoulder. Then, for the first time, I heard that clarion peel of laughter which, as I was later to learn, could herald spontaneous mirth and break the tension of any fury at rehearsal. I quickly realised that Fred's conspirator in laughter was Ninette de Valois, Director of the Vic–Wells Ballet.

The programme that afternoon contained a ballet, *Adam and Eve*, that was choreographed by my stern mentor, Antony Tudor, with Prudence Hyman as Eve and Anton Dolin as Adam. Constant Lambert had contributed the music that had been partly used in his ballet for Diaghilev, *Romeo and Juliet*. The whole event was a fitting tribute to the Camargo Society, to which the future of British ballet owed much, providing as it did many outstanding productions such as *Job* by Ninette de Valois with music by Vaughan Williams, Ashton's *Façade* to William Walton's music and *Rio Grande* to that of Constant Lambert. As a result of all of this wonderful activity, programmes of ballet featured English names at last; and it was because of the work of these English choreographers that we saw the birth of what came to be known as the English style, a fact always strongly emphasised by its principal exponent, Ninette de Valois.

It was only a few days after this famous matinée that Madame Rambert took me aside after class and said, 'My dear, the de Valois is short of a boy for one of her productions at Sadler's Wells. I would like you to go and see her tomorrow after class. I don't suppose you'll do, but go and see her anyway'.

And indeed I did go. I made my way to the theatre for a 2.30 appointment. As I had recently seen Miss de Valois with Frederick Ashton, she was no stranger to me, but this was the first time that I was to meet her personally. Her secretary took me through the pass door to where a company rehearsal was in progress, led me over to Miss de Valois and introduced me. She did no more than look me up and down and asked me straightaway if I could be in the production of *The Enchanted Grove*, which she was currently rehearsing. On my saying 'Yes', she told me to go to the office, where her secretary would give me details of the rehearsals and performances. It was as quick and direct as that. I remember the date, 12 December 1932.

Rehearsals started the following week; what is more, we rehearsed over Christmas. One of my first reactions was that, now I was to be earning a little money, I could begin to discharge my debt to Madame Rambert for my training. So began my career with the Vic–Wells. My first performance of *The Enchanted Grove* was on 3 January 1933, and it marked the beginning of an association that was to last over 60 years. Happily for me, Madame Rambert's doubts were proved to be ill-founded.

The first of my many journeys to Sadler's Wells Theatre involved taking a train from Teddington to Waterloo on the Southern Railway in one of the green-painted carriages that I was to get to know so well. Then the number sixty-seven bus took me over Waterloo Bridge through Holborn to the Dickensian atmosphere of Chancery Lane and Rosebery Avenue, which complemented *Bleak House*, my travel reading at the time. As the bus turned right into Rosebery Avenue I saw written on the wall of a café, 'Gentleman's portion 1/6d, Lady's portion 1/3d'. On reaching Sadler's Wells Theatre, further down Rosebery Avenue, I saw again written on the wall, this time by the stage door, 'Opera and Shakespeare in English'. Such simple inducements to eating out and theatregoing must have been the equivalent of what today is the more grandiose process of 'marketing'.

After seeing the writing on the wall, as it were, I was, with the production of *The Enchanted Grove*, to enter a world that contained so many of the ingredients that were to contribute to the future greatness of the Sadler's Wells and later of the Royal Ballet. There was the music of Ravel's *Le Tombeau de Couperin*, the choreography of Rupert Doone, the costume designs and décor of Duncan Grant. Doone, besides being a stylish and excellent dancer, had a close association with the Bloomsbury Group, as did Duncan Grant, and he was also the producer of W.H. Auden's and Christopher Isherwood's *The Ascent of F6* at the Mercury. This milieu was important and valuable in nurturing the ballet as a whole; for without the economist, Maynard Keynes, and his wife, the former Diaghilev ballerina, Lydia Lopokova, two very distinguished members of the Bloomsbury Group, it might not have advanced as rapidly as it did. In the event, Miss de Valois was to produce her first full-length classical ballet, *Coppélia*, then given in the shorter two act version, for the company, with Lydia Lopokova in the rôle of Swanilda.

Coming back to what was my first professional rehearsal, I discovered that I was to play one of four courtiers. One of the ladies in the ensemble was a lovely dancer called Hermione Darnborough, who later left the ballet to marry the conductor, Muir Mathieson, closely associated with film music. At first I found some difficulty in dancing to Ravel's music, which was of a different order from *Rustle of Spring* of the Mrs Hepworth Taylor days; but, as time went by in rehearsal and performance, I grew to love it then as I do now, when it always invokes memories of my first performances with the Vic–Wells Ballet.

I found it glorious to be on the stage. When I started rehearsals I hadn't realised how many important artists were to be there with me, notably Ninette de Valois, dancing an elegant Japanese lady and demonstrating her precise and intricate footwork as she made her entrance with my teacher, Antony Tudor, and Rupert Doone as Japanese courtiers. The principal rôle was danced by Wendy Toye, partnered by Stanley Judson. I was aware of the importance of this performance, my début with a professional company, and of working with Ninette de Valois and dancing in this historic theatre. I shall always be grateful to the three prominent young dancers, Travis Kemp, Guy Massey and Toni Repetto, whose dressing room I shared and who showed me, a nervous newcomer, such understanding, helping with my make-up and costume, and fixing my eighteenth-century wig. They were later to become great friends of mine in the company. The fact that we were called the Vic–Wells Ballet was brought home to me in practical terms when we all packed up our make-up and costumes and went over the river to the South Bank to dance a repeat performance at the Old Vic Theatre.

Following the elation and excitement of my début at these two theatres, I settled down once more to my classes at the Ballet Club. Almost immediately, it seemed, Madame Rambert told me after class, as was her wont, that I was to appear at the next programme to be given in the tiny Ballet Club theatre. These performances usually ran for four consecutive Sundays; in this particular case the programme was to include *Carnaval*, an old Diaghilev ballet choreographed by Fokine with music by Schumann, plus a divertissement of popular numbers from *The Sleeping Beauty* under the title *Aurora's Wedding*. All this filled me with a feeling of achievement; first the Vic–Wells and now the Ballet Rambert.

In *Carnaval* I was to be part of the ensemble called '*Valse Noble*' and in *Aurora's Wedding* one of the cavaliers supporting the ballerinas. I was rather taller than the other men in the company and it was disconcerting at the first stage call to have Madame Rambert shrieking out, 'Leslie, you are too tall. Bend your knees'. It always amazed me that no one in that tiny theatre seemed to notice that one of the cavaliers in the *Grand Adage* walked forward on bended knees whilst supporting his ballerina. I can only think that my partner's tutu covered my predicament. However, the day following this performance Madame Rambert's after-class pronouncement to me was somewhat surprising: 'Leslie, my dear, you are not at all bad on the stage.'

About that time, we heard that the Vic–Wells was going to produce its first big classical ballet, the two-act *Coppélia*, which was full of mazurkas, csárdás and ensemble numbers, so Miss de Valois would certainly be needing more than one extra male in the cast. Antony Tudor then told me that Madame Rambert had given permission for us both to be in the new production. Thrilling tidings, indeed. *Coppélia*, with its beautiful score by Delibes, would be in the hands of a former *régisseur* from St Petersburg, Nicholas Sergeyev, and Lydia Lopokova would dance the leading role of Swanilda.

Having appeared already with the Vic–Wells Ballet, I felt one up on the new people who were engaged, and greeted in familiar tones the regular members of the company. While making my way to the rehearsal room and talking to a founder member, Claude Newman, I saw a dancer I had not encountered on my previous visits. He was standing by the noticeboard and had a compelling appearance, wearing a brown trilby hat at a jaunty angle over one eye, a camelhair overcoat over his practise clothes, and red Russian boots, the essential footwear for male character dancers in those days. He seemed to me to epitomise the theatrical personality and to be on a par with Jack Buchanan, whose photograph I had seen in *Theatre World* (he, too, resplendent in camelhair coat). I turned to Claude and said, 'Who is that?' In his rich tones he replied, 'Oh, that's de Valois' new colonial wonder'. 'Wonder' was the appropriate word; from this first moment Robert Helpmann made a tremendous impression on the entire company. This production of *Coppélia* was to be his début as a dancer in England; when he burst onto the stage in the mazurka, he drew every eye to him. This was not only on account of his vitality but also because every light on the stage was reflected in the mirror-like hair, jet-black, to which he applied a generous coat of vaseline – a trick he had learnt in the theatre in Australia, where he had had, in fact, a great deal of experience.

As well as making a rapid advance artistically in the company, Helpmann quickly established himself as a forceful member of our relatively small, pioneering group. During the one-hour break between the morning and afternoon rehearsals, we all squashed into the small canteen at the back of the stalls which, during performances, served soft drinks to the public. This room was a setting for Helpmann's sharp wit and quick observation. No one escaped those great, searchlight eyes, no one's cherished foible was lost on him. He became the leader of the pack while also cultivating the lifestyle of a star performer. Not for him the journeys back and forth to Rosebery Avenue on the number nineteen bus, but a taxi to and from the theatre; and one felt that there was already a table earmarked for him at the Ivy restaurant, the West End bastion of theatrical *hoi ristoi*. All that seemed natural to him; and indeed, as he was the son of a wealthy Australian, it was. Frederick Ashton, who shared the then-popular view that all Australians were, in one way or another, connected with sheep farming, attributed the extravagance to the fact that funds would be readily forthcoming from this lucrative source. In keeping with this image Helpmann would never buy one of anything, but always a quantity: half a dozen pairs of shoes, a whole rack of ties. And oh, how he could make us laugh.

Most important, however, was his growing popularity with the public. Soon after his arrival, Miss de Valois astounded us all by giving him the leading rôle of Satan in her ballet *Job*, previously danced by Anton Dolin.

He then triumphed in the first part that was created specifically for him, the Master of Tregennis in *The Haunted Ballroom*, also choreographed by Ninette de Valois. From then onwards, for season after season, he appeared in virtually the whole repertoire of works choreographed by de Valois and Ashton and in the full-length classical ballets, when he became the partner of Alicia Markova.

This first *Coppélia* in which he was to appear was scheduled to open on 21 March 1933. Antony Tudor and I duly joined the other male members of the company; we were on loan, as it were, from Madame Rambert. Looking back, it was astounding how quickly Miss de Valois had managed to find eight men to partner her eight girls and equally astounding that Nicholas Sergeyev could manage to get us all dancing the mazurka by opening night. It was a considerable achievement for us, although second nature for a Russian, and it took endless rehearsing, entering the stage from the right and then, at the command 'Other side' from Sergeyev, from stage left. We became thus proficient at 'reversing', but not before some anxious moments had been overcome. A few of us, needing to add extra tuition to rehearsal, would go upstairs to what at the Wells was called the Board Room, which had within it a section partitioned off to serve as Miss Baylis's office. Its incumbent bore the necessity of our practising outside it with great fortitude, but there were occasions in the midst of our heavy pounding on the floor when she would pop her head out and in her inimitable voice say, 'Try to make a little less noise, dears'.

Our special tuition was given by Ursula Moreton, the Ballet Mistress of the Vic–Wells Company. She had been a member of the Diaghilev Ballet and had appeared in their production of *The Sleeping Princess* at the Alhambra Theatre in 1921. A close friend of Ninette de Valois, to whom she gave unswerving loyalty and valuable assistance in the running of her company, she was herself a wonderful artist who both featured in and created many important rôles for the repertoire. She always showed me great kindness and gave me encouragement in those early years, and was someone with whom I felt a special affinity.

Throughout the rehearsals for *Coppélia*, the proceedings were greatly helped by Lydia Lopokova, a great artist, who was to dance Swanilda. Being Russian, she was able to ease many difficulties with regard to language, since Sergeyev's English was limited to the command 'Other side'. She was enchanting in her rôle, inspiring all the young dancers with her charm and the artistry of one nurtured in the Maryinsky Theatre tradition at St Petersburg. The ballet was an outstanding success, the audience as enchanted with her Swanilda as were the whole company who performed with her. She was at one with us all. Later, her rôle was danced by

Ninette de Valois, who excelled not only in the impish humour she brought to the part but also in the classically exact execution of her intricate footwork.

For those early performances I received ten shillings a week minus the fifteen per cent repayment to Madame Rambert for my classical training. I did not receive any payment for performances at the Ballet Club, but the experience that I gained in that volatile atmosphere was invaluable. There I was, in that tiny, triangular dressing-room at the top of the stairs, making-up with my companions Frederick Ashton, Antony Tudor, William Chappell and Walter Gore; it might be occupied by the luminaries of British ballet, but the conditions of the room were somewhat primitive. There was only one mirror, on the wall above the make-up table, at which I would never have dared to sit. I always occupied a corner of the triangular space, burying my head in my own make-up mirror and hoping not to be noticed, but listening attentively to the general conversation.

This was not necessarily confined to the world of ballet, for matters of the theatre in general featured largely. All four had danced with the Camargo Society, but this was a time when there was no regular ballet company in England to offer regular employment and income; so musical comedy, revue, cabaret, films, in fact any form of entertainment that required dancers had to fill the gaps that inevitably occurred. Ashton would talk about his days with Ida Rubinstein's company in Paris, where he first met the choreographer whom he admired and who influenced him greatly later in his career, Madame Bronislava Nijinska.

His experience in various revues and musicals had also given him a repertoire of wonderful impersonations of the stars he had worked with. Later, when he had made his first trip to the United States, we were regaled for weeks with stories about the production of *Four Saints in Three Acts* that he had been invited to choreograph. This introduced us all to the reputation of Gertrude Stein, who had written the libretto and had already become famous, not least for having early recognised the art of Picasso, whose pictures she subsequently collected in large number. Ashton had found the production of *Four Saints in Three Acts* difficult, possibly because he was dealing with dancers outside his usual orbit of the Rambert; but he seemed to have enjoyed working with Miss Stein, who, discarding her habitual laconic style, declared him to be a genius.

He certainly had a great time, particularly on his trips to Harlem, where he would join the fashionable world 'putting on the Ritz' and dining and dancing in the clubs, where he shimmied until dawn with the best of them. No one could move as Fred could. We all roared with laughter at his graphic descriptions of the 'Miss America' contest, with its array of petulant, provocative or just plain saucy contestants, each wearing a ribbon across her chest emblazoned with the name of the state that she represented. Our tiny triangular room saw the re-enactment of these events, amazing and exotic to us because this sort of thing had not as yet reached Blackpool or Morecambe Bay.

While in America he naturally 'wowed' the Astors and fell easily into the high-society lifestyle of the Hamptons, East and West. But then, the Ashton charm was always formidable, almost like an additional talent. That first trip marked the beginning of his life-long love of the States and of the reciprocal love that Americans have continued to show for Fred and his ballets.

William Chappell was already an established theatre designer as well as a dancer. His mother was an actress who had introduced him to the theatre while he was very young. He would contribute remarks about the then-current performances in the West End, never cynical or unpleasant but knowledgeable and constructive, and at times he saw fit good-naturedly to chivvy the others when they got a little beyond themselves. It was then that I first heard him use his favourite phrase, 'You're too jolly clever by half'. I loved him dearly. He seemed to be the only one who understood what a tremendous culture shock all this sophisticated talk must have provided for me with my very suburban background and *naïveté*. Climbing nervously and quietly up the stairs to the dressing room, I once heard Chappell saying to its inmates, 'He's not sly; don't you see he's terribly shy?' My being intent on self-effacement had clearly produced the wrong impression.

I don't want to leave the dressing room without mention of its other occupants, Frank Staff and Hugh Laing. Together we made a cast of seven, and when we were all on in a performance the triangle was crowded indeed. Sometimes the fairly sophisticated dialogue was above my teenage head, but I listened and found the discussions unending in their interest, and for me a valuable source of practical wisdom in relation to my future career.

Chapter 3

The repertoire of the early days at the Vic–Wells, now becoming my second home, multiplied at a great rate, in spite of the fact that Miss de Valois had only one room in which to rehearse. In addition to the current programme there were the classical ballets produced by Nicholas Sergeyev in the full-length versions, new works of her own creation, new works by Ashton and the ballets for the Opera Company – *Faust*, *Carmen*, *Eugene Onegin* and *Tannhäuser*. The Venusberg music, having been choreographed by Ashton, was danced by the whole company. Before the foundation of the Opera Ballet as such, we did it all.

The architecture of the one rehearsal room added to the constraint. The two pillars near the doorway had to be carefully negotiated, both in classes and in rehearsals, but this was, in a way, a good preparation for the many exigencies to be faced in life on tour or indeed for stage life in general. Apart from giving classes herself, Ninette de Valois invited guest teachers: Anna Pruzina, Margaret Craske, Derra de Moroda, Stanislas Idzikowski. Then there was the business attached to the running of the company, no mean task in itself, and from the desk in her small office she saw to every detail that this involved. There was no doubt over who was in charge, although she had the very able help of Ursula Moreton, whom I was later to have the honour of partnering in *The Gods Go a-Begging* and *Casse Noisette*.

An example of how rapidly the repertoire grew is shown by the fact that I made my debut with the Vic–Wells Company in *The Enchanted Grove* on 3 January 1933, and on 21 March I was in the first night of *Coppélia*. Ninette de Valois had managed to put it on in two-and-a-half months, alongside all her other commitments to the current repertoire. This was also the first time that the public saw the company give a full-length classical ballet.

The whole way of life in those early days was a natural progression of hard work. There was no time for theorising or for the luxury of long sessions in committee; it was a case of getting it done. In another tiny office on the floor above, the same policy was being adopted by Lilian Baylis. The two ladies were very different in character, but each acknowledged the other's importance in the whole organisation. We all respected this founder of the Old Vic, no one more so than Ninette de Valois. She was now Miss Baylis of the Old Vic and Sadler's Wells and make no mistake about it. Her Shakespearean Company comprised most of the stars of the day, who were proud to follow their West End successes and work for her in the Waterloo Road; it put a special seal on their stardom. They, with the opera singers and the young dancers of the Vic–Wells Ballet, were all part of her family and to her it was natural and right that they should be so.

She always brought us all together for a tea party at her house in Stockwell at the beginning of each season; over a cup of tea and a bun we all became friends, talking about one another's work. There was no question of being a Montague or a Capulet, for we were all members of her team and she had an instinct for its management. There were various extra-mural activities with regard to her favourite projects in which we willingly took part: tea parties at Christmas for the old ladies living around 'The Cut' in the Waterloo Road, visits by bus to the leper colony outside London and activities connected with the Church, for she was a deeply religious person. The bus journey to the colony was an entertainment in itself; when the time came for the necessary stop enabling the travellers to pay a visit to a convenient copse of trees, the company alighted, gentlemen one way and ladies the other. Miss Baylis meanwhile remained on the bus, adopting a sentinel's stance. A group from the ballet and opera companies had produced a concert-party entertainment for this leper colony. Memorable among the numbers was Joy Newton, a dancer, singing with one of the leading tenors 'If You Were the Only Girl in the World', and Stanley Hall, another dancer, giving full rein to his latent talent for musical comedy in a spirited rendering of Gershwin's 'Nice Work if You Can Get It', followed by a vigorous tap dance.

Lilian Baylis was always the first to realise when something was amiss with one of her 'family'. Once, when she greeted us as we arrived at her party, she added, 'Go and have a word with Jill, dears. She's feeling a bit down'. The Jill in question was the distinguished actress, Jill Esmond, who was in the middle of the crisis of the break-up with her husband, Laurence Olivier. In the face of this 'cause célèbre', Miss Baylis's simple and natural approach was a refreshing understatement of affairs.

An incident during a production of *Faust* demonstrates her ultra-practical side. Members of the ballet company were dancing to the famous waltz in the first act; the momentum was accelerated because of the steep rake to the stage and a moment came when one of the girls found herself propelled over the footlights. Miss Baylis, who was sitting in her box adjacent to the orchestra pit, leaned over and said to one of the string section, 'Any of the fiddles damaged, dear?'

Later on, the rake was responsible for another mishap, during a performance of *Giselle* at the beginning of the second act. When the curtain rose, I was discovered with three young colleagues; we were a group of huntsmen carousing and toasting one another in a drunken fashion near the grave depicted in the scene. It transpired afterwards that one of the prop-men had inadvertently stuck one goblet into another, so that, as we raised our arms in a toast, the spare goblet flew into the air, landed on the stage and because of the fearsome rake quickly rolled onto the footlights and over into the orchestra pit. There was silence and then 'boom' as it hit the big drum. After several noisy rebounds and consequent titters from the audience we had to make our exit, supposedly fleeing in terror before the fury of the Queen of the Wilis, which was actually nothing to the fury of Madame Markova who was about to make her tragic and moving entrance.

The 1932–3 season was ending, but it was not a time for regret, because I had received a letter from Miss Baylis to say that Ninette de Valois had recommended that I become a member of the company for the following season of the Vic–Wells Ballet. Then, suddenly, I received a postcard from Miss de Valois asking if I would be free to take part in a gala at the Royal Opera House, Covent Garden, organised by the Camargo Society and comprising the two-act *Coppélia* and Act II of *Swan Lake*. I was to telephone her about the details of the rehearsals. These were essential because of the different conditions that obtained in the Opera House, its size and the consequent need for extra dancers to fill it.

The cast was to include Frederick Ashton, who was to partner Ursula Moreton, and Wendy Toye. Wendy I remembered well from the early days of competitions, as she always caused a sensation with her Mexican Hat Dance and her extraordinary versatility in all forms of classical and character dancing. If Wendy was in any competition, she won. Frederic Franklin, who was a great friend of Wendy's and who later became a notable principal of the Ballet Russe de Monte Carlo, was also among the number. I found them all somewhat sophisticated, and remember their singing constantly the hit tune of the time, 'Stormy Weather', destined to become a standard. I also met for the first time a dancer who remains a close friend to this day, Richard Ellis. Most amazing of all, we were joined by Robert Stuart, who went back to the days of Madam Bromova and whose subsequent progress in the Ballet Rambert was a source of cryptic comments by Naggie.

The two dates for the performance were in the middle of June, and we rehearsed in the Royal Opera House for a week beforehand. Entering it we would pass the eagle eye of the stage-door keeper, the formidable Mr Jackson. He had achieved the unique distinction of intimidating Miss de Valois, who subsequently gave us ample warning to mind our p's and q's when entering his domain. We were all staggered by the size of the stage; to my short-sighted vision it looked as vast as the acres of a cricket field. This would need some covering in our mazurkas and csárdás. It was, of course, the first time that I had danced on such a stage, and the memory of that baptism of fire, still vivid, was what I spoke of after my final performance in 1993.

In September, after the summer break, Miss Baylis assembled the company and gave her usual tea party. Then on the first night of the new season I experienced the tradition of her visits to every dressing room in her two theatres; a knock on the door and there was Miss Baylis, accompanied by her secretary, Annette Prevost, handing out to each of us a little bunch of white heather and offering her good wishes for the coming season. This, in fact, proved to be a highly successful one, opening with a revival of Ninette de Valois' *Job*, with Robert Helpmann in the part of Satan, followed by her *The Haunted Ballroom*, again with Helpmann in the leading rôle.

During this season I had my first taste of rehearsing with Miss de Valois. Unlike Madame Rambert she wore her everyday clothes when giving us classes, but when rehearsing she dressed in brick-coloured trousers and blouse, and then we knew we were in for it. When she showed us any steps, her demonstration, in her red character shoes, was powerful and exact. This was invaluable experience for me and was complemented by my continuing at the Ballet Club, dancing in their Sunday night performances, which started at nine o'clock in the evening and ended too late for me to catch the last bus back to Teddington. There was a rich vein of choreography in the Ballet Club as well as at the Wells, and I was proud and lucky to be taking a part in both.

Andrée Howard was giving proof of her original talent – it was remarkable how well she could create a great atmosphere on that tiny stage. *Our Lady's Juggler*, with choreography by Susan Salaman, was one of the ballets from the early days of the Rambert Company and had made the reputation of a fine young dancer, Harold Turner. It was to be revived with choreography by Andrée Howard. Howard's *The Mermaid* became a popular success; the limitations of the stage did not deter her from creating a shipwreck and a phantasmagoria of Spanish dancing. I especially remember the exquisite performance by Pearl Argyle, stepping over the cardboard waves and dancing tentatively forward on to dry land.

This was followed by *The Rape of the Lock*, a one-act version of *Cinderella*, *Death and the Maiden* and Andrée's most highly acclaimed *Lady into Fox*. In addition to handling the choreography, she often designed the costumes and scenery herself, and most effectively.

All this work pouring out of the Ballet Club was immensely important, and Madame Rambert's contribution in revealing the potential of the English choreographers should never be forgotten. Many ballet companies of the future were to draw upon her pioneering work. She also had what is now termed a hands-on approach, and would chivvy us all into making the most of our appearances on stage. Appearing as a huntsman in the famous Camargo Society gala at the Opera House, I had to wear an unfortunate costume of grey tights, fashioned from material that was prone to wrinkling, topped by a black-and-grey jersey of the style made popular by the football stars of the day. The final injustice was to have to wear a blond-fringed wig on which was pinned a square of black velvet resembling a sort of skullcap. We must have looked a treat.

The next day Madame Rambert's regular pronouncement to me after class was, 'Leslie, my dear, at the Opera House last night you looked like a knitting needle'. But after so dealing with this thin and gangling youth, she set about foraging in the wardrobe and found an old white cricket pullover belonging to Antony Tudor. In future I wore it under all my costumes. Thank goodness I appeared in an age of wearing costumes that had a multitude of imperfections; I don't think I would have survived the arrival of all-over tights. I took heart, however, when I realised that I was not alone in requiring some additional padding-out, and was eternally grateful to Madame Rambert for her practicality in this respect and for all the thumping she gave with the accompanying remark, 'Oh my dear, straighten back'.

When the next (1933–4) Vic–Wells season opened at Sadler's Wells Theatre, I was a member of the company. On the first night that autumn, Stanislas Idzikowski was a guest artist, dancing with Alicia Markova in *Le Spectre de la Rose* and in the Bluebird *pas de deux*. Ninette de Valois revived *Job*, which continued to be a success withRobert Helpmann dancing the rôle of Satan. I was one of the sons of Job. Early on in the season we all had the great pleasure of seeing Idzikowski dancing with Alicia Markova and Ninette de Valois in the *pas de trois* from *Swan Lake*, and noticed that Idzikowski was wearing a circlet with a feather placed upwards from it as a head-dress. It transpired that this was according to the Maryinsky tradition, and we were to see this style again years later when it was adopted by Nureyev in *Le Corsaire*.

Later in the season Ninette de Valois revived her ballet *La Création du monde* with music by Darius Milhaud. This was of a somewhat more esoteric style and subject matter, but demonstrates the fact, not always recognised, that a wide range was offered to the company's audiences at that time. Furthermore, the ballet was a success. On a less serious note, there were three male dancers in the cast, all of whom had to paint various hieroglyphics on their body. Claude Newman, who was one of them, was worried lest, with this camouflage, his girlfriend sitting in the stalls would not recognise him. He contrived somehow to intermingle the word 'Claude' among the hieroglyphics in the hope that it would be clearly seen in the stalls but not in the circle, where Miss de Valois was sitting.

During Idzikowski's time as a guest artist, he was asked to give classes to the men in the company. When he did so, the company pianist did not play for class, being substituted by a charming lady called Madame Evina. She had been a member of the Diaghilev Company; one of her rôles in it had been that of the little American girl in *La Boutique fantasque*, choreographed by Léonide Massine. With the help of Idzikowski she had also produced *Carnaval* for the Vic–Wells. We all enjoyed the classes and grew very fond of Madame Evina, loving the colourful tunes that she played.

As I had done in the production of *Carnaval* at the Ballet Club, I danced in '*Valse Noble*'. I regretted that we didn't use the famous Léon Bakst designs for the costumes and sets in this new version at the Wells, but the situation was remedied when these were restored to the production of the ballet some years later.

Towards the end of 1933 Frederick Ashton choreographed *Les Rendezvous* with its enchanting music by Auber (arranged by Constant Lambert) and splendid designs by William Chappell. It was an instant success. The public loved its joyous style and the company loved performing it. I was the understudy for one of the six male dancers in the ballet, but because of an injury to one of them I was on for the first night of the production. This was perhaps the most exciting thing that I had experienced since first arriving in the company.

Immediately after the first night, Ashton left for America to produce and choreograph *Four Saints in Three Acts*, with the triumphant reception for *Les Rendezvous* still ringing in his ears. I remember seeing him off on the early boat train from Waterloo to Southampton; thinking he might, at this early hour, be leaving alone, I popped up before class from Teddington, conveniently situated on the Waterloo line. He was very surprised that anyone had turned up so early to see him off and sent me a letter, written on board ship, vividly describing the grey, grim January seas. He said that he had taken a number of books to read on the Atlantic crossing and that as he finished them he cast them overboard and watched them being devoured by the sullen, wintry waves.

On 1 January 1934, in equally inhospitable weather, the first night of *Giselle* took place at Sadler's Wells Theatre. This was a revival for the Vic–

Wells Ballet of the first modern British production, which Sergeyev had staged for the Camargo Society's season at the Savoy Theatre in 1932. Outside the theatre and, to a certain extent, inside it as well, was the thickest pea-soup of a fog in living memory. I had managed to make my way through it from Teddington by Southern Railway to Waterloo, thanks to what was known in the Thirties as a 'fog service'. I arrived at the stage door, after groping my way across York Road, just in time to get ready for my entrance in the first act. The swirling fog creeping into the auditorium made the harvest scene in Act I seem somewhat unseasonable but was totally appropriate for Act II. Though the audience that day might well have, in Ira Gershwin's words, 'viewed the morning with alarm', on that foggy London evening they turned up to show their appreciation of this classic romantic ballet that had now been added to our repertoire.

At the end of January, again with Sergeyev's help, we put on *Casse Noisette*. This was the first and traditional version of the many productions of the ballet that were to follow, including that of Rudolf Nureyev in 1968 and, later most notably, of Peter Wright for the Birmingham Royal Ballet. An amusing feature of this 1934 production was the group of young boy singers who acted the parts of the little mice; they were known as 'The Lord Mayor's Boy Players' and were formed at the instigation of King George V. They scurried on and entered the battle scene in Act I against the toy soldiers with great gusto. I always loved the entrance of *Les Incroyables*, of which I was one, and of *Les Merveilleuses*, and being received by the Hostess, so beautifully played by Ursula Moreton, who made the party seem real and her welcome warm. It was altogether very special for me, this first *Casse Noisette*, and it was always one of my favourite ballets to perform.

Then suddenly there was a great sadness in my home life. Pat died. Naggie, his wife, who had always hated any kind of emotional fuss, didn't shed a tear, at least not when I was with her; but her faith and her love for Pat were as simple as they were enduring, and I knew that not a day passed without his being in her thoughts. Through the years that followed, we often talked about him quite naturally and mostly with affectionate humour, as when we remembered the cool, late August evenings in Brighton when he would wear his striped Fair Isle pullover that we said made him look like Tiger Tim, a famous character of my childhood comic books.

Chapter 4

During the 1933–4 season, *Giselle* and *Casse Noisette* were produced in rapid succession, as well as some newly choreographed works; this balance of the classic and the innovative was always considered an essential factor in the repertoire. Because Frederick Ashton was working in the States, most of the new productions fell to Ninette de Valois, most notably *The Haunted Ballroom*, the ballet that had put the seal on Robert Helpmann's success. It can be said that these early works did not entirely find favour with the major critics of the day, but, in spite of the ungenerous criticism they received, many showed great staying power. This was true of *The Haunted Ballroom* in particular; many years later, after the War, it was being performed with success by the then Sadler's Wells Theatre Ballet.

Meanwhile, at Notting Hill Gate Madame Rambert was keeping busy. I was appearing regularly in her Sunday night programmes at the Ballet Club. Included among them was the new ballet by Andrée Howard, *The Mermaid*, in which Pearl Argyle managed, with a minimum of material, to simulate the movements of the waves and create the illusion of the shipwreck of a boat with its rust-coloured sail. I was one of three sailors keeping up a gentle rowing motion until a storm arose and tossed me overboard in its tumult – in stage terms, into the blacked-out wings of the tiny theatre. These were the days of extreme simplicity but great invention, and the audience's suspension of disbelief was willingly given. The music contributed to this and was of the first importance; in the case of *The Mermaid*, Andrée Howard chose Ravel's music to great effect.

In April the season ended at Sadler's Wells, with no performances due until the autumn and therefore no pay. I was very fortunate to land a job to help tide me over, dancing in a production at the Royal Albert Hall organised to celebrate the four hundred years of the life of Parliament and called appropriately *The Pageant of Parliament*. Pageants were a popular form of entertainment in those days and one for which the Albert Hall was ideally suited. In this case there was a cast of actors and singers, and for the crowd scenes a large number of amateur residents of the various London boroughs. Surprisingly for those days, there was also a group of dancers, led by Mary Skeaping and Harold Turner. The male members were mostly from the Vic–Wells and Ballet Ramberts and included Antony Tudor, Richard Ellis, Frank Staff, Rollo Gamble and myself. Most important among the girls' group was Peggy van Praagh, later to become a very distinguished dancer, teacher and Director of the Australian Ballet. The choreographers were Margaret Craske, a well-known teacher and dancer, and Quentin Todd, who had made a name for himself in revues and musicals. The entire production was to be compèred by Robert Speaight, the actor to become most closely associated with the part of Thomas à Becket in T.S. Eliot's *Murder in the Cathedral*.

On the first night, various distinguished society figures graciously consented to appear, among them Lady Diana Manners, a great beauty famous for playing the rôle of the Madonna in Max Reinhardt's *The Miracle*. On this occasion she was appearing as Elizabeth of York to Cecil Beaton's King Henry VII. Their young attendants, led by me, were boy dancers who scattered red roses in the path of the King while the girls attendant on the future Queen scattered white. We all rehearsed together for this scene with the exception of Mr Beaton, who did not appear, much to the agitation of Mr Todd, its choreographer. He was very put out by the absence of the famous photographer and asked Lady Diana if it was a habit of Mr Beaton's not to turn up on these occasions. To this anxious enquiry she replied frostily, 'I am not aware of any of Mr Beaton's habits'.

At our final dress-rehearsal at the Albert Hall, as we were making our way towards the arena for our first scene, we found ourselves in the midst of a group of agitated guardsmen supervised by their Staff Sergeants. They were bewildered by the fact that their costumes appeared hopelessly ill-fitting and impossible to fasten. Once we noticed the coat-of-arms splendidly emblazoned on the back of their coats instead of the front, we realised that they were trying to put them on back to front; unlike normal tunics, they didn't fasten down the front but needed to be buttoned at the back with the help of a dresser. All was well when this conundrum was resolved, but as there were 300 guardsmen appearing in the Wars of the Roses, the poor Staff Sergeants had a job on their hands before the coats-of-arms blazed forth as designed. This task paled, however, before that of the Military Police when they were called in to break up the brawling that extended the Wars of the Roses on a Saturday night when the guardsmen had had a few jars at the local hostelry before the performance. This incident somewhat dispelled the intended feeling of serenity at our entrances that followed, when we scattered rose petals on the marriage bed to symbolise the union between the two halves of the country previously split by the contentions of the Houses of York and Lancaster.

It is a relevant and interesting point of theatre history that it was Queen Victoria, no less, who, during visits to the Royal Opera House, noticed the slovenly marching of the various soldiers' choruses in operas and insisted that all such marching on stage must be done by her guardsmen. This tradition has lasted almost to the present day – for instance, in the early performances of Kenneth MacMillan's ballet *Romeo and Juliet*, the stalwarts carrying on the sedan chairs in the ballroom scene were played by genuine guardsmen. This military contribution also obtained whenever any regimental proficiency was needed in a production, an admirable arrangement that continued until Equity, the British actors' union, failed to come to terms with it.

We dancers were next needed in a scene commemorating the freezing over of the Thames in the reign of James I. We were skaters, the men partnering very decorous ladies across the supposedly icy surface of the arena, which represented the frozen river. On the first night our partners were distinguished members of London society who featured regularly in the *Tatler and Bystander*. I enormously admired my lady partner; not only was she charming and pretty but she took the whole matter seriously and appeared on more than just the first night. She was called Mrs Peter Rodd. I discovered many years later, when I encountered her as an author, that she was also Miss Nancy Mitford.

Although the arena was the main performing area, there were permanent rostra at the organ end of the hall. These were of various heights and were used intermittently during the pageant, notably during the finale, which was produced in the manner of the then-popular radio programme, *In Town Tonight*, during which a personality of the day would make a guest appearance. The Wimbledon Championships were going on at the time, and on the penultimate evening, the Friday, the guest was the winner of the Men's Singles, the great Fred Perry, making his entrance with the smiling and delighted girls dressed in tennis frocks and simulating the players' movements on court. We boys mounted our rostrum in bathing costumes of the thirties and danced a routine representing swimmers at the Lansbury Lido in Hyde Park, named after George Lansbury, a famous Labour politician of the time and grandfather of the equally famous actress, Angela Lansbury.

The entire company entered the stage arena for a final tableau, led on the first night by a cortège of actual Members of Parliament from both Houses, the Peers of the Realm making their way on to the top rostrum, which this time represented the Upper House. The procession was accompanied by the singing of the massed choirs and fittingly glorified the Mother of Parliaments.

On subsequent nights this distinguished company was replaced by extras wearing morning suits by courtesy of Messrs Moss Brothers and Maurice Angel. Attached to the back of each coat was a label assigning it to a particular player. In many cases this had evidently not been noticed when the suit was put on, with the result that the dignity of the procession, again to the accompaniment of the appropriate climactic music, was somewhat marred by the sight of labels from the backs of Honourable Members' necks blowing gently in the wind.

Chapter 5

We started the 1934–5 season in October, and in November *Le Lac des Cygnes* was produced under the direction of Nicholas Sergeyev, with Alicia Markova and Robert Helpmann dancing the leading rôles. As usual, the male members of the company doubled-up, particularly in the third act. I started the run being in the mazurka and understudying the Spanish Dance; very shortly afterwards one of the two men in this left. This necessitated my changing costumes, wigs and all, very rapidly in the wings, an exercise made possible only by the fact that helping my dresser was any available young swan who happened to be watching backstage.

There were two important events during this time: one that Pamela May made her début as a soloist, and the other that, in the *corps de ballet* of swans, there appeared the young Margot Fonteyn. Later on, she was to cause a sensation when, in the ballet *Rio Grande*, her youthfulness was disguised by the sullen looks of a Creole girl from a hot, southern port and she was further characterised by black hair frizzed out in an appropriately exotic style.

Rio Grande had a wonderful score by Constant Lambert and was based on a poem by Sacheverell Sitwell; it was sung on stage throughout by the chorus of the Vic–Wells Opera Company. After the first night William Chappell, who had partnered Margot Fonteyn, invited a few friends, myself included, back to his flat, and I well remember that Chappell turned to Frederick Ashton, the choreographer of the ballet, and said, 'Mark my words, Fred, that girl's going to be a star'.

In *Rio Grande* there were rôles one would not have associated with the Vic–Wells Ballet at the time: the men came on as rough stereotypes and sailors, and the girls, dancing with considerable abandon, as the ladies of the port. Miss Baylis, however, waived any scruples about all that and simply said, 'I know what my girls are supposed to be, but I don't mind, because they do it so nicely'.

In the spring of 1935 we were told that the Vic–Wells Ballet was to give a gala performance in Cambridge to celebrate the opening of the new Arts Theatre, part of an enterprise due largely to the efforts of Lydia Lopokova and her husband, Maynard Keynes. It was a cold, wintry day when the dancers with Miss Baylis and Miss de Valois travelled down in buses from Sadler's Wells Theatre to Cambridge for this event. We didn't realise how literally the term 'newly built' was to apply, for we arrived at the theatre to a loud orchestration of hammering and sawing, last-minute fixing of doors and final nailing of planks to the stage.

We left our practise clothes and make-up in the dressing rooms, but noticed that these seemed in short supply: two large rooms only for the girls, and one for the boys. The principal dancers were packed into very small 'star' dressing-rooms. But we didn't mind, being full of youthful excitement and enthusiasm at the thought of performing in this new theatre.

With time to fill in between our arrival and the pre-performance class, a number of people decided to have a sightseeing walk round the town. Miss Baylis said that she was going to attend evensong at King's College Chapel and invited any of the dancers who wished to do so to accompany her. I am very glad that I joined her small group. As we made our way from the theatre through the town to the Chapel in a slight sprinkling of snow, we took a quick look at the Backs before entering that most beautiful of buildings. During the service of evensong, the last of the wintry daylight faded and the glimmering candlelight accentuated this beauty. Sitting in those glorious surroundings with Miss Baylis and my fellow dancers, I had feelings compounded of happiness, wonder and thankfulness. Looking back, it seems to me that this service was a dedication to all the wonderful times that we were to have in the city of Cambridge. It was an experience that encapsulated the magic of that moment, as well as being an intimation of my future life and that of many of the dancers who took part in the performances that evening. The happiness was simply to be sitting with Miss Baylis and my fellow dancers and to be conscious of the warmth that her presence seemed, at this moment, to engender among us all.

The gala performance was a great success, and afterwards the general company was given a meal laid out on trestle tables at a nearby hall. Later, we got in our buses, joined once more by Miss Baylis, Miss de Valois, Constant Lambert, Frederick Ashton, Margot Fonteyn and Robert Helpmann, who had been dining as guests of Lydia Lopokova and Maynard Keynes in the newly opened restaurant in the theatre. We all made our frozen way back to London. It was the early hours by the time we reached town and our respective homes but nevertheless we had to be hard at it the next morning, rehearsing Frederick Ashton's *Apparitions*.

Early in 1935 and shortly after the production of *Rio Grande*, we read exciting reports in the newspaper that the Vic–Wells Ballet was to make its first provincial tour – an important step in the history and development of the company and, as we now know, one that was to establish a permanent pattern for the future, enabling the dancers to reach a far wider audience throughout Britain. This first tour was to be organised by

Vivien Van Damm, already famous for his Windmill Theatre, just off Piccadilly Circus, which was to foster the early careers of many a star of 'stage, screen and radio', as the blurb had it in those days. It was to be financed by Mrs Laura Henderson, who was also the angel for the Windmill.

The prelude to all this was a season of two weeks of ballet at Sadler's Wells Theatre, led by Alicia Markova and Anton Dolin, as they were to do also on tour. These two weeks were followed immediately by a week at the old Shaftesbury Theatre, which was then situated, appropriately enough, in Shaftesbury Avenue. I was particularly delighted to be performing at this theatre, which had a rich record of musical comedies such as *The Belle of New York* and *The Arcadians*, beloved by local operatic societies everywhere. It was here, too, that Fred Astaire and his sister Adèle had made their first appearance on the London stage in 1923, dancing and singing in a musical called *Stop Flirting*. In one of their numbers, 'The Which-ness of the What-ness', they danced what was called the 'Oompa Trot'; this caught the eye of a very young member of the audience, Frederick Ashton, who used it many years later in *Cinderella* to accompany the exit of the Ugly Sisters (himself and Robert Helpmann) after they had made a circuit of the stage in the ballroom scene. But a really important event at the Shaftesbury that week was that for the first time Margot Fonteyn was dancing Alicia Markova's rôle in *Les Rendezvous*.

Then followed the first two dates of our tour, strongly contrasting, at Blackpool and Bournemouth. I shared theatrical digs with Richard Ellis in both places; in Blackpool they had been recommended by the stage manager at Sadler's Wells Theatre, Henry Robinson, known to us all as Robbie. He and his wife stayed with us there, as did a rather pretty blonde from the chorus of one of those many summer shows that were a great feature of Blackpool. This particularly cheered Richard Ellis, who always had an eye for the girls.

Balmy Bournemouth had a somewhat enervating effect after breezy Blackpool. The weather along the South Coast was glorious, and the young ladies in the company were tempted to lounge in deckchairs on the sands, in between classes and rehearsals. Although they had their summer dresses on, their bare arms caught the sun. When preparing for the performance that evening, they realised that to disguise the effects of the afternoon they would need an extra layer or two of theatrical wet white, which all ballerinas in those days put on to add an ethereal look in the classical ballets. But, alas, the blue light in the second act of *Swan Lake* brought a curious purple look to their *port de bras* and a right wigging later from the powers that be. The next day sunshades were to be seen on the beach.

In both towns, although we didn't exactly pack them in, the full-length *Lac des Cygnes* proved to be popular. Moreover, the audience liked Ashton's *Les Rendezvous* and were impressed by Ninette de Valois' *Job*. Everyone was excited at seeing a famous ballerina in the person of Alicia Markova, and all admired the vitality of Anton Dolin in his interpretation of Ravel's *Bolero*. It was very reassuring to notice the public's enthusiasm for the young dancers, Margot Fonteyn, Pamela May, June Brae, Mary Honer, Elizabeth Miller, Harold Turner, Walter Gore, William Chappell and Frederick Ashton. Michael Somes had yet to make his mark as a principal. It was in fact a few years before male dancers in the company received the appreciation due to them; the theatrical emphasis in those days was almost exclusively on the ballerina.

During our time in Bournemouth, Miss de Valois with Constant Lambert and her top principals, Frederick Ashton and Robert Helpmann, stayed at a rather posh hotel on the cliff top; but, in the socially-conscious thirties, even they were put in a wing of the hotel known as the 'Pro's Annexe' and reserved for residents who were in the theatrical profession. We lesser mortals managed to find accommodation in one of the more modest of the many holiday boarding-houses, and the boys were able to be a little freer than the girls on the sunny beach and venture in for a dip, as we had to be anything but ethereal on stage.

After the summer break we continued our tour with Glasgow. In view of the long train journey there and our consequent late arrival, you would have thought that we would have had enough sense to make sure that we had somewhere to stay. In those days Glasgow on a Sunday night could be rather dour and forbidding, but Richard Ellis and I boldly set off from the station, walking along the streets of tall, grey-stone tenement houses, with smell of cats in passage ways, occasionally venturing, as the locals say, 'up a stair' and knocking on a few doors, but with no luck. We were beginning to get desperate, dragging our luggage along, my Revelation case seeming to get heavier by the minute.

I had noticed earlier that we were being followed by a young man who would shrink back into the shadows and who appeared not to want to be recognised by us. Finally, I realised that it must be someone we knew and that he was in the same plight as we were; I beckoned to him to join us and I saw for the first time, through the gloaming, that it was the new boy in the company, Michael Somes. Indeed he, too, had nowhere to stay, so we joined forces on our search, the three of us limping tiredly until, down a side street, we saw a dimly lit sign, 'Bath Street Commercial Hotel'. We timidly rang the bell and the owner appeared, was very sympathetic and showed willingness to help three poor, stray lads. The best he could do, the hotel being full up, was to offer us a basement room, with three single beds in it, for thirty shillings for the week. We accepted it immediately and thankfully. Oh, the bliss of finding somewhere on that dark, dismal night – it could have been the Ritz. With this unpropitious beginning, Richard Ellis, Michael Somes and I began a friendship that was to last many years, starting with all our youthful laughter in our 'dorm' in the Bath Street Commercial Hotel.

In Glasgow we performed at the Alhambra Theatre. On first enquiring about its whereabouts, we were met with the uncompromising and unforgettable reply of a passing Glaswegian, 'Oh, you mean that hoos o' hell'! But it turned out to be a splendid place, with stage curtains embellished with a myriad of sequins, which caught the roseate flow of the footlights. We all enjoyed performing there, as we later did at the very elegant but somewhat smaller King's Theatre in Edinburgh, where we went next.

We were all enamoured of Edinburgh's beauty, and became real tourists, walking down Princes Street and popping into McVitie's, where, to accompany our coffee, we made inroads into the tiers of cake stands with their delicious pancakes, scones and, of course, rich shortbread. Well stoked up, we made our way up the twisting route to the Castle and had the splendidly rewarding view of the Firth and the docks at Leith. For a shilling the wonders of the Camera Obscura were revealed, and we had a tantalising glimpse of the community below us within its range, our guide pointing out a much-observed nosy parker pulling aside her lace curtains to spy on the passers-by. It brought to mind possibilities of a Hitchcock thriller. We clambered up Arthur's Seat and caught our first sight of Holyrood, which we later visited, after walking down the Royal Mile and paying our respects to John Knox as we passed his house. I simply loved it all there, and delighted in sending postcards to my friends, writing their addresses with the addition of the word 'England', feeling as I did so that, for the first time, I was really abroad.

Our touring repertoire seemed to meet with as much approval north of the border as it had done in the south, and this was especially so with *The Rake's Progress*. The houses, again, could have been better, but then these were early days.

From all the tours we did before the War, one memory stands out in sharp focus, that of the great cross-section of the theatre world converging on Crewe on Sundays en route for their next week's engagements. Every company that was on tour in England ended up there. A succession of trains arrived at different times of the day and remained for intervals of indeterminate length. The waits seemed endless but were relieved by the varied interests of the passing pageant on the station. Every possible facet of theatrical life was represented. There were members of variety shows, including high-kicking chorus girls in touring revues, whose rather theatrical apparel, complete with high-heeled shoes, contrasted sharply with that of our girls in their neat twin sets and tweed costumes, their balletically turned-out feet in sensible shoes, as approved by Miss de Valois. There were members of companies touring straight plays, the women wearing equally sensible felt hats and brogue shoes, while all the men wore statutory flannel bags and Harris tweed sports coats, mostly from Montague Burton's 'Fifty Shilling Tailors', with now and then a pork-pie hat worn at a suitably jaunty angle. There was always a quick raid on the tea-rooms of the type later made famous in Noël Coward's *Brief Encounter*, with people hoping to catch a cup of tea before the urn ran out and to grab the last of the Banbury cakes.

Constant Lambert would be deep in his crossword puzzle and Miss de Valois making interesting observations on the passing scene, pointing out to Frederick Ashton, who was glumly slumped in a corner, missing his country house weekends, anyone she thought looked remotely Irish. Joy Newton would wind up her portable gramophone in her compartment and she and her companions would be deep into Delius.

The trains in those days consisted of separate compartments for eight people, four sitting on each side, and during the long waits at Crewe Station one could go 'compartment hopping', hence the moving crowds on the platform. Then, at the sound of a whistle, a lucky trainload would move off, to a flurry of last-minute shouts – I remember a cry ringing out from one of the Tiller Girls to her friend Renée, who, having a pleasant exchange with one of Billy Cotton's Dance Band boys, was in danger of losing her connection. Then, at last, it was 'All aboard' for us and off we went, much to our relief, to the next town in which we were to perform.

Once arrived, there was always the dread moment when, having located one's digs, the door would open and one would come face to face with the landlady. The hall that greeted one was covered with linoleum, from the state of which could be judged the quality of the accommodation for the week ahead. No house was heated overall; there was only the one fire in the communal sitting room. In winter what was most dreaded was the icy touch of the lino in the bedroom and the shock as one's feet met the floor in the morning, exceeded only by the refrigerated feel of the bathroom floor. Some of the houses of theatrical digs were divided into separate units, each room catering for sleeping and eating. They were known as 'combined rooms'; a double room at the front of the house was called a 'double front combined' for two people, and the same went for a 'double back combined'. Baths depended on how well the geyser worked – it was apt to explode – and no hot water was allowed in the basin in the bathroom until the landlady had finished washing up the breakfast things. Woe betide you if you disobeyed this rule. Sometimes we had simply a Victorian washstand with bowl and jug for the hot water that was provided in a kettle brought up by the landlady. It was primitive and rough, maybe, but we were young and the company was burgeoning and beginning to attract larger audiences, which was all that mattered. It was well worth the linoleum chilblains.

It was not just the members of the *corps de ballet* who went into these digs, but also principals such as Ashton, Helpmann and Chappell and even Constant Lambert, until one day, Chappell, with reference to his large and imposing figure, said to him, 'Constant, you're too big for digs', so Constant was banished to a hotel! On one occasion when we were playing in Hull at the New Theatre, Michael Somes and I were staying in the same digs as Frederick Ashton. When we were ready to go to class at the theatre we went to Fred's room to rouse him, because we feared that he was going to be late, loth as he always was to get up in the morning. We found that he was still in bed, but the landlady came into the room and said, 'Don't worry Mr Ashton, boys. That's a lovely comfy bed, isn't? I always had a terrible trouble to rouse the Siamese Twins 'cos they found it so comfy too'. The Siamese Twins had been top of the bill at the New Theatre the previous week. Hardly had the words left her lips when Fred was up and on his way. After the performance that evening Fred pulled rank, and Somes and I ended up in his 'front combined' while he rapidly took over our 'back combined'.

Even this, however, fades into relative insignificance when compared to the memories of where we stayed in Manchester in what was the Mecca of all theatrical digs, Acker Street. It had a row of tall, redbrick houses on both sides of a cobblestone road that harassed the feet, especially on a hot August afternoon. Throughout its long history, it had been frequented by all the great stars in their early days, from Noël Coward to Morecambe and Wise. And now here I was in Acker Street, sharing digs with Michael Somes, Richard Ellis, Jill Gregory, Molly Brown and other members of the company.

The landladies ranged in temperament from the fiendish to the absolute dears. Our first landlady had her head encased for most of the day in a mob-cap, but when she served supper, on our return from the theatre, the cap had gone and her hair was a mass of henna-coloured curls, while her face had a thick coating of white powder, with an ample application of popular Tangee lipstick. She looked rather like a poor man's Mistinguett, but could she cook a mean shepherd's pie!

I knew from my avid reading of *Theatre World* that Manchester was one of the most important towns on the pre-London run, known in those days as the 'try-out'. It became a household expression that 'What Manchester thinks today, London thinks tomorrow', a judgement respected by everyone including C.B. Cochran and André Charlot. In fact, on our first trip there a revue was being tried out at the Princes Theatre, later to be bombed in the early part of the War. It starred Douglas Byng and, most fascinating for me, an American silent-film star called Mary Brian, who had played Wendy in a film of *Peter Pan* that I had seen in my early cinema days in Teddington.

By this time on our tour the houses had much improved, but Mr Van Damm, our impresario, organised a few publicity stunts to boost the sale of tickets. One of these was a trip on the Manchester Ship Canal. For us this engendered as much excitement as if it had been a trip on the Grand Canal in Venice. We all made a great effort to look our smartest; Somes wore his Oxford bags and I my checked plus-fours, and the girls were in their prettiest summer frocks and hats. We all assembled down by the canal and then went aboard the boat. The great moment arrived when the car came, bearing the two stars, Alicia Markova and Anton Dolin. Miss Markova, always a fashion plate, her tasteful elegance admired by everyone in the company, looked wonderful in a pearl-grey ensemble and matching hat and gloves. Mr Dolin was sporting a white camelhair summer overcoat; complete with nonchalantly tied belt – very wisely, as we discovered later on, when it turned rather chilly on the water. Here we were, dressed to the nines, floating down the Manchester Ship Canal, weaving our way through the various dredgers and coal-laden barges; never mind the dust and smuts, we felt we were at last in the big time. Looking back, I think it seems genuinely touching that this simple excursion should have meant so much to us all.

Our week's performances were at the Manchester Opera House, and at the back of my mind was the thought that this was where *Bitter Sweet* first saw the light of day and all those tremendous productions of C.B. Cochran and his protégé, Noël Coward. Ballet was not at all unknown to Manchester. Many distinguished companies of those early days had danced there, including that of the immensely popular Madame Pavlova, who had a huge following, not only there but throughout the world. Naturally this more knowledgeable audience had a bearing on our performances and made us feel very much at home; the general ambience was very sympathetic, for Manchester was well in the vanguard of the performing arts. It was indeed a theatre town.

However, since this was our first provincial tour, every town seemed to have its own excitement and individual attraction. At Nottingham it was the Castle, and we all went on a guided tour, starting at the famous medieval inn, The Trip to Jerusalem, traditionally held to be the final mustering point for the Crusades before leaving en masse for the Holy Land.

We performed at the charming Theatre Royal, which was built back-to-back with the local variety theatre. My strongest memory of this is of the time when we returned there at the beginning of the War, when the variety house featured a bill of circus acts, including among the performers an artist called Koringa, who, in the course of her act, writhed upon a procrustean bed of nails. Also on the bill was a turn involving elephants; one night as we were leaving the stage door of the Theatre Royal, one of the elephants was being exercised in the alleyway between the two theatres. Very careful footwork was therefore wise whenever we left our stage door in the blackout, and it was always advisable to make sure that the number eight battery in one's torch was fully charged.

Among the other acts on that occasion were the Flying Arabs, who we discovered to be our fellow lodgers at the digs. They were very charming and quickly allayed the fears of the young ladies among us, who had earlier been somewhat apprehensive about them. Although exotic in appearance, they proved to be delightful companions at the breakfast table, amidst the Shredded Wheat and packets of Force.

Chapter 6

So much for the excitements of our first provincial tour. When we returned home we were happy to have extended our boundaries beyond Rosebery Avenue and to have offered to a wider public the opportunity of seeing our artists and our repertoire of ballets. From the beginning of the new 1935–6 season at Sadler's Wells Theatre, life was never the same again. When I look back at the sudden flood of activity that engulfed my professional life in the mid-thirties, I am amazed that I took the rapid escalation of my career so much for granted – perhaps there was no time to do otherwise. I was seemingly unaware of the rapid development so soon to take place within the Vic–Wells Ballet that would affect me; in addition, there was the involvement with the Ballet Club which took me each Sunday night to Notting Hill Gate to work with the Ballet Rambert. By this time, Ninette de Valois had made Frederick Ashton resident choreographer at the Vic–Wells, but, in spite of this, he still produced new ballets for Madame Rambert, along with Antony Tudor and Andrée Howard. I danced in these as well as in the new productions at Sadler's Wells. It was clear to everyone that Madame Rambert had lost none of her remarkable powers of recognising latent choreographic talent and, with her typically indomitable spirit, she saw to it that the Ballet Rambert also forged ahead.

At this juncture the cold, sober fact was that Alicia Markova had left us, to start the Markova-Dolin ballet company. We all realised what a loss this was and knew that she would be greatly missed. No one felt this more than Margot Fonteyn, who is often quoted as saying at that time that it would take anyone else a considerable while to achieve the status of a ballerina. It is wonderfully ironic that these words were spoken by the one person on whose shoulders this responsibility would fall. She herself had absolutely no idea at the time that she would be the one to fulfil that rôle.

Hardly had the new season begun when, in October, Ashton produced his Sitwell/Walton *Façade*, which he had first choreographed for the Camargo Society. This was followed in November by *Le Baiser de la fée*, to music by Stravinsky and most distinguished décor and costumes by Sophie Fedorovitch. It featured a guest ballerina, Pearl Argyle, as the Fairy and Harold Turner as the virile young bridegroom. Both these artists had worked with Ashton in the early days of the Ballet Rambert. Pearl Argyle made a beautiful, remote fairy, as befitting an ice-maiden coming to claim her human lover.

The third member of the cast was Margot Fonteyn. She entered in the village scene as the young bride-to-be, searching, with shy apprehension, for her bridegroom among the crowd of villagers. The inventiveness of Ashton's choreography was especially to be seen when the six brides-maids helped the bride to dress, arranging her long veil and weaving a wonderful pattern of dance movements, and in the superb *pas de deux* for the engaged couple that was the culmination of the scene. Margot Fonteyn was unforgettable as the radiant bride-to-be, and it was in *Le Baiser de la fée* that one saw her establish an authority on stage as an artist developing a rôle's character.

I have a fond memory of the creation of this ballet when Ashton invited Michael Somes and me to watch him work out one of the *pas de deux*, on strict condition that we made ourselves inconspicuous in a corner of the famous small room that served for board meetings and rehearsals. We sat still and motionless; Hilda Gaunt was at the upright piano, while Ashton choreographed a moving *pas de deux* for Harold Turner and Margot Fonteyn. It seems a miracle to me that he could produce such a master-piece in that confined space, but perhaps the fact that he had for years learned his craft on the minuscule stage at the Mercury Theatre stood him in good stead. A considerable time later, when dealing with a fledg-ling choreographer who feared that the lack of large space might fail to show his choreographic talent to the full, Ashton, in his direct and cool way, said that one could choreograph on a kitchen table and yet show genius.

Another incident in connection with *Le Baiser de la fée* serves to demon-strate the *esprit de corps*, literally, that was essential to the company at that time. In order to make up the required number of couples in the village scene, Robert Helpmann, who was already a principal with a large public following, danced away happily among the *corps de ballet*. And no fuss!

In May, at the end of the season at Sadler's Wells, we were most excited to hear that our one-day visit to Cambridge to open the new Arts Theatre had paid off, for we had been invited to dance there for eight perform-ances in June. The company then broke up for a three-week holiday, but Madame Rambert asked Frederick Ashton, Harold Turner and me to join our old 'alma mater' for a short period at the Repertory Theatre in Bir-mingham, then under the management of the famous Barry Jackson.

His company were rehearsing in the theatre at the same time as we were, and often the young actors and actresses would come to watch our performances from the wings. One night an extremely good-looking young actor asked me jokingly if I could leave behind in the dressing-room the eighteenth-century wig that I wore in the *The Rape of the Lock*, so that he could use it in his rôle in *The School for Scandal*. I said that I didn't think Madame Rambert would be very pleased at that idea! Some time later, when the Vic–Wells were on tour in Bournemouth, Robert Helpmann, who was also making a film called *Caravan* at the time, introduced me to the star, who was lunching with him at the Norfolk Hotel. After Robert made the introduction, the star said, 'I've met this character before, but he doesn't remember me'. I replied 'I'm so sorry, Mr Granger, but I don't recall when'. This to the wide-eyed astonishment of Helpmann that I could treat the matter of celebrity so coolly. It was then that I realised that the unknown actor who had wanted to de-wig me at the Birmingham Rep. had been none other than Stewart Granger.

After our three weeks there, Fred, Harold and I made for Cambridge to rejoin the rest of the Vic–Wells Company in our short season at the Arts Theatre, after which the next event was to be the second provincial tour.

Chapter 7

The 1936–7 season proved to be the most progressive artistically that this band of closely knit dancers had yet seen. We now realised that we were a real company and one that had achieved an identity. Audiences were sitting up and taking notice in a more emphatic way, and it was to be a time of immense advance in choreography and presentation. As a team we felt, not surprisingly, that it was like being in a hive of intense activity, inspired by the personality of Miss de Valois, who saw to it that no one, including herself, sat still for a minute!

The cast of most ballets comprised the whole company, so that in the rehearsal room we came to know one another and, most importantly, learned how to react to one another on stage. The rehearsals mirrored the performances in that we danced full-out in both. We were served by two great choreographers, Ninette de Valois and Frederick Ashton, and given a plentiful supply of one-act ballets full of small supporting rôles, which we had to perform with the closest attention to detail. We liked having to make the most of them, in gesture and nuance of character, while not neglecting the technical execution of the steps. For Ninette de Valois, 'marking' was a cardinal sin, and from day one full attention to all these aspects of technique, style and interpretation was demanded. There was a constant cry of 'Do it!', a favourite method of cajoling that informed the whole attitude and philosophy of her theatre life.

She choreographed *Prometheus* for the first part of the season; it was not a very convincing production and did not remain for long in the repertoire. This was rapidly followed by Ashton's *Nocturne* to music by Delius, a composer much loved by Constant Lambert, and how splendidly he conducted it. The ballet was well cast; Helpmann played a cynical, rich young man partnered by June Brae, equally rich and sophisticated. Margot Fonteyn, supplying the pathos, was a poor little seller of violets. The scenario was by Edward Sackville-West and the décor and costume design by Sophie Fedorovitch, whose pattern of columns and balustrades framing a view over the city of Paris reflected the title of the music, *Paris, the Song of a Great City*. Full evening dress was worn, the men complete with 'toppers', while a group of strangely dressed maskers mocked the unravelling of the plot in the manner of *Le Bal masqué*. Ashton's rich choreography reached its climax in the enchanting solo by Margot Fonteyn with her basket of violets. Later, sadly jilted by the rich gentleman, she was comforted by a lone figure, played by Ashton himself, who was first seen looking over Paris, lifting his arms to welcome the dawn and then turning to walk downstage. Bending over the flower-seller, he offered her consolation as the curtain fell to end the ballet. The *mise-en-scène* was superb and Sophie Fedorovitch perfectly matched Ashton's style of choreography, bringing a sense of elegance that had not thus far been seen on the Sadler's Wells stage.

At this time in the thirties, television was in its extreme infancy when the Vic–Wells Ballet made its first excursion to Alexandra Palace, the original home of television transmission and commonly known as 'Ally Pally'. The company, having assembled outside Broadcasting House, was taken there in buses to give a live performance of excerpts from the ballet *Job* on 11 November, to form part of a tribute for Armistice Day. When, having changed into our practise clothes, we trooped into the studio to rehearse, there in the middle on a table was a model of the Cenotaph with people blowing smoke around it to simulate the pea-souper fog outside through which we had just travelled. This was to be used as a prelude to the serious subject of Miss de Valois' work. We were all very pleased to be pioneers of ballet on TV, and, although at this time only a few sets were owned by private individuals, the public could always pop into the basement of Selfridges or go to Imhof House on the corner of Tottenham Court Road to watch a demonstration model. We were very impressed by this new method of entertainment and gazed at the huge camera, mounted on a trolley, that followed every movement.

This performance was the first of several televised over the next three years, including *Les Patineurs* and *Checkmate*, and the series concluded just before war was declared with the transmission of a version of *The Sleeping Princess*, as it was known in those days. The technicians found it a strain to cope with such a big work involving the whole Company and having many scenes in three acts, even though this time more than one studio was put at our disposal. All went well, however, until the hunting scene. After we had all made a quick change from Act I, we lost our way back to the appropriate studio, different from the one we had just left, arriving only in time for the last chords of the farandole. As we entered, looking rather dishevelled, it was only then that Robert Helpmann and Ursula Moreton, who were leading the dance, realised they had performed the entire scene alone. However, the watchers on their tiny sets might not have noticed, or perhaps might have thought that they were missing the rest of the dancers as a result of the misty snowstorm effect that in those days was apt to cause interference to the picture at frequent intervals.

To reflect for a moment on the economic conditions that prevailed then, we four males, Michael Somes, Richard Ellis, Paul Reymond and I, felt moved to protest when we were offered thirty shillings as the fee for rehearsing and dancing in two performances of *Les Patineurs* on television at Ally Pally, and asked to see Miss de Valois in her office. We decided that Richard, who was thought to be the toughest of us all, should speak on our behalf and ask if we could possibly have this amount raised to two pounds. We all trooped in together to be told that this was not possible and that, as a result of our impertinence at making this request, we would not do the performances. We subsequently heard that a fresh cast of four members of the company was preparing to take our place. However, Ashton objected to this cast change, whereupon we were summoned to Miss de Valois' office. In her most endearing manner, she told us that in adopting this rather unpleasant commercial attitude we had been led astray by some of the older members of the company, and that she was willing to forgive us and allow us to do the performances. We left the office, forgetting our rôles as negotiators in the delight at being re-instated. In all honesty I cannot remember whether we actually got the increase or not.

Les Patineurs had been first put on at Sadler's Wells Theatre on 16 February 1937. Ashton had created one of his most scintillating ballets, with a score by Constant Lambert from music by Meyerbeer, which he had shaped perfectly, as always, to suit each episode in the work, from the entrance of the skating couples going round the rink to the exciting finale. There was a lively succession: the virtuoso dancers in blue, Elizabeth Miller and Mary Honer; the white *pas de deux*, Robert Helpmann and Margot Fonteyn; the red girls, Pamela May and June Brae; and, making a great impression, the young Harold Turner with his splendid elevation, his pirouettes ending the ballet and continuing as the curtain fell and then lifted again, while the audience greeted the whole performance with tremendous enthusiasm. Adding to the excellence of the choreography, music and dancing was the set designed by William Chappell, a perfect foil to his enchanting costumes for the skaters. *Les Patineurs*, in fact, became a popular success, and from that first night onwards until the present time has been performed by many companies, both here and abroad.

Then followed one of those outstanding collaborations within a team of distinguished figures: Lord Berners, who had written a score for Diaghilev; Frederick Ashton; Constant Lambert; and, on top of this, a libretto adapted from a work by Gertrude Stein. The result of this collaboration was *A Wedding Bouquet*. In the first production, the words were sung by the chorus of the Sadler's Wells Opera Company in the orchestra pit; later, during World War II, they were recited by Constant Lambert, sitting in the stage box. I found the rehearsals fascinating, and they were attended in the final stages by Gertrude Stein and her friend Alice B. Toklas, who always followed three paces behind in a large, shady hat. Gertrude Stein, a very distinctive figure with her well-sculptured head topped with a grizzled Eton crop, seemed to favour wearing waistcoats, her thumbs firmly placed in the pockets. Lord Berners would sit at the piano with Constant Lambert while he hammered out a point or two of the score, and for me it was riveting to see this work in progress with such dynamic personalities. I admired the whole production, with members of the company dancing every rôle, whether large or small, to perfection.

We all played it straight and the humour inherent in every provincial wedding came out, but not without a certain pathos. Margot Fonteyn again provided this element as she sat with her little dog, Pepé, danced by Julia Farron, who guarded her against any intrusion on her grief at having been rejected by the Bridegroom. June Brae was wonderful as Josephine, another guest, who, having taken one sip too many, was asked to leave. 'Josephine may not attend a wedding'.

The company seemed to find the ballet very comical, as indeed they might, the pace being set by Ninette de Valois, entering at the beginning as the maid, Webster, 'a name that was spoken, that was spoken, that was spoken' – the reiterative accompaniment being part of the Stein method. During rehearsals, however, Fred asked me how I liked it all, and I replied that, for me, it had moments of great sadness. 'You're right,' he said. But I personally, was very happy, because he had given me the small rôle of Arthur, an obsequious character. As the guests were lining up for the rumbustious waltz at the wedding reception, Arthur advanced to the footlights and mimed to the words, 'Everything is going on nicely, nicely, nicely', which could have been an appropriate Stein-like comment on my career at that moment.

Things had been going on nicely for me at the Ballet Club as well. Early in 1936 I was fortunate to be cast by Antony Tudor in his *Jardin aux lilas*. The trials that this choreographer suffered, one way or another, are well chronicled, but I was not much of a help; for, at the same time as *Jardin*, I was rehearsing two new ballets at the Vic–Wells and was able to spare only the briefest of time to rehearse at the Ballet Club. On the Sunday night when this celebrated work made its first appearance, Antony fought to put the finishing touches to it until curtain-up. I remember how he came on the stage, wished us good luck and, for good measure, sprayed it with lilac perfume before proceeding, as usual, to turn the capstan-like wheel that opened the curtain, and the ballet began.

It wasn't the smell of lilac blossom that made the atmosphere so potent but Antony's choreography, combined with the music of Chausson, played with such feeling by Jean Pougnet on violin and Charles Lynch on piano, and I felt immense gratitude at having been part of that memorable night. Shortly afterwards, two of the principals, Maude Lloyd and Hugh Laing, left for Manchester to dance in a pre-London try-out for a play with music called *The Happy Hypocrite*, also choreographed by Antony Tudor. Consequently, at the Ballet Club, Maude's role was danced by June Brae from the Vic–Wells, by permission of Ninette de Valois, and Hugh's role was given to me. The fact that I should follow him in this part of the lover so relatively early on in the proceedings still fills me with disbelief.

Back at the Wells, owing to the constant drilling of Ninette de Valois and her insistence on proper attention to footwork and to exact placing on stage, a precision was to be seen that would one day establish the ensemble's international reputation, when there would be spontaneous applause for the work of the *corps de ballet* during our tours abroad.

It is interesting, too, to look back at that period when there was no public funding to support us. But there was no lack of enthusiastic support from various societies such as the Vic–Wells Association; and money came, in more modest guise, from their members' annual subscriptions and from donations made as a gesture to Miss Baylis. At the end of the season, representatives from these Societies would come on to the stage carrying their Dorothy bags, and the clinking of coins could be heard. Miss Baylis gratefully received them before giving her yearly rallying call to the audience to turn up in force in the season to follow, for, if they did not, the whole enterprise was in danger. There was also a note of reprimand if there had been a falling-off in attendances for *Hamlet*, for instance, but all of this was taken to heart and in fact helped to strengthen the bond between theatre and audience and form a close association that reinforced Miss Baylis's idea of one large family. The Vic–Wells Association, in fact, has lasted to this day and is a much-loved adjunct of our two companies.

Audiences, however, seemed subtly to be changing. We were attracting a slightly more affluent section of the public, and from parts of London distanced from the Cut and Islington. We still retained our loyal followers from the early days, including gallery-ites such as the staunchest of our supporters, Miss Pilgrim, who, pilgrim by name and by nature, had made her way from the Old Vic to Sadler's Wells, becoming the doyenne of the 'gods'. Her reedy soprano voice, giving vent to 'God Save the King', floated down to an otherwise silent house at the end of every season. But now, in the Dress Circle, one glimpsed Lady Oxford, always a keen balletomane, and a well-known American heiress, Alice von Hofmannstahl, née Alice Astor, who lived in a splendid house in Regent's Park near to Barbara Hutton. It was here that she gave the party on the first night of *A Wedding Bouquet*, at which, of course, the guest of honour was her country-woman, Gertrude Stein; and it was Alice who introduced the Duchess of Kent to our performances and especially to those on the last night of the season. At the beginning of the War, Constant Lambert lived in a cottage in the grounds of the house until, during the Blitz, a bomb fell that caused damage and sadly killed Alice's chauffeur.

To return to 1937. In spite of this evidence of the wealth of some members of the audience, finances were still a bit tight with Miss Baylis. In this Coronation year, she decided to send the company to Bourne-mouth during the actual week of the Coronation because she feared that, with the whole of London *en fête* celebrating this great event, the houses would be empty. This was a serious mistake, since, as it turned out, the crowds flocked to the theatres in the evening, giving an extra roar to 'God Save the King' at curtain time and I am sure that they would have been as happy to fill the Wells as they did the Palladium, the freezing cold weather of that week being an added incentive to come inside. The crowds at Bournemouth went to the Pavilion Theatre on the pier with their sticks of Coronation Rock, and the audiences where we played were very sparse; in the end we gained nothing by the move from London, but in spite of that we enjoyed ourselves. Margot, Pamela and June all looked very festive, wearing white satin scarves with 'Coronation' embroidered on them in red thread. As we made our way after the morning class towards the pier to join the throng, we thought of the procession of King George VI and Queen Elizabeth making its way to the Abbey and of a monarch whose reign we were so relieved to welcome after the anxieties of the Abdication.

A friend of Fred had sent him a case of champagne and some tins of caviar, and Fred invited a small group of us to join him in the Pro's An-nexe of the hotel following the evening performance. Afterwards we gath-ered on the Solent cliffs and watched the fireworks display exploding out to sea. Constant said that the mass of stars falling from the rockets made the sky seem full of incandescent tresses of eighteenth-century wigs, their beauty being reflected in the sea. Although we were all missing the Coronation revels in our beloved London town, I, perhaps mellowed by the champagne, felt that there was nowhere better to celebrate the new reign than high up on the cliffs with this band of Vic–Wells dancers. It was a lovely night, even though we weren't in London.

1937 was also the year of the Paris Exhibition. This had already been hailed throughout the world as an important event. Pavilions would be built on both banks of the Seine, *Droite et Gauche*, and every country would be represented, demonstrating the merits of its culture and industry. Much was made of the fact that, even in this arch-Stalinist period, Russia would be included, rivalling Germany and America. The visual arts, theatre, music, dancing and general lifestyle of the many countries were to be featured, and visits paid by many famous theatrical companies. When it was announced that, under the auspices of the British Council, the Vic–Wells Ballet were to visit Paris to represent Great Britain, our excitement knew no bounds.

Arthur Bliss was to compose the music for a new ballet called *Checkmate*, choreographed by Ninette de Valois, and a selection of our successful one-act ballets would also be performed. This being our first tour abroad, we set to work with a will. Ninette de Valois's choreography was highly evocative of the stratagems of the chessboard, and every member of her company was involved. Margot Fonteyn, although already becoming an important member of it, was merely a black pawn in the powerful finale of the attack upon the Red King. Claude Newman was a Bishop encased in stiff buckram material, and there was a tense moment when, always apt to be a bit truculent, he complained that he couldn't move his head enough to see where he was going. William Chappell found his headdress 'so bloody heavy' that it gave him a headache. These costumes were the work of the well-known poster designer, McKnight Kauffer, and did indeed prove to be a little difficult to dance in, though Ninette de Valois dealt with the difficulties with suitable despatch.

Wearing a headdress shaped like a castle, I, along with a fellow-sufferer, John Nicholson, was a Red Castle in the first scene. As usual, owing to the shortage of male dancers, a certain amount of doubling-up had to take place. This meant that after leaving the excitement on stage as the defeated Red Castles, John and I had to rush into the wings, change our costumes during the voluptuous tango danced by June Brae as the Black Queen, who was finally to settle the old Red King's fate, and come clattering back as Black Castles. Apart from the boots and headgear, our costumes were large surcoats from shoulders to ankle in the buckram so much favoured by the designer. Every movement we made as we stormed in and out in our stiff encasements was accompanied by a loud clanking noise, but, thanks to the tumultuous Bliss score, the audience was unaware of a single clank. The whole production was planned with great theatricality, starting with two figures, Love and Death, poring over their game of chess in front of the striking drop-curtain, which was lifted to reveal the *corps de ballet* of Red Pawns standing motionless on the floorcloth painted as a chessboard, before breaking into their distinctive staccato movements. The story then unfolded dramatically, the dramatis personae being the Red and Black Knights, the senile Red King and his attendant Queen, all governed by the ruthless strategy of the Black Queen.

It was decided that the ballets that we were to take to Paris in addition to *Checkmate* would be *Les Patineurs*, *Façade*, *The Rake's Progress*, *Nocturne* and *Pomona*. There was also to be something of a bonus for me in that, together with Michael Somes, Paul Reymond and Alan Carter, a very promising young dancer who had just joined the company, I was to stay on in Paris for a further two weeks to attend classes given by Alexandre Volinine, a former partner of Anna Pavlova. We were told this by Ninette de Valois a week or two before we left. The company would pay for our classes, but we would have to move out of the hotel provided by the British Council for our short season and find other accommodation. We would look out for a suitably inexpensive hotel as soon as we got to Paris and save what francs we could to pay for it, with some supplement from our Post Office Savings Banks. Paul arranged to stay with friends he had there.

Everything in preparation for this was exciting, such as queuing in Petty France for our new passports, when even the surprise shock of our passport photos seemed fun. How wonderful finally to be crossing the Channel and disembarking at Calais, besieged by voluble porters in their blue smocks and then *en voiture* for Paris. Our initial taste of French cuisine was on the train and was a revelation. For most of us it was our first trip abroad, this time for real, and everything was foreign and different.

In Paris Michael and I, in accordance with the management's arrangement, were to share a room in a hotel called the 'Avenida' off the Champs-Elysées. When we arrived there, we immediately opened the French windows and stepped out on the little balcony to stare down for the first time at the bewildering surge of taxicabs, with the music of their 'squeaky horns' and passengers clinging for dear life to the platform at the rear of the buses. In spite of our long journey we couldn't wait to start sightseeing and to make our first excursion to the Exhibition.

No one's first impression of Paris ever fails to thrill, but at this time of the 'Expo' we were completely overwhelmed by it. Every bridge over the Seine was beautifully decorated, and music gently serenaded you as you crossed it. At night everything was floodlit. The whole effect was splendid yet unobtrusive and seemed to encapsulate all I had ever dreamt Paris to be like. We arrived in June but, even though the official opening had taken place in May, parts of the Exhibition were still not ready because of strike action, and in fact it seemed to us that every day a new pavilion opened with suitable aplomb. At our first visit we were impressed by the beauty of the whole setting but somewhat startled by the sinister aspect of the German Pavilion, with a huge swastika, daringly placed in front of the Russian Pavilion. The latter was flanked by two huge concrete figures of a man and a woman armed with a hammer and sickle; much was made of the fact that this gave the impression that they were placed there in order to smash the swastika. I personally was very touched by the Polish Pavilion, constructed like a huge column that had been hollowed out. Stark in its simplicity, it contained a few artefacts simply displayed with a soft accompaniment of music by Chopin. Within two years this arrangement of pavilions was to be remembered as prophetic.

One result of the strikes was that the specially constructed theatre for the visiting companies was not ready in time for any of them. Instead, we would perform at the famous Théâtre des Champs-Elysées. It was while making my way there that I met Robert Helpmann's mother (whom I had previously seen in London), his sister, Sheila, and his brother, Max. Mrs Helpmann, Sheila and Bobby were as like as three peas in a pod, while Max, the odd one out, must have taken after his sturdy Australian father. Anyway, the first thing his mother blurted out when we saw each other was that 'Bob's got a boil on his bum and won't be able to dance on the first night'. This was a staggering announcement on the Avenue Montaigne, and it was awful to contemplate that our leading dancer would be missing from our first important performance in Paris. However, it transpired that he could manage to mime and shuffle on as the senile Red King in *Checkmate*, a rôle in which he was supreme, and that Claude Newman would have to dance Helpmann's role in *Façade*. That news made me prick up my ears, as I was Claude's understudy in *Façade*. This meant that in the opening programme I would be in all three ballets: as a skater in *Les Patineurs*, as a couple of Castles in *Checkmate*, and in the opening number in *Façade*.

The first night seemed to go well, and the friends who had come over from England to cheer us on regaled us later with descriptions of the audience in front, the ladies resplendent in the *haute couture* of Chanel, Lelong and Balenciaga. After the evening was over, we trooped back for a set meal provided by the British Council; very plain, but at least French and more exciting than a meal from the days in Acker Street.

Nonetheless, we felt rather low-key; it would have been nice to have had some sort of reception after all that excitement and effort. It made us rather angry to read in Constant's *Times*, bought next day on the street corner, of the grand occasion at the British Embassy, brimming with exalted guests gathered to celebrate the first night of the Vic–Wells Ballet. However, there was a footnote to this article saying how odd it was that not a single dancer from the company was asked, not even the Director, Ninette de Valois. This was a poor reflection on whatever powers were responsible for organising that important event.

We saw as much as possible of the truly great Exhibition, but the performances and life around our theatre seemed very muted. That could have had something to do with the fact that we could find only one poster advertising the Ballet, and that was down a side street near our hotel. It was not, therefore, surprising that *le tout Paris* didn't accord us a welcome, because *le tout Paris* didn't know we were there.

However, we were invited to one reception, a luncheon party given by a well-known hostess, Lady Mendel, an American married to an Englishman, Sir Charles Mendel, at their house in Versailles. It was on the Sunday of the last day of our season, but, because this was France, we were performing that evening. The whole company was invited and was welcomed most graciously by our hostess, dressed in elegant navy blue to complement the pale blue of her hair. She was charming and friendly, and personally showed us round her garden, the grandeur of which reflected that of her house. Among the splendour of the flowers she had placed full-length mirrors at the end of the paths, backed with well-manicured box hedges, and these caught one's reflection during the stroll; a strange notion but somehow a captivating one, in keeping with the fact that she was a well-known decorator to the upper crust. As it was a glorious June day, the luncheon was held in the garden on beautifully set tables with a staff in attendance. There was champagne to accompany the delicious French food and I tasted my very first *fraises de bois*. This certainly made up for the anti-climax of our first night, and after this sumptuous hospitality we returned to Paris feeling like a million dollars. We gave a rip-roaring performance at the Champs-Elysées that night which Paris did not easily forget.

In between dancing each night at the theatre and exploring Paris and the 'Expo' during the day, Michael and I searched for an inexpensive hotel for the second part of our stay. We were told that there would be many such in Montmartre and, wandering round there, we went into one with the word 'Hôtel' in flickering red lights over the door. We tried to explain what we needed in very poor French to a rather dubious-looking man behind the desk in the dim foyer. At this moment we longed to be 'up a stair' in Sauchiehall Street, which then seemed to be highly desirable by comparison. It was not until we came back to Paris after the War that we would discover the fascination and charm of the *Quartier Latin*; on that first acquaintance we two found it rather intimidating. The Manager at the 'Avenida' suggested, with great understanding, that we try Montparnasse as being more in our line of country. We followed his advice and found the small 'Hôtel de Suède' wholesome and well scrubbed, and booked a room with a balcony and a view that seemed to belong more to Purley than to Paris. The manager, too, spoke passable English, which would prove to be a great help.

It was extraordinary to what extent, in that week's season, the company seemed to take on a more cosmopolitan air. During the stage rehearsals at the theatre we would be invaded by a horde of photographers, chief among them being Iris. I looked on in envy as he was taking shots of the principals in *Checkmate*, but John Nicholson and I, encased in buckram and wearing our castle head-dresses were, perhaps with good reason, not included. It was a pity that this activity and enthusiasm among the photographers did not extend further to cover adequate general publicity for our visit and for a prodigious repertoire. As we have seen, there were few if any advertisements in the press or on posters, and possibly the worst omission was a failure to invite the all-important critics. There is a certain procedure attached to a company's tour abroad, which it is disastrous to ignore, especially for a city like Paris. Nevertheless, if at this time we didn't win it over, Paris, with its wonderful and unique atmosphere, certainly won us.

Contributing to this atmosphere as residents of Paris were three Russian ballerinas of great renown: Olga Preobrajenska, Lubov Egorova and, most glamorous of all, Mathilde Kschessinska. The first two lived their life of exile in comparative simplicity, especially Olga, who was the poorest of the three; but all had been great dancers of the Tsarist days in St Petersburg. They were to become teachers of our own Margot Fonteyn, Pamela May and June Brae, who would go over to Paris to study with them during the long summer break, accompanied on the visit by their mothers.

Margot and Pamela favoured both Preobrajenska and Egorova, but June and her mother were much taken with Kschessinska; beautiful, vivacious and full of charm, she had gained the affection of the last Tsar and become his mistress, which must have put her in good stead in the Imperial Ballet Company. Many years later when we were dancing at the Maryinsky Theatre in St Petersburg, I was fascinated to be shown a small window, high up in this famous building, out of which Kschessinska was allowed to wave her lace handkerchief as the young Tsar-to-be arrived in his carriage for the performance. Many legends have grown up around her and I was also told how she was protected by the Grand Duke, Serge Mikhailovich, who showered her with jewels and built for her a small palace, the balcony of which was used by Lenin for his famous speech to the crowds at the start of the Revolution.

On the Royal Ballet's second visit to Russia I was able to visit the theatre museum in St Petersburg (or rather, Leningrad). The woman guide spoke excellent English and, when I pointed out a photograph of Olga Preobrajenska performing her renowned Sailor's Dance, I told her that I had had mime lessons from this ballerina in Paris after the War. She became very friendly and spoke of Olga with warmth; I sensed that she felt great sympathy for her. A little further along was another photograph, this time of Mathilde Kschessinska, but then, as I was told about Lenin's speech-making on her balcony, her manner hardened to reflect her disapproval. It seems that this ballerina had sided with both parties during the Revolution and, when she came to Paris in 1917, had found space in her luggage for a tray or two of jewels.

Perhaps that was part of the legend, but the facts were that she had become La Princesse Romanovsky-Krassinsky and lived her exile in Paris in the fashionable Passy district with her husband, the Grand Duke André of Russia. I was included in the small group from the company whom they invited to dinner during that first week in Paris, and I still remember the charm of their villa; it was as I imagined such a one would be in a play by Chekhov or Turgenev. The small round tables covered to the ground by cloths were crammed with silver frames containing pictures of the Russian nobility. The food was wonderful and served from huge silver tureens, brimful with a succulent meat dish, and this was of course preceded by a soup to which I felt many a carcass had contributed its stock.

Oh, what a night of wonder that was, so redolent of Tsarist Russia that, in spite of the warm evening, one felt one could hear the bells of the sleighs in the snow of St Petersburg as they swept in line along their paths on the Nevski Prospekt. This evening, together with the lunch party on the last Sunday at Versailles, provided two highlights amongst the more muted colours of the picture of our Paris season. In the 1950s I was to be reminded of that night, when Madame Kschessinska gave a class to the company on stage at the Royal Opera House in Covent Garden; she was still vivacious, her eyes sparkling, and I remember being fascinated by the fact that she wore a hairnet, a rather pedestrian adornment that could not but make one think of Ena Sharples, except that Madame's net was clearly of a finer mesh.

As far as the teaching of these three ballerinas was concerned, I think Margot favoured Olga above the other two – a good thing, as she was the one to instil strength and style in her pupils. She had not the grace of the other two, but she had achieved her success by applying herself with intelligence and hard work.

After seeing the company off to England, Michael and I took our luggage to the new hotel. We had been told to report to Monsieur Volinine's studio and to get details of our classes there and, having met Paul at the Métro, we set off, to find that the studio was in an apartment building near the Etoile. It was large and airy with good-sized windows; on the walls were many pictures of M. Volinine, photographs with and without Madame Pavlova.

Just around the corner we found a small restaurant with prices that were within our means. We knew that we could afford only one substantial meal a day, and decided that this would be lunch, following our morning class. Not wishing to slip up by experimenting with unknown dishes, we settled for a regular regime of a small steak, fried potatoes and a glass of beer, very welcome after a strenuous class; but we did discover a marvellous cheese to end our meal – Fontainebleau. We sat at a table outside on the pavement in the summer warmth, lingering as long as we could in the way normal to a Parisian, but unfamiliar to the patrons of a Lyons Corner House.

Miss de Valois had told us that we must write down the complete class, step by step, and so after lunch we returned to the hotel and, on the foolscap notebook brought from home, recorded the whole works. It was a very trying chore. Thank goodness Michael, who was not a schoolmaster's son for nothing, helped me a great deal; I am a poor speller even in English, but battling with the French of the classical ballet vocabulary was too much. However, after spending most of every afternoon doing our homework, we made a welcome escape to the Exhibition, first popping into the patisserie to have a huge, gooey pastry, which, we noticed, was cheaper in Montparnasse than elsewhere.

The evenings were our own, and we wandered leisurely round the different pavilions while studiously including the sections devoted to the traditional foods of the country in question. Here there were plentiful free samples to be tasted, much larger and certainly more in the *haute cuisine* category than were those to be had at the Ideal Home Exhibition at Olympia. So that saved us a few francs. There was a large notice in our room to the effect that no food was to be taken up to it; this was rather a blow, as we'd planned on doing just that if we were staying in. However, we cheated a bit and took some slices of neatly wrapped *jambon* and one of those long baguettes, broken in half and smuggled in the inside pockets of our jackets. But we openly carried an apple or banana, as did most of the other guests, and this seemed to pass unchallenged.

Alas, the fruits of our afternoon labours were also unchallenged, for Miss de Valois never mentioned our classes with Volinine or asked to see our records of them when we returned. But, then, that was part of the wonder of her personality; Paris had been dealt with; it was now history and so full-steam ahead towards an even more successful and exciting season at the Wells.

During this fortnight we managed to see performances at the Folies Bergère and at the Casino Theatre – standing room at the back of the stalls. This being 'Expo' time, these were very lavish and featured international stars, Josephine Baker at the Folies and Maurice Chevalier at the Casino. Miss Baker was a star in every sense of the word, appearing in the opening number wearing a train of pink ostrich feathers that seemed to go on for ever – when she came on stage, every light in the auditorium went on to heighten the general excitement. Next, she was a ragged *gamine*, singing and dancing cross-eyed, her favourite gimmick, to the music of an organ-grinder; then a Louisiana woman, singing a lullaby to rock her baby to sleep. It hardly had time to drop off when the stage was besieged by brigands who made away with the cradle and set fire to the handsome Southern home. When Miss Baker returned to her baby, she found it gone. The clever stage effects in all this involved enough dry ice to do justice to the fire in Atlanta in *Gone With The Wind* and produced a great deal of coughing in the stalls during the interval.

But the most sensational number, *'Nuit d'Alger'*, came in the second act. The curtain rose to reveal a back street in Algiers. The star entered at the top of the stage wearing a voluptuous red cloak, singing in a very melodious voice about the hot, tempestuous, Algerian night. As she made her way downstage, four huge, black male dancers entered, the last one ripping off Miss Baker's cloak to reveal a lack of costume that would not have been allowed by the Lord Chamberlain at home. There followed a dance, very dramatically choreographed, for the five of them; the four men lunged at Miss Baker, threw her about the stage, lifting her with unbelievable acrobatic skill. No ballerina had ever received such indignities. It brought the house down. Margot told me later that she had been to see the show with her mother and that, at the end of this number, Mrs Hookham had turned to her and said, 'Oh, I do hope Fred hasn't seen this', no doubt fearing for her daughter lest she be the victim of his choreography next season, newly inspired by this Folies number.

It was great to see Maurice Chevalier, the famous film star, in the flesh, but, unlike Miss Baker, he did not appear throughout the show. The second half was his alone, though, when he was heralded by the Bluebell Girls, all wearing straw hats, who made an entrance in front of a black cloth depicting one huge straw hat.

After finishing our morning class towards the end of the first week, Monsieur Volinine's secretary told Michael and me that there were two gentlemen who would like to speak to us in her office. We went in to find L. Franc Scheuer, an American living in Paris and familiar to us by name, since he was the Paris correspondent for *The Dancing Times*. His friend was a ballet critic for a newspaper called *Candide*. They explained how, on hearing that a few of the dancers from the Vic–Wells Ballet had stayed behind in Paris to study with various teachers, they had tried to track us down. Having found out that there were English boys taking classes with Monsieur Volinine at his school, they asked us if we would have coffee with them, when they would explain their mission.

So off we went to one of the many cafés surrounding the Etoile, where they told us of their great admiration for the work of the Vic–Wells Ballet; its inventive choreography, the superb musical direction of Constant Lambert and the general *mise-en-scène*. For them it had been the most exciting production of ballet to be seen in Paris for years, and this delight had been shared by those who had managed to find out about our short season. But they were, in equal measure, dismayed at the way we had been presented. When they had seen the brilliance of the principals and the excellence of the *corps de ballet* it had clearly come as something of a revelation to these two knowledgeable gentlemen, and what was so sad was that they had had no chance of telling Ninette de Valois what they and other like-minded people thought. They made us promise that we would convey their feelings to her and generally to spread the news of the company's actual success.

They were anxious that we should enjoy the rest of our stay in Paris, and offered us seats to see Serge Lifar dancing at the Opéra in his new ballet, *Alexandre le Grand*. We accepted gratefully and arranged to meet at the Opéra *en smoking*. In spite of our rebuff at the British Embassy, it now appeared that we hadn't, after all, taken our dinner jackets in vain; we joined the audience in the stalls with every man among them wearing a black tie. Michael and I were elated by our first visit to the great Opera House, majestic in every particular. Our seats were next to those of a very elegantly dressed American lady and her daughter, and we became quickly attuned to their soft and cultivated voices. Hearing us talking, the mother turned to us and said, 'Are you two boys from England?' When we said that we were, she continued, in a sympathetic way, to accord with our Englishness. 'We think that what that dreadful woman did to your King was simply awful.' We were a bit taken aback and embarrassed on that subject, but put as brave a face on it as possible and stared intently at our programmes, inwardly pleased that they were on our side, since Mrs Simpson was after all an American. It was a brief but fateful reminder of the unfortunate happenings at home during the period of Abdication.

Nevertheless, there we were, Michael and I, sitting in the stalls in our dinner jackets talking to sophisticated ladies from New York and feeling every minute more cosmopolitan.

The performance was most impressive; to us the company seemed a little wild, but we had noticed while with Monsieur Volinine that the French students were more extrovert – I had a feeling that they found us rather the opposite. On that huge stage it was not surprising that the artist was trained to show considerable panache, as we were to realise when it was our turn for an opera-house stage. It was exciting to see the great Serge Lifar in performance when only a short time before he had been a fellow guest at the dinner party in Passy. We knew of the rôles he had created in the Diaghilev Company and that in London he had been in a Cochran revue, in a ballet, *Luna Park*. This had been choreographed by Balanchine with music composed by Lord Berners, later to be used by Frederick Ashton for his *Foyer de Danse*, representing his view of Degas. *Alexandre le Grand* was what could be called a vehicle for Lifar, and what's wrong with a good vehicle? I recall that I was impressed by his stylish dancing and exotic appearance and by the way he could walk across that grand stage with such majesty, particularly when he went the length of a high rostrum that stretched right across it, representing a wall in Alexandria, wearing a cloak with a tremendously long train. Trains seemed to be in fashion that year of the 'Expo'.

We made our way back to Montparnasse on that warm summer night, dreaming of dancing in the opera houses of Europe and of international fame. Alas, soon our trip would be over; the following Sunday we were due to leave for home. However, there was yet to be a glorious finale. Our benefactors told us that there was to be a gala of dancing at the Grand Palais in the Champs-Elysées on the Saturday before our return. They had been invited in their official capacity as critics and had obtained two extra tickets for us. So it was on with *le smoking* again! The setting indicated that it would indeed be a grand occasion, with most of the countries participating in the 'Expo' being represented by their dancers. The Paris Opéra Ballet were to perform to the famous ballet music from *Faust*. Germany was sending its most controversial modern dancers, demonstrating a Central European style and heralding what we now call Contemporary Dance, in which they led the field. There were to be artists from Italy, Holland and Spain, in spite of the political turmoil in that country at the time. Denmark would testify to the stylish Bournonville tradition and the United States were sending the Rockettes, all the way from the Roxy Cinema in New York; in the event, this turned out to be the most exciting item of all.

When our last day *chez Volinine* arrived, we felt rather sad and not a little disappointed that we seemed to have made little impression on our brilliant teacher, but I didn't then realise, as I did much later on, how right it was of Ninette de Valois to send us to him and to what extent Michael and I had gained by these lessons. At the time I was, however, greatly impressed by his style and dignity as a teacher. There was an effortless grace about him with the black velvet court trousers, stockings and patent-leather practise shoes, a sense of style shared by Pavlova, whom he partnered in the famous '*Gavotte Pavlova*'. They demonstrated this quality whether they were performing in a bullring in Spain or in the Golders Green Hippodrome. I realised, too, that we could not expect much individual attention in this crowded class of young French dancers of various ages, but I do remember feeling the benefit of our two weeks' work there, in gaining greater breadth and freedom of movement. What happened to all those class notes that I copied out so diligently I don't know, but years later I did hear former members of the Royal Ballet School saying that Michael had taught some of what he called 'Volinine steps', and I often wonder if our great teacher in Paris even knew that Michael returned there after the War as partner to Margot Fonteyn in a season of *The Sleeping Beauty*. For all we knew, we too might have been in class with future Roland Petits or Jean Babilées.

The gala at the Grand Palais that Saturday evening, our last night in Paris, exceeded our wildest dreams. The building was decorated with flowers to a lavish extent known only in that city; a large stage was constructed at one end of the great salon and we had excellent seats. At Sadler's Wells we did our best with limited resources to produce an adequate ballet to the last act of *Faust*, but the version performed that night incorporated the entire Opéra Ballet company, interpreting all the different moods and nuances of that beautiful music and including a tempestuous bacchanal, with young members from the Opéra Ballet School running about, serving goblets of wine. The German contribution was stark, vainglorious and nationalistic.

Then came the number one hit of the evening with the Rockettes. Back home I had, of course, seen the Tiller Girls and just previously in Paris the Bluebell Girls, all excellent in their way, but the Americans were a revelation. There were so many of them that their line stretched from one side of the great proscenium arch to the other, and those kicks were so regimented and precise in height; it was as impressive as Trooping the Colour on Horse Guards Parade. Many years later, when television was in full swing, I saw a documentary of the 1930s that included the Paris Exhibition of 1937 and a wonderful shot from an old newsreel of the Rockettes' performance at the Grand Palais; the commentator said that they were the sensation of Paris. At the end of their performance that evening, folding doors were peeled back from one side of the auditorium to reveal tables groaning with glorious French food, which we all fell upon with gusto. Champagne flowed as the Seine itself. What a way to end our first trip to Paris. We said goodbye to our two benefactors, who had contributed so generously towards our personal enjoyment during this stay, not least in the encouragement that they had given us in respect of the Vic–Wells Company.

The following day we made our way to the Gare du Nord, still feeling full of *joie de vivre* and happy to know that we were leaving with the certain knowledge of the high reputation the company had gained. But, alas, we quickly came down to earth when we noticed many couples, mothers and sons, young wives and husbands saying obviously sad farewells. When we enquired as to what was happening, we were told that they were people saying goodbye to their loved ones, who were on their way to fight as volunteers in the Spanish Civil War.

Chapter 8

On my return from the never-to-be forgotten trip to Paris, there were still a few weeks before we started on our third provincial tour. By now this had begun to seem almost routine, but, much to my delight, Pearl Argyle rejoined us this time. Then it was October and back to Sadler's Wells Theatre to begin our new 1937–8 season. We still retained a glow from our Paris experiences, kindled by the fact that we presented *Checkmate* for the first time in London. There was even a lingering scent of backstage at the Théâtre des Champs-Elysées to accompany its success; and, as well as the choreography, décor and costumes, the music of Arthur Bliss received much praise.

From our point of view the performances seemed to have an added confidence, and, if we had not drawn the crowds to overflowing down the Avenue Montaigne, we noticed a great difference in those making the trek down Rosebery Avenue. These had increased both in number and in the interest they were showing in the Islington Dancers, as the patrons of the Royal Opera House were apt to call us in our early days. With *Checkmate* we became aware that we were attracting a more knowledgeable audience, helped incidentally by the fact that Bliss's score for the film *Things to Come* was becoming very popular. There was an ingredient now that had not been there before, and we felt we were being accepted by a wider public. It was splendid, too, that it was largely the success of Ninette de Valois' ballets *Job* and *Checkmate* that had brought this about, particularly since she was never one to relish success for herself but only in so far as it increased the progress of the company as a whole. The spirit of endeavour that she engendered spread to her dancers, and we all felt that we were on our way.

There was a revival of an Ashton ballet first produced by the Camargo Society called *The Lord of Burleigh*, with music by Mendelssohn arranged by Edwin Evans, and designed by a young artist of distinction, Derek Hill, replacing the original work of George Sheringham. I was overjoyed because I was to dance a *pas de trois* with Pearl Argyle and Richard Ellis. He and I were two beaux who wove ourselves around the lady. The choreography had great charm and was full of Ashton's expressive *ports de bras*. Pearl wore a very fetching Pre-Raphaelite bonnet, while Richard looked, as always, very handsome with his finely sculptured head; but I had to wear a hat that was rather a trial. John Hart, who had just joined the company as a young lad fresh from winning the Genée Gold Medal of the Royal Academy of Dancing, said, probably to console me, 'Well, only you could get away with that'. Some time later, when Ashton revived this number for Fonteyn for a charity performance, with two leading dancers as her admiring partners, I noticed that the hat had gone, so maybe Jack Hart was right. He, of course, later had the distinction of becoming one of the three young directors, along with Michael Somes and John Field, whom Frederick Ashton appointed to help him run the company. Performing in *The Lord of Burleigh* gave me great pleasure, but unfortunately not lasting pleasure to the public and it did not have a very long innings. Nevertheless, it was part of a great season and of a period of real recognition for the company, justifying the faith of all those who had supported the Vic–Wells Ballet in the beginning.

It was a sad irony that, at this moment of success, one of the main architects responsible for it, Lilian Baylis, died on 25 November 1937. The story goes that, knowing there was trouble with a production at the Old Vic and that a first night might have to be postponed, something she always dreaded, she went to the theatre to deal with the problem while suffering from a heavy cold, which later proved to be fatal.

It seems extraordinary that the memory of her is constantly with me even though I knew her for so short a period. Many times I think of her humour and her wisdom, which still applies to so many facets of our life today, when her down-to-earth common sense is sorely missed. Most of all I am proud that I became one of her artists. I treasure the letters that she sent when re-engaging me at the beginning of each season, even quoting Miss de Valois' remarks about my progress. These letters could also contain unequivocal comments on how to behave in the coming season, laying down rules about wearing apparel and the obligatory prac- tise clothes – black tights, white shirts, white socks, one set to wear and one in the wash, black practise shoes; all these to be purchased oneself. She really did believe that cleanliness was next to godliness. One was also reminded that there was a no-performance, no-pay clause in operation!

On 26 November we performed an evening of ballets at Sadler's Wells Theatre, ending with *Job*. When this finished, there was a minute's silence and the curtain fell. The audience left the theatre quickly and when I came out to the stage door there were a few fans, but no Miss Pilgrim. The following night there was another performance of ballet, and there after- wards, huddled in her accustomed corner outside the stage door, was Miss Pilgrim. I said to her, 'Miss Pilgrim, I missed you last night', and she replied, 'Oh, I didn't come last night; I just sat at home and thought of that wonderful woman and of all the beauty she had brought me'.

Towards the end of 1937 the building fund, which had been organised by the company to raise money for extending the premises through giving yearly galas, had enough in the kitty to purchase the two houses next to the stage door of the Sadler's Wells Theatre in Rosebery Avenue. The aim was to make space for two rehearsal rooms, extra dressing rooms and wardrobes; the whole new area was to be known as the Lilian Baylis Extension. Throughout all the rebuilding activity, with hammering and banging during the day, we carried on with rehearsals and performances, only to be released from the turmoil by going on tour. As our connection with the Old Vic entitled me to say, 'For this relief, much thanks'. The thanks were most heartfelt when, at the end of the 1937 season and similarly in 1938, we revisited Cambridge, again dancing at the Arts Theatre, where our original week's season was extended to two.

It was in 1937 that I became aware of Margot Fonteyn's great attraction to Roberto Arias. One day, when a group of us were relaxing and sunning ourselves on the Backs, Tito, the name by which we were then calling this young Panamanian undergraduate, was unaware that I had my camera at the ready. I had by this time graduated from my box Brownie to the extravagance of a six-pound Kodak, and took a couple of snaps of him, idly picking a blade of grass. When the photos were developed I gave copies to Margot; it was only when we all met up again with Tito in New York after the war that she told me that she had carried these two pictures in her handbag ever since that day.

I was always fascinated to read about the Footlights Revue performed in Cambridge during May Week, especially about the period made famous when the young undergraduate star of the show was Jack Hulbert and the costumes in it were designed by another undergraduate, Norman Hartnell. By the time that we were putting on our seasons at the Arts Theatre, members of the company had become well known at Cambridge, and Robert Helpmann, who was very much an all-rounder, was asked to produce the Footlights Revue. Bobby invited me to watch the final dress rehearsal on the Sunday following the last night of our season.

At the performance, undergraduates filled the theatre and some of the sketches in the revue drew upon the popularity of the ballet company, being written by promising young talents up at the University. In those days the cast was completely male; the talented undergraduates of the fair sex did not appear until after the war, when such as Maggie Smith, Eleanor Bron and, more recently, Emma Thompson were to participate. In the intervening years, it has been amusing to read about some august figure, perhaps a prominent man in Parliament, the Diplomatic Corps or the Civil Service, whom I remembered as performing a witty take-off of 'one of the girls who danced at the Wells' or some other rag. Tito, in fact, with one of his brothers, Modi, danced a vigorous pastiche of a South American samba. The ensemble numbers were expertly directly by Bobby and had a great reception.

We always looked back with great delight on those tours in Cambridge. On my way to the stage door I would sometimes catch a glimpse of Lydia Lopokova walking along the narrow lanes that surrounded the theatre, on her way to have dinner before the performance with her husband, Maynard Keynes. She would be in evening dress, and I remember her scurrying along wearing a pair of bright red velvet shoes with buckles. The curtain didn't go up until 8.30 pm and so it wasn't a case of high tea, as it was in our digs at home or elsewhere at that time. Madame Lopokova was known to cast a highly professional eye on the proceedings and offer rather sharp criticism on occasions.

I first met Arthur Marshall at about this time. He was in Cambridge in his capacity as secretary to Lord Rothermere, and I remember him in his sports car saying goodnight, with his characteristic laughter, outside King's College. Hardly had he finished speaking when his foot was on the accelerator and he was off like a shooting star. As the public were later to discover when he was on the panel of the television show *Call My Bluff*, he was indeed a star and famous, too, for his ready laughter. However, he had his sterner side, as I understand his pupils at Oundle were to discover when he was a housemaster there. No nonsense in the classroom! And it was no surprise that he was to become Colonel Marshall at SHAEF Head-quarters in Versailles during the war.

It was in 1937 that Bobby Helpmann, thanks possibly to Miss Baylis, had the great good fortune to play Oberon in *A Midsummer Night's Dream* at the Old Vic, with Vivien Leigh as Titania, in a production by Tyrone Guthrie, using the music by Mendelssohn, choreography by Ninette de Valois, and décor and costumes by Oliver Messel. This was all most not-able, with the Old Vic transformed by sweeping red curtains in the Victorian fashion. John Mills played Puck and Ralph Richardson Bottom. It was such a success that the run was repeated the following Christmas; but in the meantime Miss Leigh had been cast as Scarlett O'Hara in *Gone with the Wind* and was hard at work in Hollywood. Her part was taken by Dorothy Hyson, who made an exquisite Titania.

During Helpmann's absence, a new male star emerged back at the Wells – Michael Somes. After he had created a sensation with his leaps across the stage in *Les Patineurs*, he had attracted a great deal of attention from the public, and so it was decided that he would have the lead in the forthcoming ballet, *Horoscope*. The astrological theme was Constant Lambert's idea, and with the choreography by Frederick Ashton, the décor and costumes by Sophie Fedorovitch and the superb dancing of the company, this work was a perfect synthesis of all their talents. Constant's score was wonderful throughout, starting from the overture written in the form of a palindrome and played in front of a drop cloth painted by Sophie in cool, lunar colours. Pamela May was superb as the Moon, her dancing beautifully placed, and she demonstrated the unique style with which she was to be associated. Margot Fonteyn as Virgo portrayed a deceptive simplicity, tentative shyness and moments of absolute joy, to give a rounded interpretation of this role; one saw her range and the fullness of her talent, justifying the faith that Miss de Valois had had in her. What captured the audience with Michael Somes was his compelling virility and, again, extremely individual style. He was truly a Leo, a leader showing vigour and ruthlessness and, at times, tenderness. To create the richness of all this, Ashton's choreography reached new heights.

I was the understudy for one or other of the Gemini, danced by Richard Ellis and Alan Carter, and went on several times, nerve-wracked. It was jolly difficult, but I managed to get by. Sophie had earlier come to me to say that it was very awkward to paint the complicated design on the costumes that she had made for Leo's male followers. It would make it easier if she could do this while the costume was being worn by someone, and asked me if I would be a model for the complete *corps de ballet*. I adored Sophie and said 'Yes', mainly because I loved the idea that she came to me knowing that I would agree to help. So the whole of one Saturday afternoon I stood in the wardrobe room at the top of Sadler's Wells Theatre, putting on leotard after leotard whilst Sophie painted the complex pattern on each. When she had finished, I was stone cold from the water-paint. However, she invited me down to the canteen afterwards, bought me a cup of tea and we chatted on for a while. Talking to Sophie with her knowledge, common sense and understanding of what was needed in the ballet was, as always, wonderful. When she died, far too early in life, the company lost a wise friend as well as an artist and designer of great distinction.

This resoundingly successful ballet ceased to exist when, following the Nazi invasion of Holland, it had to be left behind – orchestra score, costumes, scenery – as the company, who had been touring that country with it, made their escape and managed to return to England. *Horoscope* was never reconstructed or danced again, and only a concert version of the score exists today; but for those who saw it, a perfect memory remains.

During the 1938 season, conditions at Sadler's Wells Theatre changed for the better because of the new rehearsal rooms. We had the luxury of simultaneous classes for the men and the women of the company, not having to wait for one or the other to finish and vacate the only room, as we had done before. It was also a relief that we did not have to go through the front of the house in our practise clothes to the rehearsal room; now we could work at all hours, not just when the audience wasn't there. We could warm up before a performance and even during the show, and in fact the new rooms were in constant use during the day and in the evening. Ninette de Valois made important use of this new dimension in building up classes for the future school that she always had in mind, and for which she was already assembling a knowledgeable teaching staff.

One person who benefited from this new aspect of the Vic–Wells was a young dancer called Moyra Fraser, who, at the age of twelve, came with her mother from her local dancing school in Sutton and was representative of the new intake of pupils. I first met Moyra at a company party given in the Wells Room after a first night. Her parents were friends of a Mr and Mrs Duff, friends of Frederick Ashton. They later made a name for themselves through the ciné films they had taken of Ballet Club productions. These included *Foyer de Danse*, with Ashton and Markova and all the original cast, and several other important ballets in the Rambert repertoire, now stored in their archives; when given an airing nowadays they create great excitement and interest. Pearly Duff, whom I knew well from those days at the Ballet Club, introduced me to Mrs Fraser and her daughter, who was wearing a red velvet cloak with a white fur collar over her best party dress. That was the beginning of a lifelong friendship with the Fraser family: Moyra, her mother and father, her sister, Shelagh, and, briefly, her brother, Nigel, who sadly, as a young army officer, was killed in the war.

It is strange that at this time, in spite of all the obvious portents, we were not more conscious of what was so soon to engulf us. Some portents came in strange guise; as early as December 1936 one of the firemen on duty at the theatre told Michael and me, as we were waiting to go on for the Apprentices' Dance in Act III of *Die Meistersinger*, that there was a reflection of a tremendous fire in the sky, south-east of the city. At the end of the evening we were told that the very dramatic sight was the destruction by fire of the great Crystal Palace, once beloved of the Prince Consort.

Rumours were put about that the fire was deliberate, since in the event of an air raid the mass of glass in the building would reflect the searchlight beams and, like a huge mirror, become a vivid landmark by which enemy bombers could navigate. At the same period in Teddington we would look up to see the Graf Zeppelin rounding the curve of the Thames, as it frequently did; there would be whispers that one of the briefings on these trips was the careful charting of routes for future wartime raids on London. Far-fetched as all this was, it demonstrated how people fostered the idea of the shadow of war. Then came the Munich crisis, bringing the shadow closer.

But, as everybody else did, we carried on with our daily lives and with what at the moment was an exciting event in prospect, a visit to Dublin. To Ninette de Valois this must have seemed a satisfying achievement, taking her successful young company to the city which was within easy reach of her childhood home, 'Baltiboys'. It was a pleasure to appear at the Gaiety Theatre, of which we had heard so much. We all made a special effort to make Ninette de Valois proud of her company; it was a moving experience to be part of such a group coming from London to perform to her fellow countrymen.

For most of us it was our first visit to Dublin. We explored the Liffey and I particularly liked the eighteenth-century town houses with their splendid front doors surmounted by handsome fanlights; among these was Oscar Wilde's house in Merrion Square.

Having heard about a swimming pool called the 'Forty-Foot Drop' outside the city, we took a train out to it. The journey was delightfully casual, with various stops to allow cattle to cross the line or to enjoy a friendly encounter or two with the local farmers en route. No matter, for we arrived eventually, delighted to find ourselves by the sea and, in spite of the forty-foot hole being rocky and rough-hewn by normal swimming pool standards, we thoroughly enjoyed our dip.

In those days the management of the theatre stipulated that the outgoing company had to pack their costumes, scenery and props and leave the building after the final night's performance. So after the Saturday evening show we all boarded the overnight ferry to Liverpool. Among our fellow passengers was the team of racing drivers led by the world-famous Siamese Prince Bira, who had been taking part in an international rally in Ireland that week. He had had a considerable triumph and been awarded a large silver cup, and, to celebrate this, was to give a large party on the top deck. When it came to his notice that the Vic–Wells Ballet were on board, he extended the invitation to us.

To the top deck we all went, where the huge trophy cup stood on a table and was constantly filled with champagne and Guinness to provide 'Black Velvet' for the numerous toasts to the success of His Royal Highness. We sat in deck chairs or milled around the deck on the warm summer night. There was no absence of high spirits, brought about by the magic of the night's celebration, and one or two of the partygoers took to aiming a deck chair at the waves, until there was a cortège of these chairs strewn upon the water, rather reminding me of the punts leaving Teddington Lock in my 'Melrose' days. When we finally disembarked, there was a slight mishap; while it was being unloaded, one of the racing cars veered sharply to its right, pinning a member of the team against the side of the hold and injuring him – fortunately, as we later heard, not seriously. Then on we went, sleepily, into the train for Euston.

During the 1937–8 season we added *Harlequin in the Street* to the repertoire, a ballet choreographed by Frederick Ashton and first performed at the Arts Theatre, Cambridge, in a production organised by Maynard Keynes. Michael Somes and June Brae danced the two leading rôles, and the ballet brought Alan Carter to the attention of the public. He was the young dancer who had been with us during our visit to Paris, but who did not stay on with Michael and me to study with Volinine. He had tremendous style, and excelled in a succession of very slow pirouettes performed with grace, bringing his lively personality to this work, which was very well danced by everyone and proved to be a successful addition to the growing number of ballets at the Wells.

The Sleeping Princess was performed there for the first time on 2 February 1939. The whole company were naturally delighted and suitably impressed by the addition of this great Tchaikovsky ballet, which had always been the jewel in the crown of the Maryinsky Theatre in St Petersburg in the Tsarist period. And jewels there then had been, in reality, worn by the ballerinas – rich gifts from their noble admirers, this richness being reflected in the lavish settings and costumes.

It was a different matter for us, however. We soon realised that we would not be swaggering around the set in rich apparel, for the amount of money made available for the production of this traditional masterpiece was extremely small. Nadia Benois, having the right national and artistic background, was a good choice as designer and did her best, but she must have been as disappointed as we were that the resources were so inadequate. However, despite having the look of a utility version, the production wore well and proved always to be a popular item in our repertoire, furthering the careers of so many young dancers. After Constant Lambert lifted his baton to introduce the heralding chords of the overture, which was to mean so much to us throughout the ensuing years in opera houses throughout the world and which for me has never lost its magic, the curtain went up and the enchantment remained until the final fall.

Over the years many of the titles of the fairies attending the Princess's christening have changed. I remember there being a Camellia Fairy, as I was her Cavalier. Our blond club wigs were pressed into service and we were issued with golden ribbons to tie round our heads to give the appearance of princely consorts. In Act I we discarded the ribbons and let our wigs blow about in suitably rustic fashion, joining the girls' *corps de ballet* and taking up garlands of flowers for the Garland Dance. The Princes, who arrive from East, South, West and North to woo the Princess and support her in the Rose Adage, also wore 'clubs' with the princely decoration. Ashton hated his headgear and, being who he was, constantly changed his version. I remember that on one occasion he had a sort of cloche hat worn at a rakish angle with a feather stuck in it, and, on another, a kind of turban; but he finally settled for a genuine French sailor's hat, minus the pom-pom but covered with beige satin to match his costume.

Despite the trials and tribulations, *The Sleeping Princess* proved to be to the public's liking and the company danced it beautifully and enthusiastically. It was, after all, a great challenge to inherit this classic so soon after the formation of the Vic–Wells, but its members proved their ability to meet it. The décor and costumes worked themselves in and became familiar old friends over the years; looking at pictures of Fonteyn, so beautifully posed in her rôle and photographed by Gordon Anthony, it is easy to see why.

This production was shown to great effect at a gala performance given at the Royal Opera House on 22 March 1939 to honour the visit of the President of the French Republic, Monsieur Lebrun, and his wife, in the presence of King George VI, Queen Elizabeth and Queen Mary. It was a great occasion for all of us and especially for Constant Lambert, who had the great joy of conducting the Royal Philharmonic Orchestra. We danced Acts I and III of *The Sleeping Princess*, and between these acts Sir Thomas Beecham conducted a performance of Debussy's *Iberia*. The audience was ablaze with tiaras and orders, and around the ground level of the horseshoe to the auditorium stood a circle of guardsmen, their breastplates and helmets reflecting the lights from the stage throughout the entire performance.

We were all called on stage at the time the curtain was due to go up, but we spent about an hour there waiting for the King and the President to arrive. We were intrigued to notice a very high rostrum, placed downstage just behind the stage curtains, on which stood a newsreel camera, the nozzle of which poked through the red velvet, with the cameramen ready to capture the arrival of the Royal party. The resulting film would, in those pre-television days, be shown in newsreels in cinemas throughout the world.

Many of the girls' tutus had been jollied along with an extra scattering of sequins, and for the Polonaise in Act III all the principal ladies with tutus had long lengths of cotton-backed satin attached to the back of the costumes in colours to match. This was to add a little to the grandeur, with these trains being held up by young girls in the company playing the part of pages.

It was a great and glorious night. Nobody minded the long wait, entertained as we were by Helpmann's impersonations of various members of His Majesty's Government, whom he depicted as having just one last brandy at the French Embassy, where they had been dining before the performance. Our laughter, the grandeur of the setting and the occasion, the presence of the highest in the land together with that of a whole range of diplomats from European courts, all this we thought back upon when, in a matter of months, we were at war. For the following six years the Royal Opera House was to become a place in which to entertain members of His Majesty's Forces; later, once the GIs had arrived in the middle of the war, the house would resound to their jitterbugging, competing with the even more deafening explosions of bombs, doodlebugs and V2s. Few of us on that gala night would have believed it if we had been told that the next performance of *The Sleeping Princess* that we would give in the Opera House would be in 1946 to re-open it after the war, again in the presence of King George VI, Queen Elizabeth and Queen Mary, but with the addition this time of the two young Princesses, Elizabeth and Margaret Rose. Even more incredible would have seemed the fact that the Opera House was to become our future home.

Following the production of *The Sleeping Princess* in February, a new ballet was presented on 27 April, called *Cupid and Psyche*, and destined to be our last pre-war work. It was choreographed by Ashton, the designer was Sir Francis Rose and the music was composed by Lord Berners. The whole work smacked somewhat of its country-house conception, but it gave Julia Farron her first opportunity to star, and justified Billy Chappell's earlier and accurate assessment of the young dancer's potential. She was partnered by Frank Staff, the young South African who started with me at the Ballet Club in the early thirties and later also joined the Vic–Wells. It was an excellent partnership that promised well. *Cupid and Psyche* did not, however, meet with much enthusiasm from the public or the company, but I loved it, mainly because I was given the chance to dance in a quartet of young men, representing Zephyrs, in which we wore huge wings. My three companions were very good dancers indeed; there was a great deal of twirling, whirling and jumping about and I had a hard job keeping up with them. Whether I did or no, Sophie Fedorovitch said to me one day, in her low and always confidential tones, that I danced well in this number and managed to give a feeling of flight. I never received such an accolade again. Forever after, I think I must have been grounded.

After *Cupid and Psyche* we had a short tour, which included dancing again at the Arts Theatre, Cambridge. Margot Fonteyn seemed to have an added confidence on stage and received even greater acclaim from the undergraduate audiences. Perhaps the knowledge that, like Daisy, she had pulled it off with *The Sleeping Princess* gave her that extra command.

I feel that I could be forgiven for remembering this last pre-war visit with such fondness, joy and yet, even at the time, an incipient sadness at the transience of the youthful wonderment that Cambridge always held for us members of the ballet. Michael and I managed to get rooms in a picturesque old pub in the centre of town, and I recall walking home without a care in the world after the many late supper parties that lasted until dawn. The weather seemed to be perfect, as indeed it was that last summer before the war, and no drop of rain fell to spoil outings in the punt. I think the Cambridge friends we made in those last few years before 1939 were special, and the Vic–Wells in that time had become successful and secure.

Chapter 9

After the summer break we set off for a northern tour. We opened in Manchester and then went on to Liverpool, and it was there, at the Royal Court Theatre, that we gave our last peacetime performance, on 2 September 1939. It had, of course, become increasingly obvious during the stay in Liverpool that war was imminent, but we never admitted to one another that it was inevitable. In the middle of the week a trial black-out went into operation, creating absolute confusion with trains, buses and cars, since the future refinements had not yet been effected. Apart from this, however, life went on as usual, especially in the theatres; Liverpool at that time was not only a smart city, but one with a fine repertory theatre, while also playing host to first-class touring companies. It had a very active social life, which included visits by the Sitwells, and this was augmented by the passengers of transatlantic liners that docked in this thriving port.

'The day war broke out...', as that great music-hall comedian, Rob Wilton, used to say in his monologues, the company were travelling on to our next date in Leeds, but on the way we saw placards with the words 'War Declared'. On arrival in Leeds we heard that all theatres were to be closed for the duration of the war, and this was later confirmed on the wireless. On the next day, Monday, we travelled back home and the company was disbanded until further notice.

Nevertheless, after about two weeks, we all received a letter saying that the company would start work again and that, although there were no immediate plans for re-opening in London, we would set off on a provincial tour. We would reassemble in Cardiff, and go on to include Leicester, Leeds, Birmingham, Southsea, Brighton, Cambridge and Nottingham.

This tour, confirmed by the Administrator of the Old Vic and Sadler's Wells, Tyrone Guthrie, did much to encourage us. We had at first felt, as did the rest of the country, a sense of unreality at being at war, and for us there was the threat of losing our livelihood and of saying farewell to the company and our friends. During this tour we would all receive a basic salary and, if the attendances justified it, a weekly bonus as well. In the event the audiences were very good and we thought we would be in the money. But a notice then went up at the stage door to say that now it would be possible to re-introduce contracts and to return to our regular salaries. Goodbye to all that.

Because of wartime restrictions it would have been quite impossible to take an orchestra on this tour, and so Constant Lambert and our company pianist, Hilda Gaunt, ended up in the orchestra pit playing two pianos; this they did for nine performances a week, including three matinées, and in addition they both played for classes and rehearsals. The workload was immense.

We took with us a large repertoire of one-act ballets: *Les Sylphides*, *Harlequin in the Street*, *Checkmate*, *The Gods go a-Begging*, *The Rake's Progress*, *Les Patineurs*, *Horoscope* and *Façade*. Most of us were in all of these; as far as the *corps de ballet* were concerned, there were no second casts, for we could not run to them. The girls as always bore the brunt of having a double dose of *Les Sylphides*, which was the only ballet repeated in the programming to make up the full complement.

Being back on our basic salaries we all stayed in digs, of course. I was with Michael Somes, Billy Chappell, Bobby Helpmann and Frederick Ashton when Fred made his well-publicised declaration that he would read aloud from the Bible every day, beginning at the beginning, and that when he had reached the last pages the war would end. Billy was the only one of us who had the courage to protest, but alas in vain.

Constant was much to the fore at this time, having a much more active rôle in the running of the company, and he had the idea of working with Ashton on a new ballet to be called *Dante Sonata*. His close ties with the musical world as well as with that of the ballet, established as far back as his association with the Diaghilev Company, made him an ideal partner in this collaboration. He and Fred had worked successfully with the music of Liszt before, and in this case it was to be with the sonata *d'Après une Lecture de Dante*. It was daring and enterprising to start a new ballet so soon after the company had re-assembled and with the future still much in doubt. I remember that, after he had chosen his cast, Fred asked each one of us if we were willing to rehearse a work that, who knows, might not even be produced; but as early in the tour as Southsea we had our first rehearsal.

The cast was divided into two groups: the Children of Light, led by Fonteyn and Somes, and the Children of Darkness, led by Brae and Helpmann. Constant played the piano at most of the rehearsals, which were made special by the fact that everyone involved was keyed up to make it all a success; never was there a closer collaboration among the artistic team. We used to walk along the seafront at Southsea on the way to rehearsals in the old-fashioned theatre, the beaches practically deserted and fortified by barbed wire and tank traps against a possible invasion. We all loved the ballet and were pleased to be back in harness. The principals were superb and Fred choreographed a brief but anguished solo, wonderfully executed by Pamela May.

Although Tyrone Guthrie had said earlier quite categorically that we would not return to London, in fact we did so when the theatres started to re-open there, and we began a season at Sadler's Wells Theatre in December 1939. The next month *Dante Sonata* was produced there. The décor and costumes were by Sophie Fedorovitch, and, as one might expect, in perfect harmony with the simple but dramatic message of the ballet, which was that in war no one wins. The work ended with the crucifixion of the leaders of the Children of Light and of Darkness, their followers around them grouped in sorrow. One must applaud Ashton's deft handling of the choreography in portraying the emotional climax of the work, in which it was wonderful to dance. *Dante Sonata* raised the tenor of our wartime season, which was extended by a week because of its success.

After another provincial tour we returned to the Wells in full force. On 24 April 1940, Fred's Bible reading paid off and his ballet *The Wise Virgins* was produced, danced to the music of J.S. Bach arranged and orchestrated by William Walton. By this time it had become possible to reinstate the orchestra. There was a distinguished set by Rex Whistler, who also designed costumes. Fred choreographed a delicate solo for Margot in which she wore a long, flowing, white dress; she performed this again many years later when I organised a Charity Gala at the Coliseum, and she overwhelmed the audience there by the simple perfection of a style that had by that time become the hallmark of her career.

This season had made us feel that things were relatively normal again. The war not having started in earnest, we were lulled into a sense of false security. Indeed, it was later referred to as the period of the 'phoney' war, and this feeling was reinforced by the news that we were to tour abroad in Holland, not then at war with Germany, followed by two weeks entertaining the British Expeditionary Force in Belgium and France.

We assembled at Liverpool Street Station, to travel to Harwich and there embark for the Hook of Holland. The tour was due to start on 6 April at the Royal Theatre in The Hague, a rather daunting prospect; at that time the Germans had not made a move to invade the Low Countries, while the Allies were settling in behind the Maginot Line. There were, however, many obvious signs that things could not remain that way much longer. So, as we gathered on the platform at the station with customary pre-tour 'seeing-off' groups comprising parents, friends, fans, young men mostly in uniform who were engaged to young dancers in the company, and some anxious young husbands and wives, a few of us were feeling rather apprehensive, having either heard the latest news bulletin on the wireless or read in our morning papers that there was a certain amount of agitation about a German spring offensive in the Low Countries. But apart from all that, our spirits were high at the prospect of a tour abroad and, anyway, the officials from the British Council had assured us that there was nothing to worry about. It was marvellous, too, to be dancing in Holland for the first time.

We had hardly started to cross the North Sea when we saw for ourselves the grim realities of war at sea. As our Dutch vessel, very brightly lit during the night voyage, wove its way through the hulks of half-sunken ships torpedoed in the shipping lanes, it was a cold and sobering thought to remember all the men who had died on these convoys, giving their lives to bring food and supplies to our island fortress. No wonder that, when we went below decks to have a meal from the tables groaning with food, Miss de Valois, always patriotically aware, very quietly said, 'Don't grab at the food; they'll think we're starving'.

We found The Hague entrancing, with tulips raining down on us from above during our calls at the end of the performance, a new sensation for us in those days. It seemed that they enjoyed and admired our performances of Ashton's *Dante Sonata*, maybe because of its theme of good versus evil in which neither side appears to triumph; its special success was due, perhaps, to the relevance it had to the uncertainty of the times. There was a most enjoyable party at the British Embassy after the performance.

The next afternoon we went by bus to Hengelo, a town very near the German border – so near, in fact, that we could see smoke coming from the factory chimneys of a German town. It was far enough from The Hague, however, to warrant our staying in a hotel after the performance. During our journey to Hengelo we noticed a great deal of military activity: barbed wire everywhere, heavy concrete tank-traps at all the bridges over the canals, and a heavy presence of troops, fully armed at the alert. While preparing for our performance, we heard that all military leave had been cancelled and the trains taken over by the government in this national emergency. That night we got very little sleep, as we could hear the continual rumble of lorries plus the sound of heavy hammering, which, we were told the next day, was the frantic preparation to provide some sort of air-raid shelter.

In the morning, we left for our third town, Eindhoven, with much relief at getting away from the German border, but with a great feeling of sadness for the poor doomed town of Hengelo and with memories of that packed theatre two nights before. I shall never forget the enthusiasm that greeted our performances from an audience who must have been aware of the imminent danger they were facing. It was, in fact, two days before the invasion, with all the horror that was to follow.

Entering Eindhoven our spirits lifted a little. The town was beautifully set out, with vast beds of tulips, and it was, of course, extremely important and famous for its huge Philips factory, which contained a splendidly equipped theatre where we were to appear. Our day there seemed almost a respite after the anxious time in Hengelo. On Thursday 9 April, leaving our hotel early in the morning, we started off for Arnhem. The performance the night before at the Philips theatre and the general feeling of a calmer atmosphere in Eindhoven was quickly dispelled as we reached the outskirts of Arnhem. Making our way through the town we saw barbed wire, and soldiers in full battle order with guns and drawn bayonets. All the bridges spanning the canals were heavily fortified with concrete tank-traps, and the troops guarding them examined our papers in great detail. Down every canal we could see endless queues of barges – not a surprising sight in Holland – coming from neighbouring countries, even from Germany, for the two were not yet at war. Little did we know that stacked in the false-bottomed holds were German troops, waiting for a signal from the fifth columnists before going into action. In the event, the troops would clamber out of the barges, a whole series of waterborne Trojan horses, and, supported by their airborne divisions, capture the city.

At last our visit to Arnhem was over. It had been a gruelling day: the seemingly interminable journey from The Hague, our warm-up class at the theatre on our arrival, and then the performance. When this had finished, Ninette de Valois was presented with a bouquet by a little girl who later rose to world fame as Audrey Hepburn, and she and her mother attended the party after the ballet. It was a great relief to board our buses and return to The Hague after what was to be our last performance in Holland and, for the people of Arnhem, the eve of their being engulfed by enemy occupation and war.

The journey back will live in all our memories. As our buses sped towards The Hague, we looked out to see passing lorries and tanks filled with troops going in the opposite direction. Later we were told that we were the last civilians to travel along that road until after the German invasion. We left Arnhem at about 1 a.m. on Friday 10 April, exactly two hours ahead of their entry into the town; we reached The Hague at 3 a.m., and by 3.30 German planes, evil harbingers of the invasion, were over the city.

On arriving back at our hotel we made straight for our rooms, longing at last to get to bed. Cleaning my teeth in the bathroom, I looked up at the clear dawn sky and noticed a plane approaching; with horror I saw that it had the black and white cross of the Luftwaffe on its wings. I shouted to Michael Somes, who was sharing a room with me. He rushed into the bathroom, by which time fresh planes had arrived. They were dropping leaflets telling the Dutch people not to resist the invasion. Some of the dancers found a staircase leading up to the flat roof of the hotel and watched not only the leaflets falling but parachutists dropping on the city. Hearing machine-gun fire close by, they rushed downstairs to the foyer to join the rest of the company gathered there in their dressing gowns. We were in a state of confusion and disbelief. Later, Miss de Valois found a noticeboard in the foyer and, typically, used it to pin a notice on it to the effect that the hotel roof was out of bounds. That made us feel at home!

There was another incident when two young British airmen, who had been shot down over Germany and evaded capture, were brought into the hotel under the friendly escort of Dutch soldiers. At first bewildered and in shock, as well they might be, they could hardly believe their eyes when they realised that they were surrounded by a crowd of young people whom they later discovered to be members of an English ballet company.

After this surprising and joyful encounter we relaxed somewhat, and even Miss de Valois joined Ashton and Helpmann at a table in the square outside the hotel in the spring sunshine, until the peace was shattered by the firing of a single bullet that narrowly missed them. Once over the shock, there was a good deal of light-hearted banter as to which of the three was the intended target! Inevitably, this brought forth another notice on the board: 'The square is out of bounds'. But we became more seriously aware of the grim realities of war when we heard the first bomb dropped on the city. This was one of the type that was used in the invasion of Poland; the Germans had attached a small gadget to the fin of the bomb that gave the effect of loud screaming as it fell. Ironically, the target this time was the prison, where earlier the Dutch soldiers had consigned the fifth columnists they had rounded up. It was thus a grim poetic justice.

During the long hours following the awful realisation that we were caught up in the invasion of Holland, amid the rumours and counter-rumours that flew around the hotel, first and foremost we wanted to hear the plans formulated for our escape from this nightmare. We knew that Scheveningen, the nearby seaside resort that a group of us had visited earlier, had a large and important airport; surely we could escape from there? Our hopes were soon dashed, however, when we heard that the airport was one of the first places to be captured by the enemy. The only members of the company who had contact with the Dutch authorities and with the Ambassador were Miss de Valois and Constant Lambert, and we would watch them leave the hotel on their perilous walk to the Embassy through the streets, now quiet except for the occasional burst of gunfire, and anxiously await their return, hoping for news of our departure. After one such visit we heard that a member of the Embassy staff had suggested that only the women could leave; but Miss de Valois would not hear of it and insisted that the whole company would leave or no one would. It was also thought advisable that the men should destroy the cards they carried notifying them that they were eligible for military service, for if they were caught with them on their person, they would no doubt have been treated as military prisoners of war.

This first day of the invasion was full of air-raid alarms and hurried journeys down to the air-raid shelter in the cellars of the hotel; for the rest of the time we put on a brave face, read books, played cards, talked together as brightly as we could. Helpmann recalled his early days in Australia when he was in a musical comedy called, ironically, *Miss Hook of Holland*, and gave us a spirited rendering of the first-act finale, complete with what were then called 'vocal gems'. On Friday night the company slept where they could on the floor of the hotel and even on the stairs.

The sound of German planes on Saturday morning roaring overhead was terrifying, and news came through of the beginning of the destruction of Rotterdam, only thirty minutes from The Hague by road. The Embassy told us to be ready to leave at a moment's notice. Late on Saturday afternoon Mr and Mrs Beck, our concert agents, came to tell us that we could take only one small case each; our main luggage and any other personal belongings had to be left behind. Those were the days before airline luggage, and I had only one suitcase with me, my old 'Revelation', given to me on my twenty-first birthday and very much in vogue at the time, with its expandable brackets that enabled one to raise or lower the lid as the contents dictated. I left most of my things behind and closed the case down to its smallest size, hoping that it looked as if I was not cheating by carrying more than the essentials.

At last came the time for departure, when two buses arrived at the hotel. After a security check to make sure that they were bona fide and not in the hands of the fifth columnists, we boarded and were off. As we rounded the little square and looked back, the most vivid memory I have is of the large, garishly painted poster of Greta Garbo in *Ninotchka*, which had been playing that week at the cinema next to our hotel. We were thankful to leave, but were filled with dread as to what our journey might bring. We had hardly left the hotel before we saw the wreck of a plane lying practically upright against a ruined house. Miss de Valois had divided us into groups, with a senior member of the company as a sort of

1. *A Wedding Bouquet*, Leslie Edwards second from right

2. Archimago, *The Quest*

3. Benno, *Swan Lake*

4. The Beggar, *Miracle in the Gorbals*

5. Cattalabutte, *The Sleeping Beauty*

6. The Mime (Adam's spiritual adviser), *Adam Zero*

7. Hilarion, *Giselle*

8. 'Darling Leslie, All my love, Margot'

prefect to see that we kept together; each had a list of names. Moyra Fraser, the youngest girl in the company, sat next to me and I thought wryly of her mother saying to me at the station before leaving London, 'You will look after Moyra, won't you, dear?' Little did we realise then that it would be through gunshot and fire.

It was now getting dark. We had just left The Hague when we saw a tremendous fire on our left, flames shooting up to the sky. Our guard at the front of the bus told us it was Rotterdam. We still did not know where we were making for, but we seemed to stop every half-hour, and then change direction; this was because fresh groups of parachutists kept dropping in the woods ahead. At these stops, uniformed men would join the driver to instruct him on his route. At one stop we were told to practise getting down on the floor quickly in case of firing directed at the bus, so, before moving off again, we choreographed a slick drill for a rapid drop to the floor! There was a horrid moment when we discovered that we had lost the other bus, and I suppose they felt the same when they found they had lost us.

But even more frightening was when a group of Dutch soldiers appeared and snatched one of their supposed company off the bus and started shouting at him; our driver managed to close the door and we moved off. However, the people in the rear seats, looking back, were aghast to see the guard, whom we had watched being interrogated on our bus, shot dead.

At last we arrived at a large chateau-like hotel that must have been a focal point, not only for us but for a great crowd of other refugees arriving in a queue of buses. I joined a small group who decided to walk in the huge garden. After the terror of The Hague and the claustrophobic stuffiness of the bus, the air was fresh and sweet. Then it was dawn and we saw the loveliness of our surroundings; through fresh, leafy trees paths led down to a lake, herons delicately preened themselves by the water and a herd of deer wandered in the park and then ran swiftly around the edge of the lake, splashing through the water. After the smell of war the contrasting beauty of this scene struck me so forcibly that I said to Constant Lambert, who had joined us on our walk, that he should compose a piece of music that would remind us ever after of this morning. He did so, calling it *Aubade Héroïque*. He later gave me a copy of the complete orchestral score and wrote in it in the blue pencil he often used, 'To Leslie Edwards, who suggested this piece. Constant'. During the day we managed to find a quiet place in the garden to snatch a little sleep or somewhere to rest in the crowded house where new refugees were arriving by the minute, including some Poles in the striped convict clothes in which they had escaped from a German prison camp. Amid the mêlée were groups of nuns, some elderly people and, unbelievably, three English ladies wandering about with somewhat regal detachment trying to find a fourth for bridge!

At midnight we moved off in our two buses to join the long convoy making for the port at Ymuiden and the cargo ship that was to take us back to England. It was a long, slow journey and as we neared the port the buses had to hide for a time in side streets to avoid detection by German planes. When I think back, it must have been a bright moon that night, because I remember that I could see the shadows of the low-flying planes that seemed to pursue us, making an outline against the houses. When we eventually got aboard the cargo boat we had to descend a narrow gangway leading down to the hold. The journey across the North Sea lasted about fifteen hours, but when it was light, we were allowed up on deck. It was freezing cold, but better than the stench of the hold. The poor Poles were shaking with cold in their thin, prison garb, but the worst for them was the freezing wind on their shaven heads; some of the ladies lent them their fashionable hats, and I'll never forget those poor Poles huddled together wearing them, desperate to keep warm. It was unfortunate that wartime restrictions did not allow us to carry cameras to record this scene. Then, alas, fresh planes were spotted and we had to return to the hold.

We finally arrived off Harwich within sight of the English shore, but again were doomed to wait, mainly because apparently we were unexpected and there were no pilot boats to take us in. The three would-be bridge-playing ladies were heard to declare that food should be sent aboard and, as they put it, 'The ballet girls can be waitresses'. Miss de Valois had other ideas and somehow managed to send a message ashore and contact a top member of the British Council. In no time at all, we were in two small tugs heading for land. It was wonderful to be back in our beloved island fortress, and we knew the absolute truth of there being no place like home. It was Whit Monday, a Bank Holiday, and, typically, everything was closed, including the custom house; we would have to wait until someone opened it up. But what did it matter? We were home. When we arrived in London the first thing we noticed were the newspaper placards, announcing, 'Dutch Queen leaves Holland'. We knew; we had seen her ship dock at Harwich.

Chapter 10

After the fall of Holland, some of the company volunteered to join a small Entertainments National Services Association (ENSA) group for two weeks, giving performances in the Aldershot area. The shows took on a concert-party flavour that included short, light-hearted items from our repertoire: *Façade*, 'Dance of the Tumblers' from *The Snow Maiden* and some excerpts from the classics. We also had among us two singers, Janet Hamilton-Smith and Edith Coates, favourites from the Old Vic and Sadler's Wells. Ironically, the audiences included troops who had been rescued from Dunkirk and who otherwise would have been our audiences in Belgium and France.

By early June we had opened another season at Sadler's Wells Theatre, and Ninette de Valois choreographed a highly successful ballet, *The Prospect Before Us*, subtitled 'Pity the Poor Dancers'. Michael Somes, Richard Ellis and I had a comical dance as three lawyers juggling with writs and affidavits, a masterly stroke of choreographic invention requiring considerable *leger de main* as well as *leger de pied*! Most memorable of all was a drunken solo by Bobby Helpmann, in which he brought his full comic genius to bear.

Before the end of this season Richard Ellis had joined the Navy, as had Stanley Hall. William Chappell was already in the Army, and Paul Reymond and Leo Young, a comparatively new member of the company, had volunteered for the RAF. Leo Young, an Australian, was one of the Children of Light in the *Dante Sonata* and very much liked by us all; we were greatly saddened by his death in hospital after an illness, a short time after he joined up.

In the late summer of 1940, following the start of the Blitz, we toured with ENSA to garrison theatres, in addition to our accustomed provincial bookings in towns now suffering from heavy bombing. But in December we went to Dartington Hall, situated in beautiful Devonshire countryside, and were there during the second Christmas of the war. It was very cold, with thick snow, but nevertheless the visit provided a break from the air raids in London, Birmingham, Leeds and elsewhere. Dartington Hall was the property of the American philanthropists Mr and Mrs L.K. Elmhirst, and had been the home of the Ballets Jooss for many years. It had a workshop theatre inside and a very pretty open-air one outside. This German company had won a prize in Paris for Jooss's work *The Green Table*, and, following the Nazi persecution of the Jews in the early thirties, escaped from Germany and was offered Dartington Hall as its headquarters. The inhabitants of the neighbouring town of Totnes must, I feel, have found these refugees rather avant-garde in their ways. We did hear that the young fräuleins had developed a liking for galloping over the hills above the little local railway in the most abbreviated costume or lacking any, a marked contrast to the hacking jackets and jodhpurs of the farming community; railway business suddenly boomed.

By the time we got there, the members of the Ballets Jooss either were interned in the Isle of Man or had found refuge in South America. We took over their dormitories, enjoyed having classes in their rehearsal rooms, but most of all delighted in the peace and quiet. Fred was inspired to choreograph a new one-act ballet to the Schubert *Wanderer* Fantasy. He finished it in ten days, much to the amazement of Mrs Elmhirst, who had grown accustomed to a much slower pace from our predecessors. Margot Fonteyn and Bobby Helpmann were the leads, and Pamela May and Michael Somes were given a really beautiful *pas de deux*. I was one of the four tearaways and, most interesting of all, another of these four was the new boy who had joined us at Dartington Hall, John Field from Doncaster. Later, when the ballet was produced in London, the décor and costumes were by Graham Sutherland.

By the time we returned to London, the bombing had become heavier, and this intensity of air attack spread to the big industrial towns in or near the Midlands – Coventry, Birmingham, Bristol – and to ports such as Cardiff, Hull and Plymouth. We must admire not only the bravery of the young dancers who carried on performing, even though the red 'Alert' sign had lit up in the auditorium to indicate that an air raid was imminent, but also the courage of the audience who stayed in their seats, although they were obviously free to leave the theatre and make their way to the nearby shelters. That was one of the phenomena of those war years in the theatre; the public disregarded all warnings and the theatres were packed, justifying the Home Office's lifting of the ban on them at the beginning of the war. What is more, throughout the duration, the whole theatrical profession created productions of the highest order, and the exigencies of the war brought out the best in every venture.

In order to simplify communications between the Company, now renamed the Sadler's Wells Ballet, the Old Vic and the Opera company, it was decided that there should be a combined base outside London. So for two years the headquarters were situated in the Victoria Theatre in Burnley, Lancashire. How the inhabitants found their evacuees from the Arts I can only hazard a guess, but they were friendly and welcoming and we grew attached to the little hotel where we stayed in the main square, flanked by two rather begrimed bay trees. Miss de Valois, putting a brave face on things as she always did, described the location to Helpmann through deliberately rose-coloured spectacles before we had been up there, but I could see by that expressive face of his that he was not convinced. Even so, we managed to have a good giggle about it all and were particularly grateful for nights unbroken by air raids. We were, in fact, not there all that often, because Burnley did not figure very largely in our tours; but for the administration in general this was a temporary home until the company, together with the Old Vic, moved back to London during the later stages of bombshell and fire, to the New Theatre (now the Albery Theatre) in St Martin's Lane, WC1.

It was always with a feeling of anxiety that we men entered the stage door to look tentatively at the letter rack, for that was where the call-up papers were sent. Mine arrived in June 1942 and I gave my last performance with the company dancing Arthur in *A Wedding Bouquet*. The next day I took the train to Woolwich. As I alighted at the station I was immediately instructed by Army NCOs to join a group of other young arrivals, and we were duly marched off to the Cambridge Barracks. I was stationed there for about a month and became a private in the Royal Army Ordnance Corps, before being sent to Guildford.

There I managed to obtain a late-night Saturday pass, much sought after, which enabled me to get up to town and to the New Theatre to see the last performance for that season of Helpmann's much-acclaimed new ballet, *Hamlet*. In spite of having read the rave notices in the press about the production, I was not prepared for the great impact it made on me. Its success and that of the season as a whole, with the consequent full houses, had made it possible to reinstate the orchestra; when the company had first arrived at the New Theatre, Hilda Gaunt and Constant Lambert were still gallantly playing away on two pianos. Now Constant made magic of Tchaikovsky's *Hamlet* fantasy overture which Helpmann, influenced by him, had used for this tautly knit ballet. The décor and costumes were the work of Leslie Hurry, a young artist whom Helpmann had discovered. The backcloth was painted in glowing colours, very powerful in their effect and suggesting the portent of the drama to be unfolded. Although the work was short, almost as if in deliberate contrast to the length of the play, Helpmann fully created its every character and the action that passed, as in a kaleidoscope, before the dying Hamlet's eyes. I returned to Guildford in a daze of wonder. In their *pas de deux*, Helpmann and Fonteyn as Hamlet and Ophelia danced superbly to a moving passage in the music, and I felt that the actor, dancer and choreographer in Helpmann had planted a new sense of drama in Fonteyn.

Back with my unit, I later had the good luck to be included with two other men to go to the East End of London to pick up some supplies. We made the journey sitting on the top of an open lorry. The route took us through the West End and, as we rounded Marble Arch and went down Park Lane, it still looked lovely in the bright summer weather, in spite of the windows taped to mitigate the damage of flying glass and the protecting sandbags everywhere. I pointed out the Dorchester and Grosvenor Hotels and the many fine houses still standing to my two companions: one was from Leeds, the other, who had never visited London before, from Nottingham. They were happy and delighted with the scene and the chap from Nottingham said in a thoughtful voice, 'No wonder they sing "This is the London I Love".'

Our unit was then moved to Nottingham, full of memories of my touring days, and there I spent a rather lonely Christmas, although I was asked out to lunch by a kind local family taking care of a soldier for Christmas. After this we moved to Yorkshire to be part of a small unit in a village called Kirby Moorside, the full beauty of which did not reveal itself until the spring. One night, when I was on the final watch of guard duty and thought I had called the last man in, I stood alone in an expanse of snow in moonlight. In the cold beauty of the scene I could not resist the temptation of leaving my sentry box and making a swift circle as in – what else? – *Les Patineurs*, in full guard's rig. As I was lost in the movements, every *port de bras* pure Ashton, I had not observed, making his way back to camp, one of the most formidable Staff Sergeants in the unit. One was lucky to get through the day without incurring his displeasure or being put on charge for the smallest lapse. When I saw him, I stood rooted to the spot, in mid-action, stock-still in horror. But there was silence. I think Staff could not believe his eyes. No shouting, no raving. Quietly, 'What are you doing?' he said. I thought it best to tell the truth. 'I was dancing, Staff'. He looked totally incredulous and moved away slowly in the direction of his billet. As he reached my deserted sentry box he turned and said again quietly, 'I won't put you on a charge, but I could send you to the glasshouse for this', and tapped my rifle, which I had left leaning against the box, a crime heinous beyond all other. Amazingly, that was the last I heard of it.

Shortly after this, the Royal Army Ordnance Corps was divided into two separate regiments, one to retain its old name and the other to be known as the Royal Electrical and Mechanical Engineers. I was one of those who became a member of the latter, on the recommendation of the Major in charge of the re-allocation. A more unlikely candidate one cannot imagine, as I could barely mend a fuse.

When spring arrived, Kirkby Moorside looked beautiful, and every duty that involved a trip to Whitby or Scarborough was pure delight. We were a small unit and made friends with many of the local people, but at times I wished that I belonged to a larger group where I could perhaps have organised a concert party, as so many of my theatre friends did when they were in the Forces.

However, events were to take an unexpected turn. After several months in Yorkshire my eyesight became troublesome. I was sent to a medical station in York and from there moved to a hospital in Mill Hill, where I spent seven weeks. Subsequently, my category was lowered and I was not now suitable for service overseas. After treatment and discussion as to whether there was any possible future for me in the Army, I was finally discharged for medical reasons.

My experience of life in the Army had not been unpleasant; in truth I was glad that I had found it so and had managed to come to terms, as countless others had, with an existence so different from anything I had experienced since leaving school. I was therefore in equal measure unhappy not to have been able to complete the task; a sense of unfulfilment and, with it, a deep source of regret remained with me for some years.

So in 1943 I found myself back in the company at the New Theatre. The raids over London were becoming increasingly ferocious, even if more intermittent, and later on conventional bombing was to be augmented by Hitler's new and fearsome secret weapons, the V1 and V2. I returned to my home in Teddington and, in spite of all the difficulties, the Southern Railway still managed to carry on a remarkable train service from there into the centre of London. After the war, statistics showed that the line between Waterloo and Clapham Junction, which was the first stage of the journey out of town, was the worst-bombed line in England.

This section also had to be covered by Miss de Valois, commuting from her home in Sunningdale, where she was busy looking after her house and sometimes sharing some of the routine jobs in the surgery of her husband, Dr Arthur Connell. On her journey she would deal with company matters – calls and lists of rehearsals and all the attendant paraphernalia. In fact there was a well-known episode when, immersed in all this, she turned to a complete stranger sitting next to her in the carriage and, thinking that she was talking to Joy Newton, her Ballet Mistress, asked her about the suitability of casting so-and-so in such-and-such a rôle. There is no record of the stranger's reply.

My first rôle after my return was Archimago in *The Quest*. This was choreographed by Frederick Ashton, the theme, based on Spenser's *The Faerie Queene*, having been suggested by Doris Langley Moore. William Walton composed the music, and John Piper designed the décor and costumes.

As the war continued, success came in greater measure to the company. The New Theatre was packed with enthusiastic audiences from a cross-section of the public who were becoming more and more knowledgeable and familiar with what the theatre was all about. Young people working in the war-torn capital were making their way to see the new productions, and there were Free French, Poles, Dutch and Americans all enjoying our ballets. These included another addition to the classical repertoire, *Lac des Cygnes*, with splendid costumes by Leslie Hurry, whose clever use of perspective scenery painted on the backcloth made the small stage at the New Theatre seem spacious. One was conscious of the need that the public felt for the arts during this time, and this bore out the vision of Lilian Baylis in providing the best of acting, singing and dancing for all to appreciate and enjoy; a people's art in the truest sense.

The wartime theatre world seemed to be recognising to the full the legacy of centuries of artistic talent. There were revivals of Shaw, Wilde, Ibsen and Chekhov, and the West End saw new plays of quality by such as Rattigan, Coward and Bridie. The play *There Shall Be No Night* by the American, Robert Sherwood, brought a welcome touch of Broadway, its cast including Alfred Lunt and Lynn Fontanne. Revues flourished, especially with the two Hermiones, Gingold and Baddeley, who good-naturedly satirised some of the straight plays, including Helpmann's *Hamlet*. His appearance in the play had followed his creation of the ballet. He also became a guest artist in revues, in addition to his work at the New Theatre with the company, and his act included brilliant impersonations of Olivier and Gielgud, Margaret Rawlings and Margaret Rutherford! In those days there were no barriers and artists seemed to be remarkably versatile, as indeed they were.

In the musical world there were lunchtime concerts at the National Gallery and a revival of the Promenade Concerts at the Albert Hall to vastly increased audiences. Every concert hall, in fact, seemed to be fostering new as well as established works by composers such as William Walton, Lennox Berkeley and Arthur Bliss.

All this activity and creativity was, of necessity, accompanied by day-to-day uncertainty, improvisation, shoe-string budgets and shortages of every commodity; yet in spite of, or perhaps because of this, the highest intrinsic qualities were maintained in the performing arts.

It should not be forgotten that many of the male dancers in the com-

pany were away in the Forces and that young men had to be pushed
forward who, in normal times, would still have been students at the Ballet
School at Sadler's Wells. They performed in character rôles or in those
technically more difficult than their experience would otherwise have allowed, but they gave of their best and rose to the occasion. Essentially
they were a group of dancers whose nationality made them ineligible for
war service. Alexis Rassine, for example, was Lithuanian, Gordon Hamil-
ton, Australian; David Paltenghi was Swiss-Italian and as a *danseur noble*
went on to create some important rôles. The company management was
always very grateful to the dancers who held the fort, indeed splendidly,
and when the war ended and the men returned from the Forces, most of
these temporary members of the company handed over their jobs with
good grace. Above all one must remember the women in the company,
who bravely and stoically performed through all the many hardships of
those war years.

Late in 1944 we moved from the New, for one season only, to the
Princes Theatre at the far end of Shaftesbury Avenue, not one without
association with the ballet, as the Diaghilev Company had danced there
before the war; it had also been the home of many famous musicals. At
the time of our moving, I doubled-up the rôle of Pierrot in *Carnaval*
with Bobby Helpmann, who was, needless to say, brilliant in the part.
He had discovered that, as he lay on the floor, having collapsed in a
pathetic heap of white linen and black pom-pom at the end of his solo,
there were concealed microphones connected to the rooms back-stage,
part of the intercom system. To my amazement, as I was sitting in my
dressing-room making up for the next ballet, his voice came over, dul-
cet in tone, with a selection of humorous and vivid comments, spicy in
flavour, much to the amusement of the entire company back-stage. He
was always a wag, that Helpmann, but, as Mona Lott in the popular
comedy show ITMA would say, it was being so cheerful that kept us
going!

It was the Princes Theatre that saw the first night of Helpmann's *Miracle in the Gorbals*. There were religious connotations in the miracle of the
bringing back to life of a young girl, danced by Pauline Clayden, who had
thrown herself into the river and drowned. Helpmann created a strong,
dramatic ballet, full of Gorbals characters, with an uncompromising real-
ism. He was the Stranger who performed the miracle, and looked remarkably like a figure from an El Greco painting, contrasting strongly with the
three old biddies in a pub and the crowd of louts who later bashed him up.
There was a charming *pas de deux* for a young couple, danced by Moira
Shearer and Alexis Rassine. I was very lucky to be cast as an old beggar;

after entering at the beginning of the ballet playing my violin and begging for a few coins, I slumped by a dustbin outside the pub and never left the stage until I went to the aid of the Stranger after he had been attacked. The ballet then ended on a tableau with the young resurrected girl and myself holding him up as the curtain fell.

My costume, designed by Edward Burra, was a mass of rags made up of an old overcoat and a worn-out mackintosh. Bobby told me he would work out a make-up for me to out-Olivier Olivier; there was talk of covering one eye to make the poor old man even more pathetic, but, as things went in those days, Bobby only had time to complete the ballet, let alone devise make-up for me. On the day of our one stage call, he told me to put on something or other for the rehearsal and he would make me up before the performance. Then I had the idea of going to the wardrobe and borrowing Edward Burra's sketch for the costume. I copied what he had painted; a blue stubble chin, one eye rimmed with red make-up and the other completely covered with black grease paint. It worked. What is more, for all the years later in which I played this rôle I used exactly the same make-up, and even my best friends didn't recognise me!

Chapter 11

In the Spring of 1945 the war in Europe came to an end. On VE Night there was a performance of *Coppélia* in which Dr Coppelius' balcony was ablaze with the flags of the Allies. The whole theatre audience and the company on stage were bursting with joy on this day that we had felt at times would never arrive.

We wondered, naturally, what would happen to us after this great event. Would we go back to Sadler's Wells or stay at the New Theatre, which we had grown to love? Then we heard the exciting news that the Governors of Sadler's Wells had agreed that the ballet company would dance at the re-opening of the Royal Opera House. During our tours to Liverpool many of us had got to know an important member of the artistic world of that city, David Webster, and we now learned that he had been given the position of General Administrator at the Opera House.

When, later in the year (after just one season at the reopened Sadler's Wells), we were dancing at the Manchester Opera House during our provincial tour, David Webster visited us. In an office back-stage, he interviewed the entire company and informed us individually how we would fare in our new home in Covent Garden. I, remembering our splendid gala performances there before the war, was delighted at the prospect before us. Details of our position in the company and the salary that this would carry were given to us in a very friendly and welcoming way by our future Administrator, and I knew by this that we were in for a very successful and happy régime.

We continued our regular touring programme and then, during the autumn of 1945, with the dust of war hardly having settled, we set off on a ten-week tour of Germany, organised by ENSA. The performances were given in cities such as Hamburg, Düsseldorf and, finally, Berlin, in what remained of the theatres, surrounded by rubble and the wreckage of air bombardment, with the sickly smell of death in the air from the unclaimed bodies buried beneath. We rarely found a hotel left standing and were generally stationed outside the city in one of the large houses that had escaped the intensive bombing. It was a tour very much in the charge of military personnel, who organised our billets and saw to our general welfare.

Within the theatres the German stagehands, in spite of all their hardships, were more than willing to help to run our productions, two of the most popular of which were *The Rake's Progress* and *Miracle in the Gorbals*. In the latter, one of the leading characters, the Prostitute, throws her cigarette to the ground and stamps on it; the moment her back is turned to make her exit, I would rush and pick it up, putting the stub behind my ear before walking jauntily back to my dustbin. When the curtain fell at the end of the ballet I had a habit of throwing the stub to the ground so that the stage crew could sweep it up with the rest of the bits and pieces on the stage before the next item on the programme. On this German tour I noticed that, when I threw the fag-end down, there would be a rush of German stagehands to be the first to retrieve it. Cigarettes were currency and even a stub had its worth, such were the deprivations of this time.

It was during this tour that Michael Benthall, then an army officer stationed in Germany, saw this ballet for the first time – he had planned it with Robert Helpmann back in 1944 when on leave. Another good factor was that Harold Turner and Michael Somes rejoined us after their war service, although Michael was still rather shaken as the result of a serious operation following a fall from a lorry while he was in the Army.

Berlin was the last city on our tour and, while we were there, arrangements were made for the company to visit the Chancellery, still standing amidst the ruins. Having seen this building so often on earlier newsreels, with Hitler ranting and raving on its famous balcony, I was surprised to see that, instead of this being centre-stage as I'd imagined, it was in a less significant position in relation to the general architecture. At the side was a door leading to a small suite – bedroom, sitting room, bathroom – put aside for Hitler's personal use and almost homely in contrast to the rest.

Also very interesting was another visit, this time to the stadium, famous as one of the symbols of the rise of pre-war National Socialism, that had housed the pre-war Olympic Games, recorded for posterity by Leni Riefenstahl. When we saw it, it was devoid of swastikas, of the mass of waving banners and of the ever-present military. There was a forlorn little concrete box where the great Führer had once sat in all his glory and I don't think he would have appreciated the yahoos of Bobby and myself as we ran across the vast empty space before it. What a joyous catharsis for us to be able to vent our spleen on this dread dictator; to add the final touch we took the catharsis literally and relieved ourselves in the process!

The theatre in Berlin was in pretty poor shape; dampness and dreariness were all-pervasive, as was the case throughout the city. Warmth, however, came from the marvellous audiences of military personnel, male and female, Russian, American, French and British, who crowded in to see us perform.

Michael Benthall had previously been stationed in Berlin and had written to Bobby to tell him that while he was in the city, if it was possible, he must try to visit a famous leading actor called Victor de Kowa. Bobby did indeed plan such a visit and asked me to go with him. By now the weather was freezing, and on one of our free nights we went off in the army truck accompanied by our officer, who interestingly enough was of White Russian parentage. After a search through ruined buildings on the outskirts of the city, we managed to find the actor's house, which was in complete darkness. We realised that it was no good ringing the bell, as electricity and batteries were not available for the civilian population. We hammered away at the front door, but the house remained silent and in darkness. On the point of giving up, the officer impatiently lifted the letterbox and yelled 'Fräulein!' through it.

After a brief pause we saw a flicker of candlelight in the hallway; the door slowly opened and a small figure appeared, bundled up in a huge fur coat. Our White Russian explained who we were and that we had come at the request of Michael Benthall; whereupon we were bidden inside, the little figure leading the way into a large, candlelit, freezing room. Here, in contrast to the little bundle in the fur coat, stood an upright figure wearing a heavy overcoat and muffled up with a scarf. This clearly was the distinguished actor.

After the introduction he was rather distant towards us, until a large bottle of brandy that Bobby had brought as a gift was opened. Suddenly a little warmth broke through and it wasn't long before we were being led into another room and shown trophies of our mutual theatrical profession – film stills, photographs of his famous productions for the Berlin stage and other evidence of his varied career. There were questions, too, to Bobby about the London theatrical world, all framed in very good English, and one detected a great interest in Bobby's association with the Oliviers. By now we had become friends indulging in theatre chitchat, and it was evident that the little bundle in the fur was Japanese and presumably the actor's wife. The whole atmosphere suddenly became magical. Mrs de Kowa was obviously taken with Bobby, and other famous names as well as the Oliviers' rolled round the room. Not to be outdone by all this theatrical talk of prestigious stars, the little Japanese lady broke into a spirited rendering of 'Annie Laurie' to add a final, bizarre touch to the whole occasion. Indeed it was a night to remember. But then it was time to leave, for we had to conform to the curfew, the strict factor of life in Berlin then; walking out into the intense cold, we were abruptly reminded of the grim realities that lay around us.

Before the end of our stay in Berlin, Bobby had to return to London for some theatrical discussions and I took over his part as the Rake in *The*

Rake's Progress. It was a moving experience for me to round off the tour in this little, unheated theatre in the shattered city, with the foul smell and the cold desolation intensifying the deep tragedy of it all. 'The pity of war, the pity war distilled.' I think it was the realisation of this suffering around us that enabled me to identify strongly with the situation in the last scene of the ballet; the purgatory of this prison and the cells into which people had been thrown seemed to personify all that was happening outside the theatre. I have never danced a rôle with such conviction as I did that night in Berlin; it was possibly the best performance I ever gave.

The occasion of the end of the tour in Germany seemed to me, too, to be the culmination of all that had happened previously to the company throughout the war. It was the end of an era, something to which one clung in the face of the uncertainties of a future as yet tentative and undefined.

But our worst practical and immediate concern was the weather. There was a rumour that, if the threatened heavy snow arrived, we might be unable to leave immediately because of the lack of army transport to take us to the station, since every lorry would be requisitioned to ferry troops on their extra duties around the snow-blocked city. However, luck was with us and the worst of the weather held off, enabling us to make our departure on schedule and arrive home thankfully and in time for Christmas.

Chapter 12

The first Christmas of peace spent at home that December of 1945 was the entr'acte to a new and important chapter in the history of the company. We were tremendously excited to read in the press that the Sadler's Wells Ballet was to re-open the Royal Opera House on 20 February 1946 with a brand new production of *The Sleeping Beauty*. After its long wartime function as a dance hall, this famous theatre in Covent Garden would return to its rightful place among the opera houses of the world, responding to all that was great and appropriate in both opera and ballet. With my memories of our pre-war galas at the Garden, I was especially full of excitement and feelings of hope that this would be the summit of all our achievements.

The first day of classes and rehearsals arrived and I walked up to the stage door and waited to gain permission to enter from the redoubtable Mr Jackson, the stage door keeper. I never heard his Christian name mentioned, but he was a legend throughout the theatrical world. We had earlier been told to mind our p's and q's when we dealt with him by no less a person than Miss de Valois, who had got the measure of him during her days as prima ballerina of the Opera Company under the direction of Sir Thomas Beecham. We quickly realised that we didn't demand our mail on entering the stage door, but waited patiently at the window in the door of his office until he asked one's name. If there were any letters, these would then be handed over with a searching look.

I quickly found the noticeboard on which the times of classes and rehearsals were posted and also the complete cast of *The Sleeping Beauty*. As I read down the list of characters all my joy drained away; I was cast as Catalabutte, the Master of Ceremonies. In our production of this ballet before the war at Sadler's Wells, I had been the Camellia Fairy's Cavalier and had danced away with the rest of the company. In those days, because of the scarcity of male dancers, many of the mime rôles such as Catalabutte were taken by members of the Opera Company and, I must add, very well performed too. I stifled my grief at not having a dancing rôle and hoped that the rest of the company would not comment adversely on my demotion, as I then felt it to be.

At the time, Bobby was ill in the London Clinic, where I went to see him regularly. Making my visit that afternoon after having seen the cast list, I entered the room and slumped down in a chair without even asking about the health of the patient, who then asked me what was wrong. I blurted out my news, whereupon he turned his famous searchlight eyes on me and said, 'Well, at least you're in it, so why don't you make something of the rôle as you did with the old beggar in *The Gorbals?*'

How the production was ready on time none of us will ever know. Some of the male dancers had not even been demobbed when we started rehearsing; but it was extraordinary that, after only a crash refresher course in their classes, they were back on form for the opening night, to be greeted affectionately again by the public after six years of war. There was only one rehearsal room at the Garden, and of necessity that was soon taken over by the wardrobe. The whole production staff, in fact, shared with the dancers in the scramble to complete the ballet in time. It was fortunate, in a sense, that we did not have to compete with the Opera Company for stage time as, apart from singing in the ballet of *The Fairy Queen* later that year, it was not fully launched until its first performance of *Carmen* in 1947.

The stage was stacked with wood and canvas while the stage staff were busy making the scenery. This all meant that the stage was not available for us until much nearer the first night, and we had to find rehearsal space anywhere we could outside the Opera House, such as in a partly-bombed rehearsal room in Chenies Street at the far end of the Tottenham Court Road.

When we were back in Covent Garden there was also a force to be reckoned with in the form of Mr Ballard, the technical director, a great pillar of the Royal Opera House. He was as formidable in his way as Mr Jackson and of the same school, going back to the days even before those of Thomas Beecham. His word on stage was law and he would not allow a single person on it until he gave the word, having ensured that every trapdoor and lift had its safety net in place. I well remember times when Miss de Valois would attempt to lead us on to the stage for desperately needed rehearsals and be very politely but firmly asked to leave until Mr Ballard gave the all-clear. She, understanding the situation, would then shepherd us all off until such time as everything was to Mr Ballard's satisfaction.

When we had arrived at the Opera House we were very anxious to establish our own style of family atmosphere, such as had obtained at the Wells. It was some time before we had a regular canteen, but we were well served by two friendly and loveable ladies, Eileen and Winnie, who cut good, substantial sandwiches that were accompanied by mugs of coffee and tea. This was all up in the gallery bar, to which we would make our way and then sit on the wooden benches from where the public had watched performances before the war. Later in this rehearsal period we discovered Smokey Joe's in Floral Street, practically opposite the stage door and frequented by the Covent Garden Market fraternity, of which we were to become very much a part. There we partook of the current *plat du jour*, horse steak, necessary to fortify us against the rigours of the coming season, when we would be dancing every night. As the days went on we were greeted with friendly bonhomie by the other diners who, like us, were busy putting Covent Garden back on the London map once more, whether it was the Opera House, the Floral Hall or the vegetable market.

Everything was accelerating at the approach of the first night: costume fittings, rushing down to Anello and Davide to try on boots and shoes, the wig and hat department working overtime and, on top of all this, worry at the lack of the clothing coupons that were essential at that time when purchasing material. As with ration books for food, coupons were necessary for clothing until some time after the war. This problem was partly solved by contributions from the public of their personal coupons when they heard of our dire straits, a considerable sacrifice in those days.

I personally remember the wig fittings, because the eighteenth-century wig for Catalabutte had a front section containing three false pieces of hair, which the irate Carabosse was to pluck off my head in the Prologue in her fury at not being asked to Aurora's christening. These proved to be rather a nuisance later on when, in my short-sighted way, I had to gather them up during the scene change and stick them on again for the rest of the ballet, to give the illusion at the birthday sixteen years later that they had grown back. And I had to be sharp about retrieving them before the stagehands started sweeping up.

In reply to my question as to when I would have a fitting for my first-act costume, worried because everyone else had had his or hers, I was told that there was no need, because I was to wear the same costume throughout the ballet. Feeling somewhat deprived, I went to see Miss de Valois to report this fact, only to be told that it was quite correct that there would be no change for me after the Prologue. It seemed odd that I should continue to wear the pantaloons fashionable for the christening and not the knee-breeches sported by the rest of the cast at Aurora's sixteenth birthday. The riposte came, pragmatic as ever, 'Well, you see, your costume counts as a court uniform'. 'You mean like a Beefeater', I replied. Every bit as quick was her following 'Exactly!' Later, I was to be grateful for the fact that every time I came on in my old green costume it betokened the mark of a familiar figure, from Prologue to Epilogue. The public got to know the plumed, green figure and this helped to establish the rôle of Catalabutte. To put the record straight, however, Oliver Messel designed a wonderful costume for me. Time was so short that, as late as the last general rehearsal, he sat in my dressing room and literally fashioned my hat, which he embellished with fronds of white ostrich feathers – one more feather and I could have flown!

At last the great day for the opening arrived. We were called on to the stage that afternoon after our class, where Miss de Valois gave us last-minute instructions. During the time between this and our getting made up and ready for the performance, what better to calm our nerves than a nice pot of tea? A group of us went down to Fullers in the Strand to have just this and slices of their famous walnut and chocolate layer cakes. It did the trick and, in a much calmer mood, we returned to our dressing rooms at the Opera House to prepare for the evening ahead.

The curtain rose on a packed house, with the King and Queen, Queen Mary and the two young Princesses in the Royal Box. I shall never forget the swish as it went up and I walked downstage holding my Master of Ceremonies' gold stick of office. There, facing me, was Constant Lambert in the orchestra pit and in command of an orchestra that at last was worthy of him and from which he drew the magic sound of Tchaikovsky's score. From then onwards it was a memorable night, all the dancers in the company performing superbly in every act and acquitting themselves with a professionalism that fulfilled all Miss de Valois' hopes for our début at the Garden. After the curtain came down the atmosphere was charged with success, with people talking excitedly about the whole event. The re-opening of the Opera House had been happily achieved.

David Webster announced that it would henceforth be open throughout the year, something that had not always been achieved; in fact, within living memory, there had been only limited seasons of opera and ballet, the theatre remaining dark in between. Anyway, we set the ball rolling, and this first night was followed by a six-week season consisting entirely of performances of *The Sleeping Beauty*, seven a week, including a Saturday matinée. This was made possible by the fact that Miss de Valois had prepared the ballerinas and their partners to be worthy of undertaking their taxing rôles. This is not to forget the work of the many artists in supporting rôles and of the permanent members of the company as a whole, all of whom contributed to make the season much appreciated by the audiences who filled the house to capacity every night. During this time we were also preparing several one-act ballets to be performed in varying programmes through to the summer.

As did the whole company, I fell in love with the Garden immediately. Even after we opened, life wasn't easy, for there was a lack of any rehearsal room; as a consequence we had to tramp round London to use any available church hall from Kingsway to Camden Town. But when those rich, dark red, gold-encrusted curtains swished up to the highest points of the proscenium arch and when we looked out to the depths of the red and gold auditorium, everything was worthwhile.

By this time I had got over my disappointment at playing Catalabutte. I took the advice that Bobby had given me and was much encouraged when Miss de Valois told me that, in this wider canvas of the production at the Garden under Constant Lambert's musical direction, there would be room to enhance my minor rôle. Giving me a pat on the back she said, 'You're very good at that sort of thing!' I needed no second bidding and managed things in such a way that I hardly left the stage. In fact I made sufficient impression for the well-known trade magazine *The Tailor and Cutter* to ask for an interview with me because they envisaged a possible future for men's dress in the eighteenth-century style of my costume, far more colourful than that of conventional gents' natty suiting. However, with the continuing presence of clothing coupons and the necessity to 'make do and mend', men had in fact to wait until the sixties and the Carnaby Street revolution to give those who wished it the opportunity to indulge in such sartorial fantasies.

The first entirely new ballet production at the Royal Opera House fell to Robert Helpmann, who created *Adam Zero*, with a staging akin to that of Thornton Wilder's well-known play, *The Skin of Our Teeth*. Bobby gave full rein to every theatrical possibility that the Covent Garden stage provided: the stage lifts, the trap doors, the immensity of the stage area. In fact the ballet opened with the stage bare and the stagehands setting up the scene. I came on as one of them and actually helped to move the set, until David Paltenghi, who played the part of the Stage Manager, beckoned me to join in with the ballet and mimed to me that I would be Adam Zero's spiritual self. Once again, I never left the stage until the end, having run the spiritual gamut from a newly ordained member of the Church to a decrepit old bishop blessing Adam Zero, danced by Helpmann, in the final death scene. This gave rise to what I found to be a most memorable theatrical effect, Bobby's kneeling on the vast stage, emptied and unadorned, as June Brae entered and encircled it, wearing a voluminous red cloak. When this passed over him, he, with very exact backstage timing, was able to drop down on a trap door and thus seem to disappear as the cloak moved over him.

At this time I, too, was contemplating a disappearing act; I suddenly had a brief flirtation with an old love, the Musical Comedy, which took me back to the days when I longed to become the next Jack Buchanan and to the many times when I stood in line waiting for auditions. All that, as we have seen, came to nothing; but during my first season at the Opera

House, I was offered a rôle in a revival of an old musical that had just had an enormously successful run in New York, called *The Red Mill*. I would have danced and also had some dialogue and a musical number or two, and it was this combination of dancer and actor that intrigued me. If that wasn't enough, I was also offered a part in an intimate revue at the Duchess Theatre. This took me back to the days of my seeing Herbert Farjeon's revue at the Little Theatre in the Adelphi Terrace in the Strand, in which Joyce Grenfell had made her début. Both these aspects of theatre had been very close to my heart in those pre-war days, so now the possibility of appearing in a revue or musical was a great temptation. Incidentally, my very close friend in the company, Moyra Fraser, had just had a great success in *The Song of Norway*, a musical based on the life of Grieg; this success was due in no small part to Robert Helpmann, who choreographed a ballet for it to the music of Grieg's Piano Concerto that became a major part of the production. So I was becoming very much associated with the musical comedy world.

To show how seriously I took these offers, I summoned up enough courage to see Miss de Valois and to talk the matter over with her. She was most attentive and listened to all I had to say, agreeing that it would be a very interesting experience for me. However, swearing me to secrecy, she artlessly dropped a hint that in all probability the company would be going to America in about two years' time. That did it. I knew that I would never want to miss being with the company in New York, and I left Miss de Valois in no doubt as to my feelings. *The Red Mill* ground to a slow halt. It was in fact a great relief to get this whole thing out of my system and to continue with what were really my greatest loves, the Sadler's Wells Ballet and the Royal Opera House. From that moment on and with the tenacity of my Catalabutte, I scarcely left them for the next fifty years.

After *Adam Zero*, in which Helpmann had made use of the whole range of possibility that the stage offered, Frederick Ashton's first ballet at the Garden spurned the lot, having for his *Symphonic Variations* only a simple backcloth designed by Sophie Fedorovitch. It had a small cast of six dancers, but what dancers they were: Margot Fonteyn, Pamela May, Moira Shearer, Michael Somes, Henry Danton and a very young Brian Shaw, a recent product of the school that Ninette de Valois had founded at the Wells. Danton was also a comparatively new dancer in the company and had the precise, classical line that Ashton required in his new work, which was set to the music of César Franck's *Variations Symphoniques* for piano and orchestra. As the work progressed, I sensed a very special feeling pervading the rehearsals and became aware that something of great significance was in the making.

Jean Gilbert, the young Canadian pianist, was the soloist. She had crossed the Atlantic during the height of the U-boat attacks on convoys during the war in order to be with her young English husband in the RAF, whom she had met when he was in Canada training for action. Later, as a young war widow she joined the Sadler's Wells Orchestra; for, besides being an excellent solo pianist, she was a violinist and had been on tour with the company in the provinces. For *Symphonic Variations* she played for Ashton at rehearsals and in the orchestra pit for performances. The ballet was a triumph that first season and has remained so ever since – a triumph resulting from Ashton's use of classical choreography, but with his own style and line completely imprinted upon it. The dancers held the stage throughout the entire work and, when not actually dancing, had moments of stillness that mesmerised. Ashton avoided the distraction that can be caused by moving dancers too rapidly on and off stage. He knew the importance of maintaining continuity and of allowing his dancers to inhabit the stage; their entering or leaving it was a natural part of the action. This was his particular genius.

The original cast was superb and will always be a legend, but over the years the ballet has never lost its performing power. It has been seen on many of the world's stages and been danced by numerous companies and many great artists. One sees that, in order to perpetuate the essence of a work, it is not just a case of knowing the steps but of learning the correct style, manner and execution of the choreography. This was never more apposite than with the Ashton ballets, when this rich legacy was being handed down personally by the original cast to subsequent performers.

This first season at the Garden more than fulfilled our expectations. We had the feeling that we were now part of a larger world and were following in the footsteps of such as the companies of de Basil and Madame Pavlova. We felt too that our ballets were becoming successors to the many performed as part of the great seasons of opera under the direction of Thomas Beecham at the Opera House. We were edging on to the larger international field and not just playing mostly on home ground.

I still, however, felt unsettled after my brush with the world of musicals and revue, and so did not make any plans to go on holiday when the season ended, as did my colleagues. This turned out to be to my ultimate advantage, for, during the final week of our season, the American Ballet Theatre of New York, directed by Lucia Chase, arrived in London to prepare for their season at the Opera House, which followed ours. David Webster organised a party for us to meet and welcome the American dancers, who looked wonderful – the girls in beautiful frocks owing nothing to the ration books, and the men in double-breasted suits tailored in a style known then in the United States as 'draped' and involving lavish use of material.

It was at this party that I made my first American ballet friends. Miss de Valois had a habit at all official gatherings of making sure that members of Sadler's Wells Ballet did not converse with one another but mingled with guests. She grabbed me and took me over to meet a sensational American girl called Muriel Bentley, who was wearing a large, black picture hat with a wreath of huge, red roses round the crown to accompany a svelte black dress. When we first talked, the conversation was a little stilted until we arrived at matters concerning the ballet, when I knew immediately that I had found a fellow spirit, and we then got on famously. She introduced me to a young man, John Kriza, of whom I had previously heard and seen many photographs.

Knowing that I would be in London at that time, I had already bought a ticket for the American Ballet Theatre's first night and was bowled over when I saw the ballet *Fancy Free*. Second on the bill, it starred the choreographer Jerome Robbins and Michael Kidd and John Kriza as three sailors. *Fancy Free* was the forerunner of a musical, *On the Town*, and later a film starring Frank Sinatra and Gene Kelly. Muriel Bentley was excellent in the ballet as a tough cookie.

The manager of the company, a very cheery individual called Charles Payne, gave me a pass for any evening I wished and I saw most of the repertoire. I became a fan of the company and admired them and everything they did, which included the early ballets by Jerome Robbins and a first attempt by Michael Kidd, later to become as well known as Robbins, especially for his work in films. A real bonus was that, through meeting Muriel Bentley and John Kriza, I also got to know Nora Kaye, who was very much a principal of the American company. Nora, who was well aware of the shortages we had suffered during the war, seemed to have packed a great many presents in her luggage and was always giving out wonderful things – perfume and clothes to the girls and ties to the men. I received some from a well-known shop in New York surprisingly called 'Countess Mara', with somewhat flamboyant patterns not to be seen in Austin Reed or Horne Brothers. We men were given aftershave, too, something that was at that time unknown to us.

I also renewed acquaintance with two old friends whom I had known in my earliest days at the Ballet Club, Antony Tudor and Hugh Laing. Antony, during the years that he had spent with American Ballet Theatre, had become an increasingly distinguished choreographer, and Nora was the star of one of his most successful works, *Pillar of Fire*, which was included in the programme at Covent Garden and which attracted the notice of the British public.

Suddenly London became a Mecca for ballet companies. Roland Petit arrived with his Ballets des Champs-Elysées, and the stamping of Spanish heels could be heard down the length of Shaftesbury Avenue from Carmen Amaya and Antonio with their respective companies. But in the autumn we found ourselves less exotically back on the old stamping grounds of our provincial tours and having the same life in digs, presided over by the same old landladies.

The British Council then turned up trumps again and sent us off to Vienna, a place that held the same magic for us as had Paris in 1937, although we all realised that the city would show the scars of the years of Nazi occupation. We were full of excitement at the thought of performing in a place synonymous with the whole history of musical theatre. As in Paris, I shared a room with Michael Somes, but this time at the famous Sacher Hotel which, in spite of a certain seediness that was understandable after its war-time trials, was still impressive and made me think of all those pre-war films with Anton Walbrook and Lilian Harvey, frolicking by the Danube. Michael and I had a large room with its own entrance hall, which contained a circular hat-stand crowned with antlers to accommodate the colourful hats and the indigenous overcoats of dullish green. But, sadly, from the window of our room at the front of the hotel we could also look down at the burnt-out shell of the once-glorious Opera House.

There was a grim side, too, to walking around this beautiful city, as it was then occupied by the four powers, American, Russian, French and British, and their combined presence was somewhat oppressive. Their headquarters were heavily guarded, none more so than the Russian, where the contingent of soldiers in front of the building was so dense as to make it necessary to step off the pavement when passing it. Since it was peacetime, some of the troops had wives or girlfriends with them: the American ladies beautifully groomed and smartly shod, with jaunty Tyrolean hats perched on top of the Rita Hayworth hair-dos, the French chic, the English in their best 'utilities' with sensible shoes and twin sets suitably clad for all that walking about. The Russians were generally more monotone, though one or two women sported the more colourful spoils of victory on their person by way of a fur coat or jewellery.

We danced in the Volksoper, which was in a way the equivalent of Sadler's Wells Theatre and very much to our liking. Vienna had heard very little of British ballet, but, once we started performing, we became popular and our run was actually extended. When rehearsals and performances permitted, we naturally spent as much time as possible sightseeing, taking the tram route round the inner and outer circle of the city that was one of its well-known features. It enabled us to see most of the important architecture of the Hapsburg régime, the palaces and official buildings of the court of the Emperor Franz Josef and the beautiful and legendary Empress Elizabeth of Austria.

The company was also invited to a wine harvest festival at Grinzing. We sat at long trestle tables, a small band playing, and as the evening progressed we waltzed away in true MGM-musical style. Suddenly, the grey, drab imprint of war, of which we were conscious in the city, seemed to disappear and was replaced by the happier feeling that we were in the Vienna of the *Blue Danube* and the world of operetta.

This sensation continued shortly afterwards when we were asked to attend a dress rehearsal at the Theater am der Wien of *Don Giovanni*; the production was lavish and the baroque theatre beautiful. The cast included Annie Konetzni, one of two sisters who were very popular singers at the time, both very powerful artists. David Webster, who was with us, was deeply impressed and issued an invitation to her to sing at Covent Garden.

I left Vienna with great regret. In spite of the effects of a long occupation, which started the whole chain of events leading up to World War II, the enchantment of the city had managed to survive the misery and terror and far outweighed the shabbiness that prevailed when we were there. I was happily conscious of the echoes of Strauss waltzes, of Lehar's music, the swirl of *The Merry Widow* and the scintillation of *Die Fledermaus*; only the spectre of the shattered Opera House brought me sadly down to earth again.

On our return from Vienna, the company produced a new ballet, choreographed by Frederick Ashton, called *Les Sirènes*, with an Edwardian theme suggested by Lord Berners, who also composed the music; the décor and costumes were by Cecil Beaton. Margot Fonteyn danced the rôle of the flashy character called La Bolero, probably founded on a famous courtesan called La Belle Otero, who had dallied with a few crowned heads in her time. The ballet was not a success, perhaps because it had been thought up too light-heartedly during a weekend country-house party; but I loved it, mainly because I danced with Margot. I played her chauffeur arriving in an old Edwardian motorcar, pulled by stagehands with a rope. We stopped and then whipped off the outer layer of our vintage motoring clothes. I grabbed a guitar from the back of the car and we both went into a turbulent dance known as a *farruca*.

Ashton cast himself as an Eastern potentate surrounded by a group of yashmaked dancers. It was planned that he would arrive in the basket of a balloon floating down from the flies, but after the first night, because of the height from which the balloon was suspended, he demurred and decided to have himself carried on in a palanquin. Robert Helpmann, who initially had to make his entrance in the rôle of a famous tenor, Adelino Canberra, by simply walking on stage, had no such hesitation and certainly no fear of heights. Knowing a good entrance when he saw one, he was already climbing to the top of the stage, and in a trice was descending in the basket, singing in fluting tones an aria recalling in no uncertain terms his birthplace near Adelaide.

The whole cast tried their best and we all enjoyed the bathing scene, danced in amusing Edwardian bathing costumes; but it was all too soon forgotten, except that ten years later three of these old bathing costumes were worn by Anya Linden, Alexander Grant and Brian Shaw in a *pas de trois* called *Valse Excentrique*, choreographed by Kenneth MacMillan for a gala. It was an immediate success and became a sure-fire hit at innumerable other galas and divertissements in the programmes of the Royal Ballet.

Towards Christmas the company produced *The Fairy Queen*, based on Shakespeare's *A Midsummer Night's Dream*. It used the music of the masque by Henry Purcell, a work much admired by Constant Lambert, who arranged the score and fashioned it for this production with his usual skill. The dancers were supplemented by the opera chorus, who were by now rehearsing in the Opera House in preparation for the opening of opera per se, which was due in 1947. We had some individual singers too, including Olive Dyer, remembered by the ballet company for her rôle of Gretel in *Hansel and Gretel*, which was the regular Christmas attraction in Miss Baylis's day at the Old Vic and Sadler's Wells.

The three acts of *The Fairy Queen* were choreographed by Frederick Ashton, who used all the principals of Sadler's Wells Ballet, including Margot Fonteyn, Beryl Grey and Michael Somes. It was an interesting combination of dancing, acting and singing; the actors, paradoxically, were led by Robert Helpmann as Oberon, while his Queen Titania was played by Margaret Rawlings and Bottom by Michael Hordern, then a little-known actor. Besides some telling ensembles Ashton choreographed a beautiful echo dance, performed by a trio of dancers led by Beryl Grey, and an exquisite *pas de deux* for Fonteyn and Somes as spirits of the air.

The run of the production continued into the protracted freezing weather conditions of the winter of 1947 and, as a result of fuel shortages, there was no heating in the theatre, either backstage or in the front of house. The last act included a divertissement of the seasons and I danced in a *pas de trois* with Beryl Grey and Philip Chatfield in which we represented Summer. Beryl Grey wore a diaphanous costume of chiffon, while Philip and I wore tights and had bare tops, except for a wreath of cornflowers and leaves over one shoulder. At the end of the four seasons we had to stay on stage in groups arranged by Ashton until the end of the ballet. We did ask if we could go off after the divertissement, but were told decidedly 'No', so we stood on stage until the finale, shivering from head to foot. The only 'season' who came off well was David Paltenghi, covered completely in a heavy cloak as Winter. Augmenting the orchestra for the finale was a backstage organ; on one occasion it malfunctioned – maybe it, too, was suffering from the coldest weather since records began – and instead of its usual sonority it gave out a series of explosive sounds of flatulence that reduced us, even in our frozen state, to helpless laughter. We envied the audience who sat in their overcoats, many bringing rugs to keep themselves warm.

In 1947, also, the great choreographer Léonide Massine descended upon us. He produced *Le Tricorne*, in which, dancing the rôle of the Miller, he had achieved fame in the Diaghilev Company; and also *La Boutique fantasque* from the same era. In this production in London he danced the cancan, not, as originally, with Lydia Lopokova, but with Moira Shearer. It was wonderful to work with the legendary figure, and we were to get to know him very well, as he was to contribute works for the company that included *Mam'zelle Angot*, *Clock Symphony* and *Donald of the Burthens*.

Generally speaking, 1946–7 was an *annus mirabilis* for the company and for me in particular, not least because my beloved Naggie was able to be present at so many of the performances at the Opera House, which was the theatre that she most enjoyed. She was so proud that this was where everything from my first classes with Mrs Hepworth Taylor had led. Though previously she had never been to Covent Garden, she told me one day that 'That's where I always wanted you to be', with her instinctive knowledge of what was best. Then, in February 1947, just about a year after we had re-opened at the Garden, Naggie died, very gently while she slept. There is so much that I could say about her and of my gratitude and deep love. Life at first without her seemed empty, but now I have come to know that I have felt her presence throughout my career.

Chapter 13

In September 1947 the British Council sent us on an extensive European tour, to include Brussels, Prague, Warsaw, Poznań, Oslo and Malmö. This could not have come at a better time for me as I still felt very low, missing Naggie so much. We had danced in Brussels before, but it was very exciting to go to Czechoslovakia, and Prague overwhelmed us all with the beauty of its baroque buildings. The weather was extremely hot, and on the many sightseeing trips that were arranged we were glad that there were frequent stops at bistros to refresh ourselves with Pils beer. To our amazement, ice-cold jugs of this were placed in our dressing rooms at every performance. Miss de Valois kept a discreet silence.

It was Warsaw that truly fired our imagination from the beginning, when standing on the station to meet us was one of the greatest and most famous of Polish dancers, Leon Woizikovski. He had been a principal dancer with the Diaghilev Ballet, where he had first met Ninette de Valois, who was overjoyed to see her old friend and colleague again and much relieved that he had survived the long and dreadful war in Poland. Warsaw had been bombed and shelled by both Germans and Russians and had had to endure heavy street fighting in the final stages of the conflict. We were horrified to see the damage in the centre of the city, where hardly a building was left standing. We danced in a small theatre that had miraculously escaped the bombardment and that stood out in the flattened ruins, a lone building, then being used for most of the theatrical activities in the city.

On our first night in Warsaw I went with a group of the company to see a performance in Polish of *Hamlet*, a play I knew well. Apart from having gone to many productions at the Old Vic before the war, I had helped Bobby Helpmann through his lines when we were on the provincial tour before he played the Prince at the New Theatre, where he had earlier danced the rôle in his own ballet. I could therefore follow the action fairly easily, but we all had to suppress giggles at the strange pronunciation of the hero's name, which sounded like 'Omelette'. Bobby himself was not with us on that tour to enjoy all this, because he and Moira Shearer were in England making the film *The Red Shoes*.

We were very moved by our pilgrimage to the Ghetto, bombed flat, with the clearly visible remains of the railway lines that had taken victims to the gas chambers. Yet in spite of this shadow of horror, the people we met, both in the theatre and outside, were so friendly, showing great interest in this company from the West. They enjoyed our ballets, especially *Symphonic Variations*, whereas in Prague *Dante Sonata* and *Miracle in the Gorbals* had been the favourites.

Backstage inside the theatre, a feature of the senior boys' dressing room was a row of large cupboards, and Alexander Grant, who had joined the company while we were at the Opera House in 1946, was apt, mischievously, to hide inside one, kidding us that he wasn't there for the performance. On one night we locked the cupboard door while he was inside to teach him a lesson, though it is fair to say that we released him later! When we returned to Warsaw many years afterwards in the 1960s, Alex and I looked for and found what we thought was this same theatre. The then caretaker didn't believe that it was so, but, allowing us to look around, he led us to a dressing room that still contained the cupboard in which we had imprisoned the young Alex. We were both overjoyed to find that it and the theatre were still there.

Margot and Pamela were driven round the city by two young Polish men, who, as one can imagine, were delighted to chauffeur the two ballerinas from the West. They also liked to talk to everyone in the company and spoke the excellent English necessary for their employment by the British Council. They added greatly to the feeling of friendliness that we experienced during our stay.

After Warsaw we moved on to the city of Poznań, where we danced for a week. The two drivers came with us and continued to provide a car for Margot and Pamela. While attending a reception in our honour there, I found myself sitting at a table with a group of Polish gentlemen. In some strange way we seemed, in spite of the language barrier, to make ourselves understood in the general consensus of opinions that East and West could be friends; the common denominator was the toast, raising our glasses time and time again to '*Vive* Churchill'.

With a sudden shock I realised that I had lost all sight of my colleagues; I could not have told my new-found acquaintances where I was staying even if I could have spoken in fluent Polish, as, being shepherded about Poznań in British Council buses, I had no sense of the direction or the district of my hotel. During our stay in Warsaw we had constantly heard stories about people being popped into shiny black limos and disappearing to heaven knows where. So I thought, 'Well, that's it, a labour camp in the Urals'. However, the seemingly good-natured behaviour of my new friends and the frequency of the toasts to Churchill gave me a vicarious courage; with a combination of mime from me and knowing nods from the Poles I realised that someone knew where the English dancers were staying and I found myself walking in a line of amiable gentlemen, making V-for-victory signs galore.

Suddenly we were at the doors of my hotel and I was let in by the amused hotel porter. I crept up to my room and, without disturbing Michael, with whom I was as usual sharing a room, I fell thankfully into my bed. A little while later I was woken by a torch being flashed in my eyes. It was Teddy, one of the two Polish drivers. Margot and Pamela had been worried by my disappearance and Teddy had gone back to search for me. Failing to find me anywhere, he had returned in desperation to the hotel and there I was. He, too, had been aware of the potential dangers and was relieved that all was well.

When he later left Margot and Pamela, after taking them to the train that joined up with the ferry to Malmö where we were next to dance, we could tell that he was very sad at leaving his two ballerinas. Unknown to us until much later, a friend had warned him as he was about to leave the station and drive back not to do so; his friendship with us all had been noticed and he was in danger of being arrested. He had apparently managed to hide away until he could make his escape to Canada, where he worked in farming outside Toronto. During one of our later tours to Canada we happily met up with him again. He told me that, after leaving Warsaw to evade possible imprisonment, he managed to get a message to his wife and that she, too, later escaped, disguised as a waitress on the Malmö ferry.

Warsaw at that time was the hub of political intrigue in the tug-of-war going on between East and West, and we were constantly being reminded of this while we were there. A few of us, including Ninette de Valois, were asked one evening to a late party in a flat where our Polish hostess had, despite the food shortages, prepared a marvellous meal for us. Also present was a group of Polish guests, who all spoke excellent English and who, during the course of the evening, performed a Polish song of great beauty. It was explained to us that it was quite usual for guests to contribute in this way. We unfortunately could not reciprocate in kind, although Miss de Valois was most anxious that we should comply with this custom. We were stumped. Then, in her endearing way of getting titles of things a little wrong, she said 'Surely you can manage a chorus of "Push Out the Barrel"'.

However, a somewhat brash young man from the British Council, who had accompanied us to the party, now volunteered to fill the gap, but proceeded to sing a song with an obscene lyric that even Max Miller at his most ebullient would have shunned. We were appalled and didn't know where to look. This was not at all what one expected from a member of the august British Council. Later we discovered that he proved to be a defector. As usual, Miss de Valois carried it off on that evening, and, quickly looking at her watch, said, 'Goodness, it's so late and you've got a class at ten o'clock in the morning'. We all joined her in making a gracious farewell to our hostess and so diverting attention from this unfortunate lapse. When we got into the bus we all said how upset we were at such a dreadful gaffe, but Miss de Valois silenced us with a quick, 'I'm not bothered about you lot; it's the Poles I'm worried about'.

There was another occasion when she, ever solicitous of our behaviour on these important foreign visits, brought us to heel; this was after yet another reception following a performance in Poznań. On leaving we had to make our way along a path through a field in order to reach the road. The grass was wet with the early autumn dew, which sparkled in the moonlight, and the beauty of the scene proved too much for Margot. Leaving the path, she slipped off her shoes and ran about, delighting in the cool balm to her stockinged feet, hot and tired from an arduous performance that night. Suddenly her name was being shouted, and up came Miss de Valois to give her a right ticking-off, saying that she would catch cold and worse. The joy dispelled, Margot dutifully put her shoes on again. Dear *Prima Ballerina Assoluta*, I can see her now, suddenly sixteen again and receiving a wigging. But at least this time the incident was purely domestic!

Before we left Poland, Leon Woizikovski gave the company a special class, as well as coaching some members in the rôles that he had performed with the Diaghilev and de Basil companies. He gave some excellent tuition to Michael Somes in the Miller's dance from *Le Tricorne*, created by Massine but also danced with great success by Woizikovski, which Michael was later to perform. Ninette de Valois had told us what a marvellous character this Polish dancer was – a great artist, while yet an uncomplicated and straightforward human being, he succeeded in winning all our hearts.

The tour ended with a series of performances in Malmö in what was then considered a very modern theatre with an expandable stage and several advanced technical facilities. But for us the great moment was when the Swedish film actress, Mai Zetterling, who at that time was an international star and a household name in England, gave us a marvellous party on the night before we left for home. It had been a tour of great interest and importance to us all, full of memorable occasions. We felt privileged to have been given this closer understanding of the people and the countries that we had visited in this immediate post-war era; we felt, too, that we could look forward to growing even closer to them, since there seemed to be every possibility of our returning to extend this rapport in the future.

When we returned home it was business as usual, as Ninette de Valois set about planning the rest of the season with the practicality that was typical of her. There were revivals of Massine's *Le Tricorne* and *La Boutique fantasque*, which had first been performed by the Diaghilev Ballet. The company also produced for the first time *Mam'zelle Angot*, a very light-hearted work founded on an operetta by Lecocq, *La Fille de Madame Angot*, which Massine had choreographed originally for American Ballet Theatre. Although fairly successful, it had not remained permanently in that company's repertoire. For Sadler's Wells Ballet Massine revised the choreography, and we also had a wonderful new décor and costumes by the famous artist, André Derain. He followed the example of Picasso, who had painted the backcloth for *Le Tricorne* for the Diaghilev Ballet, by doing the same for us now, working in an improvised studio in Floral Street next door to the famous Smokey Joe's. This studio is used for the painting and dyeing of costumes for the Royal Ballet and Opera to this day. I was fascinated to see Monsieur Derain on one occasion up a ladder with a long, thin-handled paintbrush, working on the backcloth of *Mam'zelle Angot* just as Picasso had done some years before for the Diaghilev Ballet.

Margot Fonteyn as Mam'zelle Angot was full of humour and danced with such joy as to reflect the spirit of the work. Alexander Grant emerged in this ballet as a wonderful and vibrant character dancer; the public took him immediately to their hearts and kept him there throughout his career. As the Barber he jumped about the stage creating a character full of charm and, when he was put down by others, of pathos. The company peopled the stage with a host of richly etched individuals, something that has always been a strong point and that was particularly noticeable in the ballets of Ninette de Valois and Robert Helpmann. This was the first work to be re-staged specifically for us, and to our delight we found that Massine much enjoyed our improvisation as long as it was within the framework of the rôle as he had envisaged it. In the first scene, Henry Legerton, John Field and I were a trio of somewhat eccentric tradesmen, Butcher, Tailor and Bootmaker. Whilst Michael Somes as a Caricaturist and Moira Shearer as an aristocratic Lady were rehearsing a *pas de deux*, our terrible trio, much encouraged by Massine, were trying to console the Barber, who was obviously enamoured of the Lady, and Grant drew all eyes to his touchingly unrequited love. But as we edged nearer to the centre of the stage, all our 'business' was not fair on the beauty of the *pas de deux*; this was redressed when Miss de Valois in one of her 'tidying up' rehearsals firmly insisted on our retreating towards the wings at this point in the action.

The first-night audience loved the exuberance of the whole thing and from then on Alexander Grant never looked back. At this time, too, inspiration was in the air and Frederick Ashton decided that he would like to choreograph a full-length ballet, *Cinderella*. We had all heard about the production by the Bolshoi in Moscow, the story danced to the music of Prokofiev, with Galina Ulanova in the title rôle; Ashton, in creating his own version, would be having to meet this challenge. It would also be the first classical three-act ballet to be created in England.

During the preparation for this task Fred revealed the fact that he had never seen a pantomime. I, who had spent every Christmas queuing up at Kingston, Richmond and Wimbledon to see the local pantos and who remembered the glittering occasion of the one at the Lyceum to which I was taken by my mother, could hardly believe it. Margot shared my enthusiasm – and so did Bobby, surprisingly, since I did not associate the pantomime tradition with down under. However, not only had he seen them but he had actually been in one, dancing in an early engagement as a wattle flower, not exactly a characteristic rôle for him. I could remember going with him to a wartime panto in York, where he joined in every chorus with enormous gusto, especially when the Dame sang 'Never Miss Your Last Bus Home'.

'The lady conductor gave the warning
There won't be another till the morning...'

It was agreed that Fred, Bobby, Margot and I should all go to the current panto at the London Casino (now the Prince Edward Theatre), and I was not surprised when Bobby did the same thing there with equal relish, so that Fred, who sat passively and seemed impervious to all the high jinks, was moved to say, 'Do be quiet; everybody's looking at us'. Nevertheless, Fred had taken in the glorious Englishness of the occasion and I felt later that this little interchange gave rise to the humorous style of the two Ugly Sisters. Throughout his *Cinderella* he seemed to have been more influenced by the old pantomime tradition, exemplified by such as Dan Leno, than by the treatment of the story in the Russian ballet.

The décor and costumes for the production were by Jean-Denis Malclès. Because of his French nationality he did not design the usual ballroom scene; instead, Cinderella and the Prince met in a garden during a *fête champêtre*, where all the guests wore daytime costumes, some of them heavy and cumbersome for such an occasion. Each had an individual design, avoiding the impression that a chorus line had been invited to the party. My partner and I had costumes of dark brown velvet, trimmed with black fur, and matching brown hats sporting cock's feathers. Robert Irving, who with Warwick Braithwaite had by this time joined our group of conductors, christened us Marquis and Marchioness Mouse. Helpmann and Ashton as the two sisters, each with such defiantly different characters, were made to seem constantly at loggerheads, both flighty with the Prince, yet united in their failure to capture him in the last act. In their disappointment they showed that they were sisters under the skin, and there was a true sense of pathos when they made their exit.

Earlier in the kitchen scene in Act I, I had to cope with a very different sort of costume. I played the part of the hairdresser delivering the wigs to the Ugly Sisters, and entered the kitchen with the rest of the purveyors. They wore heavy tradesmen's clothes and thick-heeled shoes, while I wore a white blouse, blue velvet waistcoat, pink tights and ballet shoes, entering trippingly on the toes! I feel I must have looked oddly out of place. There was not a recognisable entrance to the kitchen, the set being a simple one with a backcloth and a line of wings on each side; we came out wherever Ashton had indicated in the rehearsal room. I entered from the downstage wing and went through the upstage, but not before I had slipped in a double *tour en l'air* for good measure!

Ashton wanted those present at the Prince's reception in Act II to dance in the baroque style on which Mary Skeaping, our great ballet mistress, was an authority – she gave Ashton a great deal of help and advice and added largely to the success of the ensemble. As usual in his ballets there was a superb *pas de deux*, danced by the Prince and Cinderella, and he created a spectacular transformation scene, during which there were variations to represent the four seasons. Nadia Nerina was a sparkling Spring, Violetta Elvin a voluptuous and languorous Summer; in Autumn Pauline Clayden threw leaves above her head and whirled about the stage with great speed and Beryl Grey made a very impressive Winter, with her strong and precise technique.

In the Autumn variation I was reminded of a previous occasion when I was having lunch with Bobby at the Ivy. We passed the table near the door, the most favoured position, where Edith Evans was sitting. She stopped Bobby and said that she had recently been on a visit to Russia, something few people had been able to do in those early post-war days, and that she had seen Ulanova dancing. We had, of course, not seen the famous Russian ballerina in London and Bobby asked what she was like and how she danced, to which Edith Evans threw her head back and, in those famous fluting tones, replied, 'Like a leaf'.

For most of the rehearsals Margot Fonteyn danced the rôle of Cinderella, but, unfortunately for her, she injured her foot and Moira Shearer took her place on the first night. She not only danced the part beautifully but also brought a great deal of her own to it and was a huge success, as she was in the many subsequent performances that she gave.

Life was still made difficult by the lack of rehearsal room at the Opera House and indeed the absence of any in the near vicinity. The management had not thought of acquiring any of the bombed buildings in Floral Street, close to the stage door, which were for sale at very reasonable prices. A short time later these very buildings were renovated and turned into what became the Dance Centre by an enterprising young dancer who had appeared in *Oklahoma!*. We continued to set off with our practise clothes to rehearse in various halls all over town, and for the forthcoming *Cinderella* in the basement of the Kingsway Hall, opposite Holborn Station and still standing today. We had to make our way down a dark passage past rows of dustbins to enter a dingy hall with a floor that was anything but perfect, and the strains of Prokofiev's wonderful score were constantly interrupted by the sounds of falling dustbin lids knocked over by the cats searching for remains of someone's fish and chips. To this cacophony Ashton created his exquisite *pas de deux* and the enchanting solos for the ballerinas dancing the part of the Seasons.

We left all this behind when in 1949 we went to Italy and Florence. *Cinderella* was included in the ballets we took there and was played to great acclaim in the Teatro Comunale. Our repertoire also featured a number of one-act ballets, among them *Checkmate*, which also enjoyed a great success.

In those early post-war days, comparatively few people travelled by plane to Europe. On this occasion Ninette de Valois, Constant Lambert and Margot and Bobby, who were needed for advance publicity, did so while the rest of the company had to cope with the long journey by boat and train, in which we were not given sleepers, but sat up all night four-a-side in the carriages. It was a squash. By that date *The Red Shoes* was on the world's screens and Moira Shearer was a star sensation. No matter, she sat all night with the rest of us without any fuss, much to her credit. It was a relief, after a sleepless night in cramped conditions, to arrive in the morning in Milan, where we had a stop long enough to enable us to leave the train and make for the nearest cafés.

As we sat enjoying our coffee and croissants I noticed a young Milanese man walking past. He suddenly stopped in his tracks and looked at our table, mesmerised. He left after a moment, only to return with a companion or two and an excited frenzy of conversation began. Then I realised that they had recognised the beautiful star of *The Red Shoes*. It was unbelievable to them that here she was, sitting at a table in their familiar, everyday surroundings, and in no time, a group assembled to watch the famous actress sipping her coffee, until we gathered her into our midst and hurried back to our train. But crowds also gathered on the platform there to demonstrate their excited admiration.

Miss de Valois was at the station in Florence to meet us, and, realising that we had had a long and tiring journey, graciously told us that she had cancelled classes and rehearsals for the day. So we were free to explore the beauties of a Florence that was somewhat dusty and showing signs of wartime deprivations. It was warm and sunny, and this encouraged us the next day to discard our jackets when we walked to the theatre for class. As Michael Somes, Richard Ellis and I walked past the Grand Hotel where, in accordance with the hierarchy that then obtained, the principals were staying, Bobby Helpmann appeared and looked at us in horror, telling us that we were in a city and not at a seaside resort and ordered us back to our hotel to put on our jackets. Without a word that is what we did. *Tempora mutant...*

We were greatly taken by the beauty of the city and royally entertained there. Wine, which was hardly known at home then, flowed and the Italian food was superb. This visit to Florence was quite different from our recent previous visits to Europe, and its atmosphere suggested a coming back to life, both culturally and socially, after the war. The city was full of Americans recapturing the spirit of the Grand Tour; when they expressed admiration for the Sadler's Wells Company, we were delighted to tell them that we were due to visit the United States in the fall, on our first American tour. It was marvellous for the company to feel that they had made their mark in this famous old city, and in consequence they responded by giving their absolute best.

By this time Margot Fonteyn had recovered from her injury and was able to dance the rôle of Cinderella. To this she brought her own special qualities of warmth and pathos, particularly in the kitchen scene, where she sat patiently by the fireplace and, in her stillness, gazed into the flames.

For the summer break this year, a group of us from the company decided, having now become Continental-minded, to leave thoughts of Scarborough and Hastings behind and to book a holiday in Italy – in Positano, then still a simple fishing village and a place recommended to us by Margot, Bobby and Fred, who had been there the previous summer. We had a delightful time and, as it was full of young American lads on Fulbright scholarships who had settled there to write the great American novel, we were able to give ourselves a little advance publicity about the forthcoming tour in the United States, as we had done earlier in Florence. This was greeted with much enthusiasm and with promises to come to our performances, from New York to places West, along the 'Atchison, Topeka and the Santa Fe!' We made many friends in Positano and used to dance practically till dawn outside the little hotel to a gramophone urging us to 'Put another nickel in, in the nickelodeon', the popular hit of the day. We followed the lyric to a nickel.

While this was going on, Margot and Fred were on holiday in Paris with Nora Kaye, the American ballerina, who had stayed on in London after the American Ballet Theatre's further season at the Opera House. Margot, who was then being dressed by Christian Dior, took Nora and Fred into the hotel opposite the Dior Salon, the Plaza Athénée, at that time famous for a very potent cocktail, 'Dream Special', which proved to be much to Fred's liking. In those days the Government had imposed a travelling allowance for British citizens going abroad on holiday, so one's expenditure was strictly limited. Nora Kaye, as an American, was not affected by this and with a plentiful supply of dollars and generosity to match was always footing the bill. I was told later that on one occasion on which the waiter brought yet another bill to Nora for the replenishing of Fred's 'Dream Specials', she looked up at him and said, 'What else do you want? Blood?'

After these happy diversions and trivial pursuits of the summer break and before going to America in October, the company had to fulfil its commitments at home, which included a two-week season at the Edinburgh Festival followed by a week in a cinema in Croydon. Then, as now, there was a shortage of theatres suitable for ballet companies, and it was usual for them to dance on the enlarged stages of the super cinemas. We have, in fact, come full circle, and companies of dancers are back on the cinema circuit again.

At the Festival we performed *The Sleeping Beauty* every night with matinées on Wednesday and Saturday at the Empire Theatre, which mostly catered for variety shows. The stage was inadequate for us, especially as we had by now grown accustomed to the immensity of the one at Covent Garden; though the dancers made the best of things, as they always did, the overall quality of the performances was not up to standard, and we were aware of this. Nora Kaye, who had now become an old friend, told us later that she had two friends, well known in New York as very keen and knowledgeable followers of the ballet, who would be going to Edinburgh. She felt sure that they would make a particular point of seeing our company and would no doubt come backstage and take us out to supper. Well, they didn't! We saw not a sign of them during the whole two weeks; perhaps they had come and hadn't really liked what they saw. If that was so, then we had better pull our socks up.

It was, nevertheless, rewarding to be part of the Festival in 1948, its opening year. Edinburgh looked impressive and provided a rich assembly of attractions, plays, operas, films and exhibitions, and when we returned to London it was mainly to complete the arrangements for the forthcoming visit to America.

First of all we had to obtain our visas from the American Embassy. This was not the simple routine that it later became, but entailed submitting to a detailed questionnaire, which did not exclude a thorough enquiry into one's political views and associations, and it was with much relief that we all passed muster. We had become an international company and had toured in Iron Curtain countries, where we had made many professional friends; it was understandable in the climate of the day that this was a very sensitive area as far as the United States was concerned. For them the Red Menace was very real and was portrayed in many of the current Hollywood films; the McCarthy period, after all, was not far off. However, we were finally set to cross the Big Pond and meet our fate!

Herbert Hughes, manager of the company, posted our travelling arrangements on the notice board at the theatre. David Webster, as General Administrator of the Royal Opera House, with Miss de Valois, Frederick Ashton, Margot Fonteyn and Robert Helpmann would go ahead to New York to be present at press conferences and to cope with the advance publicity. They were to leave on a scheduled flight that coming Saturday, while the main company would travel on the following Monday in two chartered planes. This was long before the days of jumbo jets that would later accommodate everyone in a single aircraft; on this occasion we were divided into two groups, women on one plane and men on the other. In the event of any mishap to either flight, the management would have found themselves with a one-sex company!

Whilst having lunch at home in Teddington on the Saturday of the first plane's departure, I had a telephone call from David Webster to say that Miss de Valois was suffering from migraine and had decided that she would prefer to postpone her journey until Monday and travel on the men's plane. Since there was no extra seat available on that flight, a quick swap had to be made. After several unsuccessful attempts to contact various members of the company, I was the first found to be available; I was told to report at the airport at six o'clock, so I tore around, collecting shirts, shoes, everything I could think of. I was then sharing 'Melrose' with a niece of Naggie, Florence May Kathleen Croucher, affectionately known as Bon, and while I was cramming everything into my well-worn Revelation suitcase she hurried to the cleaners in the High Street and collected my suits, which was something I had planned to do later that day.

I had told David Webster that I knew that my brother Fred, who lived at Hampton, would take me to the airport. He duly arrived with his wife and picked me up together with Bon and we drove post-haste to Heathrow. I had not flown before, but Fred had frequently done so and knew the routine of finding his way round the collection of Nissen huts that in those days comprised Heathrow. He hurried me to the departure lounge, where I excitedly joined Margot, Fred, Bobby and David Webster, who looked much relieved that I had made it on time. He told me to ask at the desk for Miss de Valois' ticket, saying that he would confirm the fact that I was going in her place; but, alas, there was apparently no ticket for her. Consternation. Suddenly a thought occurred to me. 'Was there a ticket in Miss de Valois' married name?' Indeed there was, so I crossed the Atlantic not only in the seat but in the name of Mrs Arthur Connell.

Joining our flight was the lady responsible for the wardrobe that the girls in the company would wear outside the theatre during the visit to the States. The leading British fashion houses had especially designed dresses and coats for this purpose, and it provided an excellent opportunity to display their many talents emerging after the war. To ensure that there was no favouritism, the designers' names were put into a hat and all the girls, from ballerinas to *corps de ballet*, then picked one out. Needless to say, Fonteyn, with her usual sense of wanting to be treated as one of the team, packed away her Dior and wore her company model, as provided, when she arrived in New York.

Our first stop on the flight was at Prestwick, where we alighted while the plane was being refuelled for the next stage to Shannon. We were having a drink in the bar and all seemed to be going smoothly, until an announcement was made to the effect that, because of a slight technical fault in the aircraft, we would spend the night in the Grand Hotel, Troon, and continue to Shannon the next morning.

After our stopover in Ireland and another in Reykjavik, we really felt we were on our way. I was in a window seat gazing out in wonder at being high above the clouds when I noticed that one of the propellers had stopped. I turned to Helpmann and gave him this report. Those famous, expressive eyes grew even larger than usual and he said at once, 'Don't tell Fred' – this in consideration of his friend's fear of flying. But in the innocence of my first experience of air travel, I replied that there were three more propellers, so why worry? No more did Fred. Strange as it seemed to me, there was no announcement and we continued on our way. I was told much later that stopping the propeller was technically known as 'feathering' and was a procedure that could be followed if necessary for technical reasons. One lives – fortunately – and learns!

We finally arrived at La Guardia (then the main airport serving New York City), though later than scheduled. In spite of the late hour we were met by the faithful Nora Kaye together with the famous Russian impresario, Sol Hurok, who was presenting us on this American tour. I had seen him briefly in London but here he was, larger than life, wearing a wide-brimmed hat, a coat flung around his shoulders and carrying a walking stick. He asked immediately where Ninette de Valois was. Bobby stepped forward saying that she was unwell, but before he could elaborate he was silenced by what amounted to a reprimand: 'Don't ever say in a public place that anyone in the company is ill, especially at an airport. "De Valois", "Fonteyn", both foreign names, someone overhears, gets the idea that the principal is indisposed and then there are queries to be answered at the box office.' Such was the apparent authority and pragmatism of Mr Hurok.

There was a message for Bobby from Garson Kanin, the playwright, inviting him to meet him at Reuben's restaurant as soon as he had arrived, and it was decided that Margot, Nora and I should join them there. But first we three took a cab and, at Margot's request, made a detour to look at the Metropolitan Opera House, which was downtown and some way from the restaurant. In a trice we were bowling down Broadway, through Times Square past the famous Camel Cigarette hoarding, showing a man smoking with real puffs coming out of his mouth. When we arrived at the 'Met', the stage staff were removing the scenery and costumes of the company that had closed that night, a procedure technically known as the 'get-out'. As the large doors through which they carried the scenery opened on to the street, we were able to step from the pavement directly on to the stage. The curtain of the proscenium arch was up and we had a full view of the auditorium. It was with great emotion that I saw the slight figure of Margot Fonteyn, surrounded by the noise and bustle of the stage crew, silently looking out at the darkened theatre where, in only a week's time, the audience would be sitting in judgement on this unknown dancer in the rôle of Aurora in *The Sleeping Beauty*.

After this brief pilgrimage we made our way to Reuben's. Following our meal and the buzz of conversation in the restaurant, the visiting team deemed it time to go to our hotels. It seemed an age since Fred and Bon had rushed me to the airport, and a world away from Teddington. In fact it was early morning when we said goodbye to loyal Nora Kaye, who had waited all day at La Guardia airport for our arrival and was still with us.

The hotels where accommodation had been reserved for the members of our flight were all in the proximity of Reuben's restaurant in upper Fifth Avenue: the Plaza, Margot's hotel, was right on Central Park; David Webster and Fred were staying at the Gotham, opposite Tiffany's; Bobby was being entertained by Garson Kanin. But where was I to go? My alter ego, Mrs Arthur Connell, in whose name I had crossed the Atlantic, was booked into the St Moritz Hotel, but I couldn't assume her identity for a second time. David, however, who had been a long-time habitué of the Gotham, managed to get me a room there, in spite of the usual weekend influx of visitors to the city. So off we went, staggering under the weight of the Sunday papers, already on sale on the Saturday night, as they are now in London. David asked me if I had any friends in New York; I hadn't. He then told me to meet him in the foyer of our hotel the following evening, when he would take me to a party to be given by two of his close New York friends.

The next morning, waking up in my luxurious surroundings, I telephoned room service as instructed by David Webster, and a waiter duly arrived, wheeling in a table groaning with a most delicious cornucopia of a breakfast. Fortified by this, I decided to go out on what was a fresh, sunny, Sunday morning. I explored Fifth Avenue, wandered into Central Park and walked to the Zoo, having gazed at the horse-drawn carriages opposite the Plaza inviting people to take a drive around the Park, and generally revelled in the opulence of the shop window displays, such as I hadn't seen since before the war in London. In the evening I went as planned with David to an elegant mid-town house where the hosts at the party were Trumbull (Tug) Barton and John McHugh. The house was as elegant inside as out, and at a grand piano in the first-floor drawing room was a young man playing Richard Rodgers's 'Manhattan', which had delighted me when I had heard it in Croydon a week or so before we left for America. Little did I know at the time of the party that Tug and John, throughout the many years of our touring the United States, would become such close and stalwart friends.

On Monday morning I packed, left the deep luxury of the Gotham and went to the Bryant Hotel on the West Side, adjacent to Columbus Circle. The Bryant was a very different kettle of fish, but when it was invaded, after the arrival of the main company, by laughing and chattering teammates, I felt it was great to be back among them again. By this time Michael Somes had became a partner of Margot Fonteyn; in consequence his hotel was in the upper echelon and my new roommate was John Field. In all sincerity I can say that John was great; friendly, full of humour and considerate, and he, too, remained a close friend throughout the years I knew him.

But now life for us all took on a serious note; the next week was devoted to working in preparation for our début at the 'Met': classes, rehearsals, concentration on every detail in the final run-up. All this, Miss de Valois knew, was necessary to give us confidence. In spite of our nervous anticipation, though, I must admit we found ourselves loving New York. How could one resist the native friendliness, the glow of the old 'Met' and being surrounded by the ultimate in show business, Broadway, with theatres lining every street, home to long-running successes? We out-of-towners were dazzled by the displays, brightly lit day and night, proclaiming the stars who were filling the houses. We simply had to 'make it' and be part of the big parade on the Great White Way, but that long week before the opening seemed to be full of dreadful doubts.

While we remained true to our Covent Garden home, it was marvellous to experience the wide apron of the stage at the 'Met', jutting out over part of the orchestra pit and so giving us a feeling of closeness to the audience, in contrast to dancing behind the flat proscenium arch of the Opera House and having to project over a very wide pit before reaching the stalls. Outside was frantic industry, because this was the rag-trade district, where one encountered racks of dresses whizzing through the streets. The nearby drug stores delighted us with their exotic novelties, chocolate-malted milkshakes, blueberry and apple pies *à la mode*, 'eggs over', and made us forget clambering up to the gallery bar at the Opera House for the morning break. We also forgot the horse steaks in Smokey Joe's as we grappled with the huge beef steaks of various cuts in McCarthy's Bar opposite the stage door of the 'Met', which featured largely in our letters home. We even described how much we had to leave on our plates.

Interviews were much in demand and Helpmann, typically, declared that his main ambition was to see the World Series, that yearly bonanza of baseball, even declaring his favourite team to be the Brooklyn Dodgers. One evening during this first week we gave a lift to a young up-and-coming actress friend and, as she got out of the cab, Bobby told her that he had managed to get tickets for the game and invited her to join him. Her reply to this was to the effect that she would rather be seen dead than at the World Series. An expansive gesture of throwing her silver fox stole around her shoulders emphasised the dismissal as she went on up to her apartment. Our cab driver turned to us and said, 'How do you like that broad? And she's from Brooklyn!' With a touch of the Professor Higgins he must have recognised her native accent.

On Saturday 5 October we were all called to the final rehearsal, when

Miss de Valois gave us our last notes before the big night. There was a somewhat tense and solemn feeling in the theatre; a few early good-luck messages had arrived from England, which gave us a slight flicker of homesickness. As I took Margot back to her hotel, we were both silent until she asked me if I would have dinner with her that evening. I said that of course I would, but that I must first ring Fred, who had invited me to join him and a friend, Alice Bouverie, to see a revue, *Lend an Ear*, that had become a great hit on Broadway, starring a young actress called Carol Channing. When she heard this Margot said immediately that she would love to join us, welcoming a pleasant distraction from the task that lay ahead. Mrs Bouverie was duly telephoned and, having been originally Alice Astor and not without influence on the New York scene, managed to procure an extra seat for this sell-out show.

Afterwards we all took Margot back to her hotel. We watched her turn and wave to us before entering the Plaza and, in that moment, I realised that the weight of all our hopes for the opening night that was to follow rested uniquely on her slim shoulders.

Chapter 14

In New York that year, October was particularly hot, and the 6th, the night we opened at the Metropolitan Opera House, was no exception. From dawn the temperature was blistering, and the 'Met', unlike its modern counterpart, was not air-conditioned. We arrived at the theatre in time for our morning class as usual. Beryl Grey lovingly recalls how surprised she was to find Margot Fonteyn already at the barre; she had thought that perhaps Margot would be resting in her hotel room until she left for the theatre to prepare herself for the big first night. Seeing Margot already there gave Beryl great heart and confidence for dancing her own rôle as the Lilac Fairy and made things seem like a normal routine day. But, my goodness, we were nervous.

We returned in the early evening to give us extra time to get ready, which was just as well, for the heat was so great that the make-up started to slither off our faces and we had to keep applying new coats. Margot tells in her autobiography that I had established a habit at the Royal Opera House of going to see her before a performance; we would talk a little and have a laugh or two. That night in New York I hesitated, not wanting to disturb her in any way on this very special occasion. But then, I thought, not to go and see her and so make a break in the chain of normality might disturb her more. She wrote later that the fact that Pamela and I had gone to her dressing room had reassured her; this was still the Sadler's Wells Ballet and she was with all her old friends.

Finally it was time to go on. When the call came, 'Overture and Beginners', we assembled on the stage, wishing one another good luck with hugs and kisses. There was that wonderful mixture of nerves, anxiety, excitement and worry that is all part of a first night. Over and above this was the feeling we all shared, that this was an important occasion, which could prove to be a turning point in the history of the company.

When the curtain rose I made my way downstage towards Constant Lambert, miming in my usual fashion the opening of the proceedings, but when I reached the footlights opposite him there was a huge outburst of applause, which was totally unexpected and knocked me for six. It was, of course, an acknowledgement of Oliver Messel's beautiful set and a spontaneous greeting for the visiting British company. Constant noticed a momentary lapse on my part and said later, 'Well, I've never seen you taken aback before'. However, I quickly recovered and continued my promenade around the stage and my mime of accepting the scroll of guests invited to the christening and announcing the arrival of the King and Queen. The wealth of greeting went on as each artist appeared on stage, and great appreciation was expressed at each of the variations of the Fairies, especially for the brilliant solo danced by Beryl Grey. Most remarkable was a spontaneous round of applause accorded to the line of the Lilac Fairy's attendants as they travelled downstage, exhibiting the neat footwork and exact head movements typical of the Sadler's Wells *corps de ballet*. And this was still only the Prologue.

After the interval we returned to the stage for Act I, and there was Margot practising, before the curtain went up, for her first entrance. The rest of us had had our baptism of fire, but all was still before her. The curtain rose on the assembled company, the garland dancers moving about the knitting women, the princes as suitors, the King and Queen – all had established the beginning of the act. And then one heard the first notes of Aurora's entrance. The tension mounted on stage and in the audience as everyone waited for her first appearance. Then came that magical run across the stage and the burst through the arch of trees as Aurora entered to celebrate her sixteenth birthday; the princes stepped forward to claim her hand in marriage and the *Rose Adage* began. Almost immediately the whole house capitulated to the wonder of Margot Fonteyn – her musicality, the purity of her dancing and the incredible simplicity hiding the technical complexity of one of the most difficult of Petipa's passages of choreography. On top of this, and perhaps the most potent quality of all, was the way she established the character of the rôle and the charm of a sixteen-year-old girl. As the performance proceeded, the success of the company became more and more evident, and in the last act the audience witnessed the serenity and regality of Princess Aurora on her marriage to Prince Florimund. Here Robert Helpmann made a great impression, having been a fiendish Carabosse in the Prologue, he now showed his prowess as a *danseur noble*, supporting Margot in this last act.

We were overwhelmed by the ovation at the end, indicating the audience's appreciation not only of the artists but also of the company as a whole and its creator, Ninette de Valois. The evening was electrifying on stage, and outside the Opera House the crowds milling around made it plain that they had taken us to their hearts. We left the stage door and boarded our two buses with Margot in one of them as well as all the other principals, and made our way with a police escort through the crowds and traffic to the party given by the Mayor of New York at Gracie Mansion, his official residence. Once there, Margot, looking wonderful in a champagne-coloured dress, led the company down the open staircase of the building to the lawns that edged on to the river, to join the other guests sitting at supper at tables there. After the party I went on with Margot, Fred, Bobby and Nora Kaye not to Sardi's, where the theatre world always gathered to read press notices, but nostalgically to Reuben's, where only a week before we had sat rather tentatively and nervously on our arrival in New York. There we read the notices in the morning papers, which were without exception unstinting in their praise, and there was no doubt that Margot had exceeded all expectations.

Next morning I had a phone call from Johnny Kriza; he was downstairs with Muriel Bentley and they both wanted to take me out to lunch. The sentiments expressed in the Rodgers and Hart song 'Manhattan' were never so true for me as on that sunny day when we made our way in Johnny's open car to the restaurant. It turned out to be a marvellous occasion; it was also the first time that I had encountered eggs Benedict! Because Johnny and Muriel were so popular, people kept coming up to our table, and the principal topic of conversation was the triumph of the Sadler (sic) Wells Ballet, as the Americans insisted on calling it, and, of course, the wonderful impression that Margot had made on the whole city. Success is nowhere else as potent as in New York.

Since seeing Johnny and Muriel in London, we had become good friends and when Johnny, who was a first-rate dancer himself with great charm on and off stage and a rare sincerity to match, said that the company had just proved a great success in New York, you believed him wholeheartedly. Furthermore, he seemed to emanate an aura of show business, which, for me, has always been a sterling hallmark. I loved getting to know the American dancers as we met them then; their early days in the late forties seem to parallel those of the Vic–Wells Ballet in the thirties, and they too had to find other jobs between seasons to keep them going. At that time Johnny was working in cabaret in a downtown hotel, The New Yorker. Later on he invited me to see him there and he was great, especially in a number by Cole Porter, 'Too Darned Hot', from *Kiss Me Kate*, then showing in New York.

My own feelings after the previous night at the 'Met' were akin to those of receiving the keys of the city. Alas, it wasn't any 'isle of joy' for Trumbull Barton and John McHugh, the friends of David Webster whom I had met on my first night in New York. They had handed over to friends the tickets that he had given them, and spent the weekend away from the city in preference to attending the first night of this little-known ballet company from England. As they opened the front door on their return and pushed back the bulk of the morning papers, there to meet their eyes were the banner headlines, 'FONTEYN CAPTURES NEW YORK', and the inside pages had room for little else but tributes to this 'little known company from England'. Poor Tug and John, to have missed this. Throughout the many years of their subsequent deep and faithful friendship to Margot and to the company this was a favourite anecdote, which we often mulled over gleefully.

During the six-week season at the 'Met', our weekends consisted of two performances on Saturday and two on Sunday. Mostly they were the full-length ballets, *Swan Lake* and *The Sleeping Beauty*, both of which proved very popular with the New York public, who had never seen these works in their entirety before. This was a considerable task for the *corps de ballet*, but in spite of it all they scored a great success in their own right and continued to set a personal seal with their distinctive English style.

We sighed with relief when the weekend was over and we could relax on Monday, our free day. We soon learnt to make the most of this, shopping and visiting our new-found friends and, for me especially, seeing the latest American musicals. I cut my teeth on *Kiss Me Kate*, *South Pacific* and *Where's Charlie?*, the American version of *Charley's Aunt*. Terence Rattigan was on Broadway, producing his latest play from London; he, with us, became part of the British contingent and we all got on well together, which added greatly to the pleasure of the whole experience – and how we revelled in it.

It was not surprising that our two full-length classical ballets plus Ashton's three-act ballet *Cinderella* made the biggest impression on the New York audiences. They were a new experience for a public used to a constant programme of one-act ballets, brilliant though they were and choreographed by such talents as those of Jerome Robbins, Michael Kidd and Agnes de Mille, who had indeed already proved to be a success in American Ballet Theatre when they came to London in 1946. However, in addition to the three blockbusters, we took with us the one-act ballets created over the years mostly before the Royal Opera House. These met with varying success. Ashton was already known in America for his pre-war production of Gertrude Stein and Virgil Thompson's *Four Saints in Three Acts* and later *Devil's Holiday*, which he choreographed for the Ballet Russe de Monte Carlo. However, *Façade*, *Hamlet*, *A Wedding Bouquet*, *Miracle in the Gorbals*, *Apparitions*, *Symphonic Variations*, *The Rake's Progress*, *Job* and *Checkmate*, all of which we took, had not been seen that side of the Atlantic. The three latter works brought home the fact that Ninette de Valois was herself a first-class choreographer as well as being the Founder/Director of the company.

One sees now, after the passage of time, that this selection should have made more impact than it did, but in fact it was overshadowed by our full-length ballets. These had the virtue of greater novelty for audiences everywhere; previous performances of *Swan Lake*, for example, had been limited to Act II. Indeed, Sol Hurok had been worried that, when people saw it billed, they would assume we were performing the extract and not the whole work, so he decided to add *Hamlet* for good measure. This made for a late evening, and not an easy one for the critics who had to make the next morning's edition.

Façade had always been a popular feature of the Vic–Wells and Sadler's Wells Ballets, but one of the items, the Foxtrot, originally danced by Ashton and Helpmann with Pamela May and June Brae as their partners, had been deleted. It was decided to re-instate it for America, and Ashton cast Kenneth MacMillan, who had just joined our section of the company, and myself in their original rôles. This delighted me, but I knew I was up against stiff competition, for Kenneth was a brilliant dancer before he became better known for his choreography. However, I did my best and tried to make up for my lack of technique with a frenzied vivacity!

The success of Margot Fonteyn during this season has been well documented, but it must not be forgotten that the company included a number of really notable dancers; the large repertoire demanded this, and the demand was well and truly met. Each ballerina gained her own following with an individual interpretation of the great classical rôles: Pamela May, Beryl Grey, Violetta Elvin, Nadia Nerina – and Moira Shearer, who had a special rapport with the American audiences, not surprisingly, considering her success on the screen. The male contingent was headed by Helpmann and Ashton with Somes, Hart, Field and Rassine, and, as we have seen, the *corps de ballet* made their own very distinctive mark.

Our Sunday evening performances became particularly enjoyable, despite the heat and hard slog, as most of the cast of the musicals, plays and general Broadway entertainments were free that night and would take a busman's holiday to go to Sadler's Wells Ballet. Some famous figures came round to see us and would often find us still on stage, where we remained to chat together. One such occasion I remember well, although it was a Sunday on a later tour in New York; after a performance of *Giselle* Lilian Gish came and talked at length about our mime, saying that what we did on stage was akin to what she had done in the early silent films, attempting to make words unnecessary. I was in my seventh heaven talking to her, while recalling those far-away Saturday nights in Teddington when Pat would take me to the (silent) pictures. Although her most famous film, *Birth of a Nation*, was too early for me, a TV series on the days of the silent films included a clip of her floating through icy waters, clinging to a chunk of an iceberg until hauled to safety by one of the heroes of the silver screen. She was so bright and intelligent as she talked away and so knowledgeable that I was conscious that here was a great star of the cinema of any age.

As we spoke, I was also reminded of a day that season, between a matinée and an evening performance, when I went to a small party where the most famous trio of silent stars were present – Mary Pickford, Gloria Swanson and Charles Chaplin, all deep in conversation by the fireplace. Miss de Valois, who wasn't exactly a film buff, suddenly remembered being taken as a young girl to the cinema. She turned, wide-eyed, to me and said, 'Look, there's the whole three of them together!'

Our free Mondays were already starting to form a pattern to be followed on our many subsequent seasons in New York. We had daytime trips out of town to some 'very lovely home' in New York State, which was always most enjoyable, and early on we started going to regular luncheon parties given by Tug and John. To these they invited a large group of the company plus their own friends, who ranged from celebrities such as Myrna Loy, Lauren Bacall and Angela Lansbury to other people less well known but equally delightful. Margot was there, relaxed and full of laughter on her one free day, beautifully dressed as always. I can see her now in a large, black cartwheel hat to complement her outfit that day, which she wore with her usual unaffected ease.

During his days working in Australia, Moyra Fraser's father had made friends with a charming lady who later became Mrs Oscar Hammerstein. The Fraser family retained their friendship with her and, soon after the war, her daughter came over to England from America to study acting and became a great friend of Moyra's sister, Shelagh, and myself. Before I left for the tour to the States, Mr Fraser gave me a letter of introduction, addressed to Mrs Dorothy Hammerstein; one way or another I delayed posting it to her until very late in our New York season. However, when I finally did so, back came an answer, telling me that she would be attending our last night at the 'Met' and inviting me to have supper in the Oak Room restaurant at the Plaza Hotel. I felt that this would be a very pleasant way to end our stay in New York.

For me, when the curtain fell on that last night, which, as on our triumphant opening, was a performance of *Sleeping Beauty*, there was a feeling of sadness. Would I ever return to this magical city that I had grown to love so much? As I started to remove my make-up, a knock came at the dressing-room door; I opened it and there was Dorothy's daughter, Susan. While we were laughingly greeting each other she turned to her escort and said, 'You must meet my husband'. I looked up and there before me was Henry Fonda! Susan explained that she had come round to tell me that her mother and father had gone to the restaurant and that I was to follow at my leisure and join them there. Dorothy had also extended the invitation to Bobby Helpmann. This was a great relief to me, being somewhat in awe of having to meet the Hammersteins all on my own. By the time I had said, 'See you later', and the couple were leaving, there was a line of heads popping out from every dressing-room door along the corridor. I then went along to Bobby's room to pass on the invitation; but no, he was already engaged. I was appalled at the thought of having to enter the Oak Room to find the Hammersteins without Bobby's moral support. I said to him, 'I just don't know how to do this', and he replied, 'Well, you get a cab, go to the Plaza Hotel, make your way to the Oak Room and just sit down with the Hammersteins'. I went out with my tail between my legs and did just that.

When I arrived at the Plaza, at the mention of the magic name I was led by a succession of bowing waiters right to the Hammersteins' table, and I have to say that every tentative vestige of shyness left me before the charm and friendliness of Dorothy and Oscar Hammerstein and Susan and Henry Fonda. The whole evening was a complete joy, and what a way to end the season in New York.

The next morning we left for Washington D.C. It was by now 9 November, but the fine late-autumn weather still continued to accompany our first sight of the capital. With its wide avenues, government buildings and memorials to the nation's heroes, we found it very impressive, but we were captivated by Georgetown and the streets of small town houses, lived in by many distinguished politicians and powerful figures behind the public faces. As everywhere in America, the entertainment was lavish, but since we were in Washington for only two days this was limited to a luncheon party on our arrival and a grand reception later at the British Embassy. Alas, this was the time when the city had no theatre suitable for a large classical ballet company such as ours; the day was far away when it could boast the admirable Kennedy Center. We appeared at Constitution Hall, where the substitute for a stage was a relatively small platform with a floor as slippery as that at the Tower Ballroom, Blackpool, and throughout the performance dancers, including Fonteyn, measured their length on the parquet. However, at the reception at the Embassy the British Ambassador, Sir Roger Makin, made what was to be a much-quoted speech to the effect that we were not the first British to slip up in Washington.

After this we continued our tour to Philadelphia, where again our stay was for only two days. On arrival there we were shown the final summing-up of the company's season in New York, written by John Martin, the eminent critic of the *New York Times*. He was much impressed by the dancing and choreography, and was generally encouraging. Before I had seen this notice, a member of the company had told me about it and said very surprisingly, '... and you're mentioned'. Well, the mention turned out to be actually a whole paragraph. This may have been because I was the sort of artist in the more traditional style of the old, established companies, who had not been much featured in America. But it was in the States that I first felt some confidence in myself as a performer. On the lighter side, though, there was an apocryphal story going round during the time in New York that our major ballet, *The Sleeping Beauty*, was sub-titled 'Or a Hundred Years with Leslie Edwards'.

After Philadelphia we moved on to Chicago, dancing at the Civic Opera House for a week. For me this was a city steeped in legend, the result of so many Saturday nights in the cinema in Teddington spent under the spell of James Cagney and gangland bloodbaths on St Valentine's Day, long before all this was featured in the delightful film *Some Like It Hot*. Then there was the thunderous knock on the door of the speakeasy in Al Jolson's film *The Jazz Singer*, which heralded the beginning of sound and the 'talkies', and the epics about the arch-gangster Al Capone and the mob, spraying bootleggers with bullets on every street corner.

What I found, however, was an exciting town set against the beauty of Lake Michigan, so vast that it seemed more like the sea as we watched the great ships passing by. An elegant historic water tower added to the charm of that part of the city. The architecture of the apartment blocks on the lakeside was impressive and, as we discovered on later visits in the hot summer, there was a huge beach for swimming and welcome relaxation. But on this first night it was very near Christmas and we loved seeing Father Christmas outside the stores, particularly Marshall Field 'on State Street, that great street', ringing the bells rather like the ones we once had in tea-rooms to call the waitress.

We found great friendliness from the ballet contingent there, led by a fascinating and well-known dancer, Ruth Page, who had her own ballet company and a large school in Chicago. One of her principal dancers, Bentley Stone, held a special interest for me; he had choreographed for the Ballet Rambert a *pas de deux* to Ravel's *Pavane pour une Infante défunte*, first danced by Maude Lloyd and William Chappell, and this I was later to perform at the Ballet Club with a tall and beautiful dancer called Daphne Gow. I much admired Ruth Page; she was very spirited and became a friend of Margot and Fred. She married an attorney, Tom Fisher, and they were both popular and important members of the Chicago community.

Ruth invited the company to marvellous parties in her lakeside apartment, and years later the two of us used to take the floor in what were known in those days as exhibition dances in the style of Astaire and Rogers when in their elegant and romantic mood.

The Civic Opera House was dedicated to a famous singer of Scottish extraction from the early part of the century, Mary Garden. I have a feeling that the beauty and personality in the interpretation of all her rôles might have outweighed the power of her voice, but no matter; she could claim and rightly so the title of prima donna. Entering the stage door at this Opera House I was immediately confronted by a full-length portrait of Miss Garden; while most paintings, busts and statues of prima donnas, ballerinas and conductors generally grace the foyers of the great opera houses, Miss Garden's presence backstage seemed to indicate a desire for her likeness to calm the performers and wish them good luck. We all felt this every time we returned there, and we greeted her as a friend.

The main company stayed at the Sherman Hotel, which various members of the hotel staff told us was well to the fore in the days of Prohibition. Indeed, there were still many people in the windy city willing to tell you of the gangster era, and they would vouch for the fact that 'Legs' Diamond met his end outside the bank on the corner next to the hotel. Whether it was true or not didn't matter; by that time we were susceptible to every legend, many of which later became the subjects of films and television series featuring the federal agent, Eliot Ness.

The hotel was right in the middle of the city and at the heart of everything, cinemas, theatres and shops; but what was wonderful was that there still remained portions of the old elevated railway, known affectionately as the El. We loved whizzing around the city on that, having climbed up a staircase from the street to reach the station. On these elevated short tours we really felt as if we were in the movies. The Sherman was unashamedly jazzy, its rooms decorated in the strong, primary colours much in fashion at the time and unlike the more subdued tones back home in England; but it was friendly and had a splendid coffee shop where we would congregate before leaving for rehearsals and performances at the Civic Opera House, within easy walking distance. We would hurry back after the curtain fell to have supper in the hotel restaurant called the 'Well of the Sea', which had an excellent cabaret in the form of a revue. I loved this and we all became friends with the cast. All in all we had a most enjoyable time in Chicago and hated having to leave it.

Our next engagement was at East Lansing, a nearby university town, where we gave two performances in the college auditorium. Sadly this was to be our farewell to the United States, and we were due afterwards to leave for Canada and Toronto. Since leaving New York we had travelled by train – no ordinary train, but one that was known as the 'Sol Hurok Special' and was advertised as such on the front of the engine. It left each town in which we had been appearing at about three a.m., following the evening's performance, and was special in that it carried the company, the orchestra, the scenery, the props, the costumes and, with them, the stage staff. It took some time to load up all the effects, hence our uncongenial hour of departure. As can be imagined, the conditions were somewhat cramped and there were occasions when we left so late that we only just arrived in time for our next engagement. However, this was all part of life's rich touring pageant.

Toronto was in fact one such occasion; we were to appear at the Royal Alexandra Theatre, but we had a job to get there, trudging through the deepest snow after our arrival at the hotel. This was of the small, hick-town variety and, on the weekend before we left, the trappers had been at the liquor. As you walked down the corridor to your room, other bedroom doors would open and an empty bottle or two would fly through the air. Over the years Toronto has become very dear to my heart and I have many loyal friends there; the city is now magnificent, but it was rather on the primitive side in the late forties. I well remember seeing on our last Saturday morning, while walking down one of the principal streets, Yonge Street, a number of Indians wearing their long, feathered head-dresses and riding up to City Hall. They looked splendid, and their dignity was in keeping with one's traditional ideas of Canada and the Rockies.

In Toronto Bobby met an Australian friend who, years before, had stage-managed a show with him back home in Sydney. He had settled in the city with his Polish wife and two daughters, and offered to take us to see Niagara Falls. Pamela, Margot, Fred, Bobby and I squeezed into his car and off we went. It was freezing cold and even the long grass was covered in ice, as were the coin-operated binoculars that were there for visitors' use on less rigorous days. We managed to unravel ourselves from the car and slither over to the railings from which one could look down at the Falls. Typically, Fred, at his first sight of them, said, 'Oh, how disappointing'. Bobby just managed not to hit him, his friend having taken us all this uncomfortable way. However, when we later made our way, dressed in oilskins and sou'westers, across the passage constructed immediately behind and underneath the mass of water falling from its great height, it was anything but disappointing.

Our kind chauffeur and his wife asked the five of us to dinner at his house; they had two daughters who studied at the local ballet school run by Rita Warne, and she and her husband, Aylmer Macdonald, were also guests at this enjoyable party. I liked them both and Mrs Macdonald even offered to help with the washing-up. Imagine the delight to find that Margot was doing the drying!

Ottawa followed Toronto. The Governor General of Canada at the time was Lord Alexander of Tunis, who won us all over with his charming manner – and, of course, his distinguished war record was already a matter of history. When we arrived, the temperature was subnormal and the pavements covered in ice; as we left our buses to enter Government House, where we were entertained during our stay, we practically took the Cresta Run. But once we were inside and defrosted, we were given a buffet luncheon in the grand dining room. During this we were all amused to hear conductor Robert Irving, true as always to his Wykehamist code ('manners maketh man'), turn to the wife of Lord Alexander's aide, Lady Clutterbuck, an extremely impressive and statuesque person, and ask her if he could pass her a roll. She replied in sonorous tones, 'Oh, Mr Irving, I always enjoy a roll'. I have to say that this became one of the favourite catchphrases of the tour.

It was a short visit and a freezing one, but there we were at the seat of Government in Canada – another milestone on this journey. The final stage was Montreal, where we had a week of performances before returning to London. We were conscious of the French influence in the city, which gave it an elegance, and everywhere were glimpses of the snow-capped Laurentian Mountains, to which we made visits in horse-drawn carriages, the popular thing to do.

As the week progressed, the weather deteriorated. On the day we were due to leave, the girls' plane – we were still working on the single-sex travel pattern – managed to take off on schedule in the morning; but, alas, by the time the men were due to leave a freezing fog had descended, the airport was closed and we had to stay on for another night in Montreal. We had all run out of cash by this time, but Bertie Hughes, our manager, gave us an extra day's pay to enable us to survive the twenty-four hours. The next day we were able to depart, but unfortunately were still dogged by unfavourable weather. Unable to make London Airport, we were diverted to Prestwick, where we had to spend yet another night sleeping on the floor of the airport lounge – an uncomfortable contrast for me to that earlier outward delay at Prestwick, where, travelling as a VIP, I had been put up at the Grand Hotel, Troon.

To add insult to injury we were at the mercy of the dour customs officers, who spared us none of the rigours of their examinations, ripping open our presents for loved ones at home and, in so doing, leaving a heap of shredded gift-wrapping on the floor. There was further gall in store: while lying uncomfortably trying to get some sleep, we heard on the wireless the news from London, with an announcer talking about the arrival of our ballerinas and their having earned much-needed currency for the country, a matter of great concern in those austere post-war days. He quoted the nickname newly coined for them – the 'Dollarinas' – and described their welcome at Heathrow, where they were allowed to sweep through customs without a hiccup.

We eventually arrived back in London just before Christmas, and on Boxing Night we opened at Covent Garden with a performance of *Cinderella*. The house was packed to welcome us after our triumph in the States, where we had been constantly applauded to the rooftops, and now we awaited the possibility of the same treatment from our own loving public. We assembled on stage behind the familiar red velvet curtain, and, before Constant went into the orchestra pit, we all discussed with Fred how we were to react to prolonged opening applause; both he and Constant agreed that we should dance straight through it. Anyway, Margot, Fred and Bobby, who were on stage when the curtain went up, would bear the brunt of it at first.

The overture ended and the curtain rose. You could have heard a pin drop. Bobby and Fred as the Ugly Sisters, sewing away at the kitchen table, first looked at each other nonplussed and then broke into helpless giggles; only the total professionalism of these artists prevented the audience from noticing this. Poor Margot, sitting woefully by the fireplace, pathetic and sad, had the worst of it; the giggling became infectious and she had to cup her face as she pretended to be gazing dreamily into the firelight. Not one pair of hands in the Opera House came together. The audience was going to behave just as they had always done, and applause would come at the final curtain. This was England and, far from being disappointed, we were treating the situation with typically English giggles. However, nothing could detract from the happiness we felt at being back in our beloved Opera House and when, at the final curtain, the applause did come and in a great wave of affection, we knew all was well and that we were home again.

Chapter 15

Having launched our return season with *Cinderella*, we quickly got into our stride and set about showing our paces with the revival of old favourites, dancing with a new-found transatlantic zest. In February 1950, Ninette de Valois choreographed a new ballet, *Don Quixote*, to a fiendish score by Roberto Gerhard. Ray Powell and I were two Spanish clerics, and the high spot of the ballet for us was when we had to rush across the stage in front of the backcloth, which had been inventively painted by Edward Burra to evoke the powerful figure of Don Quixote. We paused in the middle of the stage for a silent and statuesque moment and then, when the cacophony restarted, made an agitated exit on the other side. We spent a considerable time at rehearsals around the piano with Miss de Valois and Robert Irving, trying to fathom how best to negotiate this difficult score. Robert was a tower of strength in unravelling its intricacies; it was as if he was resorting to the navigational skills in the Fleet Air Arm that had earned him a distinguished award for his part in first sighting the *Scharnhorst*. When it became obvious that there was no easy way of coping with the difficulties, Ninette de Valois said to Ray and myself, 'Well, just count'.

Helpmann was wonderful as the Don, and Alexander Grant a superb Sancho Panza, but as this was a period when Bobby was having frequent leaves of absence in order to be in a film, his understudy John Field later took over his part. This was the time of the Festival of Britain (1951); as our contribution to it, we took *Don Quixote* and two other one-act ballets to Liverpool. In tandem, the Opera Company, with Sir Thomas Beecham conducting, was taking *The Bohemian Girl*, one of Miss Baylis's favourites and a rare treat.

Just before leaving for Liverpool, Miss de Valois told me to understudy the Don. I did my best to watch John Field during the few rehearsals of the ballet before we left, but I hadn't time to learn the rôle. *The Bohemian Girl* started the ball rolling, followed on the second night of our visit by *Don Quixote*, when disaster struck. John Field developed a contagious and severe skin complaint on his face and, on the afternoon of the performance, the doctor forbade any use of make-up, indeed telling him that he was not to appear. We had no spare ballet with us and there was not time enough to have anything sent up from London; it looked as if the whole evening of ballet would have to be cancelled.

David Webster, who was a very important figure in Liverpool, could not bear this to happen. He sent for me and, although aware of all the facts, begged me, 'Please go on and keep the curtain up'. While he was talking I was back at the Regal Cinema, Kingston, seeing that great backstage film *42nd Street*, when the producer sends on an equally unprepared member of the company, Ruby Keeler, to replace the star. Anyway, I replied to the effect that, if Miss de Valois would chance it, I would go on; and so I did.

The Don had a *pas de deux* with the ballerina, Dulcinea, danced by Margot, who ran through this with me, but time was short and I had only half an hour to rehearse the whole ballet. Alexander Grant took me through the scenes with Sancho Panza and there was some complicated business swinging across the stage on a rope. In the event, the whole company helped me in every way they could and I did manage to keep the curtain up. Miss de Valois was wonderfully understanding and said she would rehearse me in the rôle when we got back to London, and I did actually perform it subsequently at the Opera House.

But on that night in Liverpool David Webster came round to express his gratitude and said he would take me to supper at the splendid Adelphi Hotel. On our arrival the head waiter rushed up to the great and much respected Mr Webster and presented him with the menu, which David waved majestically aside, saying, 'I don't need that; I just want you to bring something out of this world'. My entrance to the Oak Room in New York paled before that!

The Festival of Britain was further made memorable for me when Margot, who had been invited to the opening ceremony, asked me to accompany her to the Dome of Discovery on the South Bank, where this was to take place. The inauguration was to be performed by King George VI and Queen Elizabeth, with Queen Mary and the two princesses, Elizabeth and Margaret, in attendance, all of whom later toured the whole site. I arranged to meet Margot at her flat in Long Acre. She had conscientiously been to Madame Volkova's class and so was somewhat late, which she was apt to be at such times; hence we also were late arriving at the South Bank and found that the main doors to the Dome of Discovery were closed. We went round to a side entrance and knocked on the door, which was opened by an attendant who, no doubt susceptible to Margot's charm, allowed us to enter.

When we finally got in we found that by chance we had the most advantageous view of the arrival of the Royal Family. During their tour of inspection in the Dome of Discovery, in which there were two escalators connecting the ground to the upper floor, we were delighted to see that the King had espied Winston Churchill coming down one of them. Standing stock-still he descended slowly and impressively on it, much to the amusement of the King, who greeted him with great good humour when he finally arrived. We all joined in to inspect this incredible exhibition, assembled so soon after the war and dominated by the old shot tower, which had stood there for centuries, now side-by-side with the Skylon and the Royal Festival Hall.

The season that followed our first American tour was, by all accounts, a great success and ended in July 1950. After the summer holiday we had a week's season at the Royal Opera House before setting off, yet again, for the United States. Sol Hurok, much elated by the success of our first visit, had decided to get together with David Webster to arrange a long coast-to-coast tour to start in September. This seemed almost unbelievable, since it was less than a year since we had first arrived in New York. We were overjoyed.

So there we were, boarding the bus outside the Opera House and making our way once more to London Airport. This time, however, we were to fly on a new type of plane, a Stratocruiser, chartered for the whole company – no single-sex nonsense this time. The first-class section was occupied by David Webster and us principals, and was extremely comfortable; the rear section was occupied by the *corps de ballet*. David had seen to it that his champagne was at the proper temperature before being happy to share it with us all. It was fun to experience a charter plane, which in those days provided several luxuries not to be found on regular scheduled flights, and to share these with one's friends and colleagues, who now seemed like one's family.

On a personal note, prompted by mention of my first-class flying status, I had already been and was to continue to be very fortunate on these tours of the United States in having several leading rôles that the audiences and critics seemed to like. Though for some time before that I had, regardless of rank, become good friends with the principals in the company, I now felt that I could meet them equally on professional as well as social terms. The new confidence that I mentioned earlier now increased to give me the assurance that I tended to lack in earlier days.

But enough of that! We arrived at La Guardia without any mishap, and then there was New York again. We were excited and delighted to be back, but this time we felt like seasoned New Yorkers, especially when a few old friends, including our great impresario, Sol Hurok, met us at the airport. After a week of rehearsals and classes and further renewing old acquaintances, we opened on a Sunday again at the 'Met', this time with *Swan Lake*. No reception at Gracie Mansion after this occasion, but Sol Hurok gave a wonderful party for us to celebrate the beginning of another six-week season at the Opera House.

Margot recaptured the American audiences as she had done on that magical first night in 1949 as Aurora in *The Sleeping Beauty*. There were also many opportunities to assess the rest of the dancers, and very successful they proved to be: Beryl Grey and Moira Shearer made an even greater impression in every rôle they danced; the quality and style of Pamela May was much appreciated; Nadia Nerina showed a sparkling, strong technique; and the Russian-born and trained Violetta Elvin had a great following.

The same warmth and kindness towards the company that we found on our first visit was once again evident. Typical of this was an incident following a party in New York during which I had a long conversation with a certain Arthur W. Kelly, who knew Charlie Chaplin in the years before he had left England for the States and became a legendary film star. It appeared that Chaplin was very taken with Kelly's sister, Hetty. During our season in New York this year, Chaplin had re-issued one of his old silent films, *City Lights*, to which he had added a musical score composed by himself, and which was having a great success on Broadway. I told Arthur that I and most of the company regretted we had not had time to see it, and that the following week we would be in Philadelphia. He at once said that he would arrange for a private showing of the film there, and gave me a number to ring when I arrived. This I did, and the film was shown for us one morning at a cinema in the city. We all loved it and emerged into the daylight red-eyed after the final scene with the little tramp and the blind girl, an ending with a rare pathos. We all appreciated Arthur Kelly's kind gesture; only in America would that sort of thing happen.

After the last performance in New York we set out in our Sol Hurok Special train once more for our long coast-to-coast tour, loaded with the now-familiar showbiz paraphernalia, which could have provided another verse for Irving Berlin's song, 'There's No Business Like Show Business'. At this juncture Ninette de Valois had to return home to mount a revival of her ballet, *The Prospect Before Us*, for the Sadler's Wells Theatre Ballet, as it used to be called. The title of this ballet as it applied to us, getting into our train, was of visiting thirty cities in the course of the tour, which included six weeks of one-night stands. It might seem a formidable schedule, but I don't think that I was alone in finding it a wonderful experience; on the occasions on which I meet the rapidly dwindling group of my former colleagues, we now have many a laugh as we reminisce about it.

We finally reached Los Angeles on the outward journey west, which was something that the film buffs among us had greatly looked forward to. The entire company stayed at the Ambassadors Hotel, which had a ball-room called the Coconut Grove, famous for featuring in many films. The Shrine Auditorium, where we would be dancing, had in its turn become a famous film location, notably in *A Star is Born* with Judy Garland, and was also the venue of the Oscar awards ceremony. The Ambassadors was a colourful and comfortable hotel and we settled in there to enjoy our stay.

There was, however, a contretemps concerning the British colony in Hollywood. Ronald Colman and his wife, Benita Hume, had planned to give a party for us on our opening night; but when Ninette de Valois, who had by this time rejoined us, heard that they intended to invite only a few principals, she said rather high-mindedly that she could not think of go-ing to a first-night party that did not include the whole company. So no Colman celebration. The press quoted the sad fact that all those frocks ordered from Bonwit Teller by the stars for the occasion would not get an airing. There was, in one sense, a happy ending, because Sol Hurok threw a large party for us in the hotel in the Coconut Grove with orchestra *et al.*; but it had been a very kind gesture of the Ronald Colmans to propose their party, and I for one sorely missed the opportunity of meeting the great British star – from nearby Richmond, Surrey, to boot!

Meanwhile, back at the Shrine, we all felt nervous when we first arrived and our thoughts were totally concentrated on the big first night there. Surprising as it may sound, the prospect of performing before all those great movie stars filled us with awe, and while we were talking together in this vein at the stage door Miss de Valois came up to us and asked, 'What's the matter with you lot?' We told her of our fears about dancing in front of that galaxy of stars. 'What nonsense', she said, 'they're only a lot of old pros who've made it'. As usual, she was right. She was also one person in the company who wasn't singing 'Hooray for Hollywood'. She left us dur-ing our stay in Los Angeles in order to lecture in Canada to raise funds for the ballet school, and rejoined us in San Francisco, our next port of call.

The railroad into that city did not pass over the Golden Gate, but took us straight into Market Street Station, in what was then rather a drab district. On the next day it was a matter of classes and settling in at the War Memorial Opera House, where we were to open our week's season. Our form did not seem to please Miss de Valois, back from her lecture tour; she perceived a certain degree of slackness, probably the result of the wear and tear of a long tour and the very large number of one-night stands. Notwithstanding, we were put through our paces thoroughly, re-hearsing the entire touring repertoire, which occupied every day of our stay. Maybe it was just as well, because, for the first time in our States tours, we had a rather lukewarm reception. Perhaps this had something to do with the fact that San Francisco had a well-established ballet company, founded by the Christensen family of brothers – dancers – who chose not to make a move of friendship towards us during our stay in the city. It was, therefore, important for us to be in top form to combat this indifference.

I was fortunate in having met at the first-night party some San Franciscans, who very kindly called for me at my hotel and drove me across the Golden Gate Bridge, from where I saw the sinister Alcatraz prison situated in the middle of the glorious bay. I also went to the Mark Hopkins Hotel to have a drink, like Josephine in *A Wedding Bouquet* – 'only one', since this was between the matinée and evening performances – and as I left I glanced back at the lights coming from high up in that famous bar at the top of the Mark. So, despite the crowded schedule, I did manage to take in something of the beauty of the city.

In November we had our halfway party. This was in Denver, where we were staying at a hotel called the Brown Palace. Of unorthodox design, it had a large foyer around the inside of which floors with finialled balustrades rose one above the other, giving the appearance of balconies onto which the bedroom doors opened, so that you could sit downstairs and see visitors entering and leaving their rooms.

The party there was strictly for the company; we all came in fancy dress, and very inventively too. Kenneth MacMillan displayed his ingenuity long before he began his distinguished career as a choreographer by managing to turn his large zip-up travelling bag into a wearable costume, and came as 'baggage'. Another figure, petite this time, came, or rather was carried on, by two members of the company; unrecognisably bandaged from head to foot, it was placed on the top of the grand piano, where it remained until judging time, soon after the party began. We were naturally intrigued and mystified by this most individual of fancy dresses, and Fred, who was the judge, had little option but to succumb to the general enthusiasm and award it the first prize. When the bandages were removed, the person of Pauline Clayden was revealed, no longer mummified; she had clearly intended to represent the result of the rigours of six months' touring, or 'One of the ruins de Valois knocked about a bit'!

After leaving Denver on 18 November, we danced in thirteen different cities, again mostly on one-night stands, finally reaching Chicago on 19 December, where we were to give a Christmas season. On all this journeying our Sol Hurok Special did yeoman service, and we got used to the two-tier, green-curtained bunks; if you had to scramble up to the top one, you got an extra dollar in your pay packet.

We had been impressed by the festive bustle on our previous visit to Chicago in the earlier Christmas season, but we were practically deafened this time by the crescendo of ding-a-lings on the eve of Christmas, which almost drowned the noise of the elevated railway. In between rehearsals and performances we had fun buying presents for one another, and even in the early hours of the morning the obliging drugstore was still open for the last-minute rush. I thought back to that other time when I had spent Christmas Day with the company, at Dartington Hall in Devon; as in Chicago it had been a white one, but then the war was beginning to bite and our lifestyle and exchange of gifts had been of a very different order.

We were staying again at the Sherman. Since the usual business clientèle was celebrating the holiday at home, we had the hotel to ourselves, and decorated our rooms as if we, too, were all at home. True to the American theatrical custom, there was a performance on Christmas night, but we were free at lunchtime. Consideration had been given, just as it had years ago in Dartington, to those without particular friends in the city, and they were asked out to Christmas lunch. I was fortunate to join Robert Irving, who had a friend, Brenda Forbes, living at that time in San Francisco but visiting Chicago for Christmas. She was a delightful person, an English actress who had appeared in films, notably *Mrs Miniver*, and we all celebrated with a wonderful lunch.

For Christmas evening, David Webster had generously sent us money to have a party in the hotel after the performance. As a further celebration, Alfred Rodrigues, a dancer in the company as well as a choreographer, and his wife, Julia Farron, had written a cabaret for a group of us to perform. Gillian Lynne, April Olrich and Greta Hamby took part, and on the boys' side Ray Powell, Kenneth MacMillan, Alfred Rodrigues – Rod, as we all called him – and myself, in our checked cowboy shirts and jeans, the first we had ever worn. In one number we added to this outfit white swans' head-dresses – we dashed on stage and then put down the luggage we were carrying and sat on it, slumped in despair at having just missed the Sol Hurok Special. To the tune from *Oklahoma!* of 'Everything's up to date in Kansas City' we sang plaintively, 'We're the swans they left behind in Kansas City'.

For all this farrago Rod was a hard taskmaster, and made us rehearse diligently every day before the evening performance, in the little room with the portrait of Mary Garden looking quizzically down upon us. The hard work paid off and the cabaret was a great success. It was in fact a foretaste of things to come, since Gillian Lynne was later to choreograph *Cats* and *Phantom of the Opera* for Andrew Lloyd-Webber, April Olrich was to make her name in musicals and films, and Rod to become a producer of revues in the West End and of programmes for television. One such revue was *Airs on a Shoestring*, starring Max Adrian, partnered by my great friend, Moyra Fraser, who was wonderfully funny in the sketches as well as famously dancing a solo, making much of her expressive eyes as she gently burlesqued the classical ballerina. She was also cast in two revues starring Joyce Grenfell, *Penny Plain* and *Tuppence Coloured*, following her success in the musical *Song of Norway*. But to go back to that Christmas night in Chicago: I felt that I, too, was at last achieving my ambition and appearing in an intimate revue.

After this marvellous time we made our way once more to Canada, now adding Winnipeg and Québec to our previous schedule of Toronto, Ottawa and Montreal. In Québec we stayed at the famous hotel Le Château Frontenac. It was winter sports time and we participated by tobogganing down the ice run. I remember that Margot loved it and looked every bit the part, in a set of ski-resort clothes that she had bought in one of the very smart shops in the hotel. She never did things by halves, and the local press had a field day photographing the prima ballerina appropriately dressed for this elegant city. She always knew the importance of setting the right note, and sensed the *genius loci* wherever we went.

The whole company was grateful to Mr Hurok for giving a wonderful farewell party in Le Château Frontenac and the following day we left for home. What must never be forgotten is that not only had we taken a very substantial amount of money at the box office, but, thanks to the efforts of the 'dollarinas' and, may I say, this time the 'dollarinos', we brought an equally substantial amount home to launch the new season at the Royal Opera House for both the Ballet and the Opera Company.

We were tired after our long tour and, despite having had such a marvellous time of it, we were happy to be at home again. For me this homecoming was tinged with sadness, because while in San Francisco we had learnt that Bobby was to leave us. I had not heard a word about this extraordinary event before it was announced, not even from Bobby himself, generally so forthcoming about what he was up to. Whether Fred, Margot or Pamela was aware of the situation I don't know, but the first and only information I received was when Bertie Hughes, our manager, told us that Miss de Valois had invited a small group of Bobby's friends to dinner on our free night, the reason for the gathering being that Bobby was returning the next day. The suddenness was such that there was not even time for the company to organise a farewell present, let alone an appropriate party to bid him goodbye. And all this in mid-tour!

There have been many accounts of this episode, none of them really conclusive. I personally think that Bobby felt the time had come for him to make his main activity the theatre and filming, in both an acting and a producing capacity. However, for all of us it was the suddenness of his leaving that understandably took us so much by surprise – and oh, how we were going to miss him. Perhaps it would not be inappropriate here to misquote the Scottish play and say that he stood 'not upon the order of his going', but went.

On the evening of the dinner party we had all assembled in the foyer of the hotel when Bertie Hughes came to tell us that, unfortunately, Miss de Valois had a very bad migraine and would not be able to join us. However, before we could get through the revolving doors to make our way to the restaurant, the lift door in the hotel foyer opened and out came Miss de Valois. 'Hello, everybody', she chirruped – typically, without a word of explanation – and off we trooped. During the dinner party we kept up a continuous banter of jokes, each one contributing to the many happy anecdotes about Bobby, and naturally laughter predominated. Encouraging this happy atmosphere, Ninette de Valois saw to it that we papered over the cracks. When we got back to the hotel she got into the lift, waved and said, 'Goodnight, everybody'. End of story.

Life went on, nevertheless, and Bobby was still to remain a brilliant contributor to the company, making guest appearances in some of his old rôles, choreographing ballets such as *Elektra*, as well as giving us a new production of *Swan Lake* and the Opera Company a *Madam Butterfly* with Elisabeth Schwarzkopf. He remained a close friend of us all.

Chapter 16

At about this time I received a letter from Rita Warne, the dancing teacher we had met in Toronto at the dinner party given by the Australian friends of Bobby's who had taken us to Niagara Falls. Rita's husband, Aylmer Macdonald, had spent a great deal of time in the wild lake district of northern Ontario at a small trappers' town called Barry's Bay. By the shores of the nearby Aylen Lake, Rita had set up a summer camp devoted to ballet, calling it 'The Wilderness Ballet Camp'. She asked me if I would be interested in being a guest teacher. In Canada, as in the United States, summer camps had long flourished, offering some educational and vocational instruction besides the outdoor activities on offer. Rita's was such a one, and popular too, however improbable the association of subject and setting might seem. I had had no experience of teaching, but I liked the idea; I asked Margot, who always gave one a considered and honest answer to one's questions, what she thought I should do. She had no doubt that I should accept, which I did.

I did not much care for the thought of another transatlantic flight without my usual air-travelling companions to share its hazards, and had always relished the idea of crossing the Atlantic by ocean liner. Rita, who was paying my fee, readily agreed to these seafaring arrangements, and I travelled to New York on the *Queen Mary*, spent the weekend there, and then took the overnight train to Toronto, where I stayed with Jack and Silvia of the Niagara trip. This longer journey and my proposed three-week stay at the camp were within our holiday period, and Miss de Valois agreed my plans. I would return in time to join the rehearsals for our season once again at the Edinburgh Festival.

Like Gaul, in those days the passenger accommodation of the *Queen Mary* was divided into three parts: first, second and third class. The last was completely cut off from the other two, and when first and second class (of which I was one) were taking a turn about the ship, they could look down at the third-class passengers in the stern, looking up at us from their lowly position. It was somewhat reminiscent of the shots of steerage on the *Titanic* in the film *A Night to Remember*. The first class was, to use the word first associated with liners going to the East, very 'posh' – black tie was *de rigueur* for dinner. We were allowed to make our way through the first-class area when we boarded at South-ampton and to see the shopping arcade with the Doris Zinkeisen art deco, pictures of which, as background to the celebrity passengers, had featured in the *Tatler and Bystander* and *The Sketch* when the ship made its maiden voyage in 1936. After this brief encounter we were then cut off from such grandeur.

However, my cabin class, as it was known, was very comfortable, and there were plenty of stewards who saw to it that the essential comforts for the week's crossing were not lacking. The deck steward would tuck the rug around one's legs to counter the stiff breeze when one was sitting on deck, and at eleven o'clock would reinforce this warmth with bowls of steaming bouillon. The bath steward would enquire as to what time one wished to have one's bath. Details were given out regularly about cinema performances and the various social highlights of the day, one of which – the fancy dress evening – filled me with horror! There was an abundance of choice for every meal, though no single tables to enjoy this gourmandising in private. In my ignorance on this, my first trip, I made a major mistake; for, when asked if I would like to sit at a table for four, six or eight people, I plumped for four, thinking this would be quieter. But after being closeted with the same three for five whole days, on my next voyage I was careful to choose a table for eight.

On the way down to Southampton to board the *Queen Mary* I thought of that day in 1936 when we were dancing at the Pavilion Theatre, Bournemouth, and Michael and I went over to watch this great ship steam slowly down the Solent on her maiden voyage to New York. Now here I was, about to travel on her myself. When, after five days, we passed Ellis Island early in the morning, most passengers were up, eager to watch for the first glimpse of the fabled Manhattan skyline. When it came into view, it did not disappoint, and the moment when we passed the Statue of Liberty became a fitting climax to the whole trip.

After a short break in New York and then the stay with Jack and Silvia in Toronto, I finally set off with Jack in his car for Barry's Bay. As we said goodbye to Silvia that morning, I could not help noticing her anxiety that Jack should on no account forget the map, and from this I suppose I should have had some apprehension about his knowledge of the route and the terrain. We were to meet Aylmer at the lakeside in the afternoon; it being summer with long, light evenings, I was looking forward to enjoying my boat ride across the lake to the Wilderness Camp.

However, it seemed a while before we left the far-flung suburbs of Toronto, and the various townships, important landmarks on our way, seemed to get further and further apart. When later on we stopped at a drugstore for a cup of coffee and to check our route, the name 'Barry's Bay' brought a blank and bewildered look to the face of everyone we asked. By this time, we had come to the conclusion that we were not born map-readers, but we pressed on.

Darkness fell and then, happily to confound our confusion, there it was. The barman at the only hostelry in the small town looked dubious when we told him we were meeting Aylmer at the lakeside. He said that Aylmer had collected the mail for the camp some hours before and had mentioned the fact that he was shortly meeting friends to row them across to the ballet camp. As we left, we were directed towards the road that led to the lake. This part of the journey was something of a night-mare, for 'road' was a loosely appropriate term for a rough, potholed track surrounded by heavy, overhanging trees. Making our uncertain way along it, our chief anxiety was that by this time Aylmer would have given up the wait; we knew that there was no telephone, and the thought that there would be no means of communicating with the camp did nothing to lessen this anxiety.

Suddenly, through a clearing, we saw the moonlit water glinting, and then to our joyful amazement a welcoming voice called out, 'Why, hello there!' It was Aylmer, sitting waiting in his boat, smoking his pipe. As I learned when I got to know Aylmer pretty well during the years that followed, his steadfast wait for us was typical of that solid, unruffled Can-adian. We then sped across the lake in his powerful motorboat.

As we neared the shore in rough water, the moon had disappeared behind clouds and it was pitch black; I could just make out some figures in the water, and then a lamplight waving. It belonged to Rita, signalling away on the shore where we finally landed. The figures that I had seen from the near distance turned out to be young girls preparing to retire for the night and cleaning their teeth in the lake water. Margot had said it would be a new experience and it certainly was, but Rita and the girls hailed us with cheery welcomes, and introductions were made.

Just before lights out, Jack, who was staying overnight and had noticed my barely-concealed surprise at this new environment, said quietly, 'If you want to leave in the morning, I'll take you back with me'. I did no such thing, and I had a wonderful stay by the shores of Aylen Lake and loved the simplicity, the quiet and the beauty of the island. I returned for many years, becoming very fond of Rita and Aylmer, who were ever gen-erous to me. A particular pleasure was the occasional trip across the lake to Barry's Bay with Aylmer to collect the mail; we would go into the one hotel and have a beer in what was picturesquely known as the 'beverage room'.

As with all buildings in this wild lake district, the Wilderness Ballet Camp consisted of log cabins. Two were of very large size, with one of them given over to a studio for the ballet classes. This studio had a good floor, and I thought back to my early days at the Ballet Club when Madame Rambert would use her little watering can to sprinkle the floor before class; Rita did the same, after two of the girls had swept away all traces of sand brought in from the beach. In the corner stood the piano, played by the pianist who accompanied Rita's classes in her school in Toronto; she was a charming woman, very professional, and we had a good working relationship. I became very attached to my pupils, a group of fine young Canadian girls, good-naturedly always willing to work hard, trying their very best to tackle what was probably a difficult technique for them.

I enjoyed the routine of my day, which began in the early morning when, after getting up, I would scrounge a cup of tea from Bella, the cook. Thus warmed up, I would plunge into the lake for my 'skinny-dip' in that end of the beach allocated to my ablutions – the girls had to go to the opposite end for theirs. The clear, fresh waters of the lake were chilly but refreshing, and the dip was an invigorating prelude to a piping hot breakfast in the cookhouse. Then it was time to put on practise clothes and take my morning class.

After lunch I was free to relax on the beach or to take a canoe out on the lake, stopping silently to watch the beavers industriously swimming about collecting twigs and branches for their lodges and damming up the watery entrance to them; or in the early days, watching a bear devour the blueberries on the hills around the lake. That was a rare sight then, but when I returned on later visits the lake had attracted more visitors, some of whom bought land and built log cabins around it, encroaching on the natural habitat of the bears, which then scavenged the rubbish dumps. This meant that these large, shiny, black creatures were then often seen shambling along what was, on my first visit, a rough track but had now become a concrete road to and from the landing stage. I was glad to be in Aylmer's solid station wagon when encountering them.

Aylmer gave the students art classes, sitting with them perched up on the rocks that surrounded the lake, painting the scene on the opposite banks. Driftwood would also be collected as a medium for woodcarving, being energetically rubbed down and fashioned into the likeness of a swan or an eagle; there were, however, finished specimens that to the eye of the beholder remained obstinately pieces of driftwood. True to the spirit of a holiday camp, Aylmer would take his boat out so that the girls could go waterskiing; they returned blue with cold but glowing with a sense of achievement in spite of many a tumble in the water, and recovered a normal temperature in the sun on the beach afterwards.

Often, however, the lake was extremely rough – too rough for Aylmer to collect the mail or make his quick social call to the beverage room. But there were compensations for bad weather: preceding supper there was what was called a repertoire class, in which I would teach the girls a variation or two from the well-known classical ballets, and then after the evening meal we would play Chinese Checkers, read or listen to records on Rita's wind-up gramophone. A particular favourite and top of the pops was 'I'm a Gnu' by Flanders and Swann – all the words learnt by heart by the delighted listeners. If the evening was exceptionally hot, Rita would light a bonfire and, armed with forks tied to long sticks, we would toast marshmallows in its glow.

I particularly appreciated the chats that accompanied my early morning tea, when Bella told me of the time when she had cooked for lumberjacks in a camp that could be described as rugged in every sense. She had made it clear that she would not stand for any nonsense if any of the lumberjacks got out of line: 'I had my gun with me and I was a very good shot'. Our worlds could not have been further apart, but we regaled each other with stories from these different worlds and she listened incredulously but intently to my experiences of the theatre and the ballet, and to what to her must have seemed an extraordinary life. She followed it all with great interest, and would later ask about people I had talked about.

She had throughout a great sense of dignity, and when Rita took the girls to church on Sunday, exchanging their T-shirts and jeans for dresses and hats, Bella would watch and appraise them as they left in Aylmer's boat, while she and I waved them goodbye from the beach. She lived by the camp all the year round in her log cabin, visited only by friends from Barry's Bay, who crossed the frozen lake in their sleighs in the snow; a high spot for her was when Rita and Aylmer did this over Christmas. She said that she never felt lonely there and that she had the same true aim for an intrusive bear as for an importunate lumberjack. I grew very fond of her and the genuinely unaffected people of that small community, and always returned home refreshed after this escape to the simple life and natural existence.

However, I did not find favour with everyone; one pupil, whom I chivvied for her inattention at the *barre*, was apt to float off into a personal improvisation that was not part of the routine of steps I had wished. After I had given her one rather sharp ticking off, she had, as Rita later told me, gone up to her and said, 'Miss Warne, do taxidermists stuff people?' I wonder what I would have fetched for Damien Hirst.

In 1953 the company toured America. It was on that tour, at a party given by the English Speaking Union in New York, that Pamela May told me we had both been asked to have dinner with Margot Fonteyn and Tito

Arias at El Morocco. 'Do you mean the Tito we all knew up at Cambridge before the war?' I asked. Pamela told me that indeed it was the same Tito, and that he had recently been in touch with Margot. In the time that had elapsed since we had all been together, he had been married and had three children, but the marriage had ended and he divorced hs wife shortly afterwards.

Our reunion at El Morocco and our reminiscing about our earlier days was fun. I noticed that Tito had become rather plump, and looked now too dignified to perform the cha-cha as he had in the Footlights Revue at Cambridge before the war, to say nothing of turning cartwheels as he had had a habit of doing on the Backs. I chided him about this, and with an immediate 'Oh, wouldn't I?' he demonstrated his somersault on the pavement outside El Morocco. In spite of the fact that he had become the Panamanian delegate to the United Nations, he was still the same old Tito. The following day he telephoned me and asked if I would join him for breakfast at his hotel; he told me then of his continuing love for Margot and that he hoped to marry her. I thought at once of the snapshot that I had taken of him that day in Cambridge when I first realised that Margot had a crush on him; I had given it to her and, as I have already mentioned, she had kept it in her handbag throughout the war, although she had completely lost touch with him.

During that American tour Tito took to visiting her constantly, and indeed organised many social events for her close friends in the company; unexpectedly he would turn up at the various towns on our route and would arrange a party. In California he took the whole company to Catalina Island on the yacht belonging to John Wayne, who had lent it to Tito for this occasion. Tito became a well-known figure associated with us, and was like one of the family. We all shared the pleasure of waiting for the next present bestowed upon Margot as the red boxes from Cartier arrived, and of seeing her radiant in diamond earrings or bracelet, enjoying this new and exciting lifestyle.

At the end of the tour, Tito invited Fred, Jean Gilbert (the company concert pianist who had become a great friend of Margot) and myself to join him and Margot for a holiday on the yacht that he and his brother, Tony, owned, called the *Edmar*. The yacht was docked at Nassau, to where we flew from New York to join her. Margot told us that Tito had also invited Danny Kaye's wife, Sylvia, on the holiday and that she would meet us at Nassau. She arrived extravagantly late, but in spite of this we liked her from the first. We had a glorious time, cruising among the islands of the Bahamas in the clear, blue depths of the ocean. On board we were entertained at the piano by Jean and by Sylvia who, besides being Mrs

Kaye, was famous in the entertainment world of film and theatre as Sylvia Fine and was responsible for many of her husband's songs and film scripts. We became good friends, on both this and future visits to the United States and on her times spent in England.

We had arranged to leave for home from Nassau, but it was suggested that we stay on the yacht, sail to Cuba and return to England from Havana. Later on, however, we experienced a sudden and violent storm and decided that perhaps the *Edmar* was not up to it. As things turned out, we flew home from Nassau as originally planned, but not before we had en route visited Cat Key Island, where we hoped to have a little flutter in the Casino. This was not as simple as we had wished; at the door we were refused entry because we three men were not wearing black ties. Tito, spying a drugstore nearby, managed to buy three of the ready-made bow variety which we attached to our white summer shirts, making this small concession to the requisite evening dress, much to the amusement of the ladies. The doorman relented in the face of this ingenuity and let us in. Sylvia was the only one to win anything at the tables, and with her generosity promptly bought presents for all of us: for the men, distinctive ties with the emblem of the island, the cat on the key woven into the silk.

The whole trip was a wondrous delight. It was given an added touch by the elderly black butler whom Tito had brought along from his father's house to look after our wants – a man of great charm, as his enormous brood of children by his five wives would testify. Tito's athletic routine in these surroundings included waterskiing, and he had a personal trainer on board to help him master this skill.

When we returned home we were at once embroiled in a production of *The Firebird*, a famous Diaghilev ballet, which one could see would be an ideal vehicle for Margot. It would be staged by Serge Grigoriev, who had been ballet master to the Diaghilev Company, helped by his wife Lubov Tchernicheva, a famous member of that company. Tamara Karsavina, always loved and admired by Margot, had created the rôle of the Firebird, and it was she whom Margot consulted about this, as well as about any other rôle that Karsavina had danced. The experience of the artists who have worked closely with the choreographers as they create rôles and are aware of the trials and pitfalls that they involve in performance is an invaluable legacy. This is especially true of the great classics, where such a traditional link has helped to maintain historical accuracy and integrity of interpretation.

I was always very fond of Grigoriev and his wife – he, tall and so commanding when he showed how to dance the various men's characters; she, putting the girls through their paces. She had played many sultry *femme fatale* rôles, and I loved to watch her at rehearsals introducing a coquettish touch to the typically English niceness. By this time, of course, she could not handle dancing the parts herself, but her expressive face and telling gestures were a joy to watch. I admired the evening dress that she wore on a first night at the Opera House, and loved it when she preened herself in the wings before taking her calls as the producer.

Serge Grigoriev was a great help to me in a production of *Petrouchka* in which I had the rôle of the rich merchant. I had a heavy costume and over that a cumbersome overcoat lined with fur, which I had to wear draped over one shoulder throughout the whole ballet. It trailed on the ground behind me and needed careful handling as I moved among the crowd of revellers at the fair and joined the gypsy girls in the short dance we had together. He showed me exactly how to handle matters and how to avoid the possibility of tripping up gypsies or revellers.

The superb *Petrouchka* of these two will linger long in the memories of older ballerinas and those others involved in their productions. For the first time, actors and actresses came on as extras, playing older character rôles that had previously been done by students, prematurely aged with a few lines of Leichner's Lake applied by the make-up man. All were carefully directed, so giving weight and verisimilitude to the crowd scenes. Many of these actors and actresses became permanent adjuncts of the company in its major productions, and became great friends of Kenneth MacMillan, who used them whenever possible in his full-length ballets.

During the fifties we were adding considerably to our repertoire and, on a personal note, there were several ballets in which I suffered a violent demise. In John Cranko's light-hearted *Bonne Bouche* I was part of a small ensemble of missionaries akin to the Salvation Army called 'The League of Light', for whom the composer, Arthur Oldham, had written a pastiche of a familiar hymn. We were shown spreading the word in Africa, where we all finally suffered dreadful fates: mine was being swallowed by a snake, the large head of which appeared abruptly round the edge of the wing. As a sea captain in Andrée Howard's *A Mirror for Witches* I had a fatal heart attack, expiring on a high note in the score in the arms of Julia Farron. In *Checkmate*, which was regularly performed at that time, I was stabbed in the back by the Black Queen. As I left the stage door one night when the programme comprised all three ballets, a faithful follower among the audience said, 'Oh, Mister Edwards, what a night you've had: swallowed by a snake, a heart attack and then stabbed to death by Beryl Grey'. In passing, literally and metaphorically, I like to recall that each of these ballets required, besides a change of costume, a complete change of make-up, which had to be effected during an interval of not a second over fifteen minutes.

It was in the middle fifties, to strike this time a domestic note, that Margot told me that her mother, Mrs Hookham, had bought a house by the Thames near Bray Lock. Subsequently it became one in which many of the members of the company were frequently and generously entertained. The cottage next door was occupied by a young couple and their small baby. When, in due course, they were about to move, Margot thought I should buy it, and asked me to go down with her to lunch at Taplow and afterwards to call on the young couple, look around the cottage and see if I thought I would like to have it. In the end that is just what I did. My brother Fred, who by that time had a very successful property business, advised me as to the best way to go about it.

I added two extra rooms and a new bathroom, putting everything in the hands of a local builder, Mr Ernest Chase, who also agreed to look after the property in my absence on tour in America. This initial commitment started a long-standing friendship with Mr Chase and his wife. I had bought two stone urns for the garden, something I had longed for, and they looked very fine when planted with geraniums. I turned to Mrs Chase, who had come to inspect her husband's handiwork, and said that I was very fond of an urn. Mrs Chase looked at me knowingly and with a slight smile said, 'Oh, so am I.' They were a lovely couple.

Bon, Naggie's niece, with whom I was still sharing the house in Teddington, was very cautious about the idea of my having a weekend retreat, but in the event approved of it and enjoyed coming down for Sunday lunch and meeting my neighbours, especially Mrs Hookham. Early on, William, with his wife Vera and small son Martyn, spent a summer holiday there while I was on tour. Bill was an excellent gardener and worked on planning my garden. Brother Fred with his wife and daughter came down frequently. Like many motoring enthusiasts of the fifties, he was very taken with the American car, and had bought an impressive one himself – the only trouble was that, being somewhat broad in the beam, it was apt to get stuck between the narrow hedgerows, so we all had to lean back against the hedge to enlarge the path to my front door. Sometimes he would bring down Moyra Fraser's mother, affectionately known to us all by her nickname, Moth, and her granddaughter, Carol, to whom I was godfather.

We became a close-knit community and, led by Mrs Hookham, had a great deal of fun. Although working hard at the Opera House at that time, I did manage to get down to Taplow for some part of each weekend. If I arrived after a matinée, I had to make sure that I did not disturb Mrs

Hookham and her sister-in-law, Margaret, in their evening's viewing of the popular TV series, *The Blue Lamp*, featuring Jack Warner as the archetypal policeman, with his 'Evenin', all'. Sometimes I was invited to dinner, and was always amused when the ladies, including a regular weekend guest, a White Russian, Countess Tania, embarked on a game of Scrabble. The Countess, who had an antique shop in Ebury Street, was not above slipping in a few words of Russian, which caused heated arguments as to their validity in the context of the game. The whole household was full of jollity, all reflecting Mrs Hookham's character and her ability to invoke an atmosphere of friendliness and enjoyment. She set the style that we were all happy to follow.

Margot and Tito were married in Paris on Sunday 6 February 1955. Having danced the previous evening in *Daphnis and Chloë* in London, Margot left for Paris early on Sunday morning with a group of her close friends: Ninette de Valois, Frederick Ashton, Michael Somes, Jean Gilbert and myself. On arrival we went to the Hôtel Plaza-Athénée, where two valued members of Christian Dior's staff, Suzanne Luling and Yvonne Minassian, were waiting in Margot's suite to help her dress. Knowing that I had shared with her the early, exciting days of the 'New Look' when she had first gone to Dior and that I had previously met Suzanne and Yvonne when we were all in Paris, Margot asked me if I would like to see the wedding dress. I readily agreed, and there was Dior himself, her great admirer, putting the final touches to the pale grey taffeta dress, making a stitch here and there and adjusting the head-dress, which was of small, grey, birds'-wing feathers, tipped with the lightest blue, and closely fitting her neat head. After this delightful preview I joined the other guests in the restaurant of the hotel to lunch with the bridegroom.

The wedding took place in the Panamanian Consulate. We watched Margot leaving the hotel to join Tito there, accompanied by her close family. It was explained diplomatically that the Consulate was far too small to accommodate all of us, and that we should wait for Margot and Tito to return and rejoin us at the reception. We were rather sad watching the car go off and waving her goodbye, until Fred suddenly rose up defiantly, declared that we had not got up at the crack of dawn to fly there and then not see her married, and called a taxi. It was a case of 'Follow that car!' to the Consulate, where we clambered breathlessly up flights of stairs and fought our way into the small room where the wedding was to be conducted. This was packed wall-to-wall with press photographers with their blinding flashlights, much to Margot's amazement and disquiet. The noise and hubbub was such that we could not hear a word of the proceedings, which were anyway in Spanish, and it was even difficult to see Margot herself in this mêlée. But at least we were there at her wedding, thanks to Fred's spurring us into action as he did; and thus we returned in triumph to the Plaza-Athénée for the reception, which was hosted by the British Ambassador.

There we were joined by Pamela May and June Brae and their husbands, Charles Gordon and David Breeden, who had all arrived in Paris the previous day. In her thoughtful way, Margot had sent a car to bring her dearly-loved dancing teacher, Olga Preobrajenska, now in her late eighties, to the reception; but, possibly feeling that the whole occasion would be somewhat overwhelming for her, she did not in fact come. Margot was naturally disappointed, but quite understood what might have prompted her feelings.

The honeymoon was to be spent on the *Edmar*. Fred and I, with memories of our cruise on that yacht, knew what enchantment that would be.

Chapter 17

An important milestone in the history of the company, the first visit to Russia, had been planned for 1956. We cancelled it following the Russian invasion of Hungary, and four years were to elapse before we would finally dance in the Soviet Union. By that time our repertoire had changed from the one we had proposed to take in 1956, for which programmes had been printed (later to become collectors' items).

We finally arrived in Leningrad in 1960 in the early summer, the best time to do so. There were the tall rows of finely-etched silver birches that one associates with the St Petersburg of Chekhov, set in a landscape that as a young man I had imagined so vividly from listening to the excellent BBC productions of his plays. The impression was still so strong that I felt we had come to the city of the Tsars rather than that of the Soviets; and this feeling was reinforced when we entered our hotel, the famous Astoria. Its furnishings were still in the fashion of 1917 – the circular tables in our bedrooms covered with plain red or heavily patterned chenille tablecloths with deep fringes, the bed in an alcove and curtained with similar material. The whole hotel was redolent of the era of gilt and plush. When the company returned in the seventies, the hotel was closed for refurbishment, to accommodate a new sense of modernity and so courting the fashions of the West – not entirely to my liking.

As far as I was concerned, this was the city that had seen the first performances of the most important ballets of our classical inheritance: *Le Lac des Cygnes*, *Casse Noisette*, *The Sleeping Beauty* and countless others that had not by then reached the West. Here was where the scores of Tchaikovsky and Glazunov were heard for the first time; and, in the history of ballet, here was the apex of the triangle drawn from the base of French and Italian traditions. It was a daunting prospect for this very young company of ours to compete with such greatness. We were treading on hallowed ground.

After we had settled into our hotel, we could hardly wait to see the fabled Maryinsky Theatre, and a small group of us decided that we would throw off the shackles of the Intourist guide and find our own way there. With the aid of a map issued at the hotel desk, we set off, travelling hopefully – and suddenly there it was. We were delighted to see our posters outside; they were largely incomprehensible to us, but we could tell the section that announced our names, albeit disguised in the Russian alphabet. A neatly dressed woman came past, seeming to like our smiling enthusiasm and perhaps thinking that we were foreign visitors wanting to go to the theatre. Brian Shaw mimed to the effect of asking her to read out our names, which sure enough she did. When she came to Brian's, he pointed out that he was that very person. She gave him a startled look, turned and hurried away at speed. Perhaps the shock of actually meeting foreign artists was too much for her; whatever the reason, it was the first time that Brian had had that effect on anybody!

When we got back to the hotel, where Miss de Valois had found an appropriate place for her usual noticeboard, we read that the whole Company was requested to go immediately to her suite. Once there we were thoroughly ticked off; my group got it in the neck for our visit to the Maryinsky, others for hiring a boat to go for a trip on the river and, worst of all, two young male dancers for using their cameras, for which they had been caught and charged. All these forbidden escapades had been reported back immediately to the company management. By the time Miss de Valois had finished with us, Siberia loomed, and we realised that everything we had been told about the restrictions of life in Communist Russia was indeed true.

It did not take us long in the hotel to realise that it was a good thing that we had brought bath and washbasin plugs with us, as well as plentiful supplies of rolls of soft lavatory paper as we had been told to do before leaving England. We had also brought ample supplies of chocolate bars and tins of coffee to give to our helpful dressers and chambermaids, and various other items of everyday use that were considered luxuries in this Communist stronghold. We noticed that our gifts were always reciprocated: a wild flower or two, a glass of Russian beer (an acquired taste). Michael Somes took pleasure, whenever he thought there might be a hidden microphone in a vase of flowers or in the glass dome of a hanging light fixture, in delivering a few sharp comments on his attitude to the régime. Fortunately, there were no repercussions.

Just before we left London, I met Serge Grigoriev in the rehearsal rooms. He was sad and almost tearful, with an exile's longing to see his country once more, and he told me to be sure to walk by the river after our performances in the evening to experience the effect of the light of the midnight sun upon the water. I did so, and long after midnight there were people walking along hand-in-hand, or swimming, and I understood what Mr Grigoriev meant by the magical atmosphere. The beauty of the city at all times captivated us; the wide avenues of evenly matched buildings, pale yellow and white, or pale green and white, as with the Winter Palace, seemed to give a colour-wash to architectural beauty.

Finally we were performing on the first night of our season, in Frederick Ashton's new ballet *Ondine*, with a score by Hans Werner Henze that was extremely advanced in style. Ashton had had a difficult time choreographing to it; Ninette de Valois was more sympathetic to the music and sought to reassure him of its suitability, making, as she sometimes did, her inimitable readjustment to an idiomatic phrase: 'It's a wonderful score, Fred, and just up your tree'.

Anyway, Fred produced a ballet of very high order, while Margot, in the rôle of Ondine, created a miracle of beauty, particularly in the Shadow Dance when this fishlike creature sees for the first time her shadow in the moonlight when she steps on land. I always remember the moment when she emerges from the sea after the shipwreck and stands still, in a position capturing total silence. A great feature of this ballet was the perfect partnership of Fonteyn and Somes; since first being seen together in *Horoscope*, these two artists had become a dearly loved team in the classical ballets and had created leading rôles in new works, especially those of Ashton. The quality and texture of the dancing of each of these artists created a harmony, while Michael's personification of the *danseur noble* made him the perfect foil for Margot. Together with Julia Farron and Alexander Grant they translated Ashton's flowing and dramatic choreography into a work of great power, while the beautiful set and costumes of Lila de Nobili must have been a revelation to the Russian audiences of that time. *Ondine* was original and a challenge to the conventional.

I played the part of a somewhat dotty cardinal and was dressed in full regalia, my red cardinal's hat painted green and given a scattering of seaweed and leaves for good measure. The designer had earlier scoured the marketplaces leading out of Oxford Street in London for lengths of old woven material for the costumes and particularly for pieces of fine lace, some of which decorated my surplice. When Ashton was choreographing the wedding ceremony, at which I was to officiate, he was very insistent that I should take this Christian marriage with due solemnity, although it would seem odd to be blessing the union of a fishlike creature and a nobleman. I told him to have no fear, as I fully realised that 'all God's children got fins!'

If *Ondine* was a challenge for the audience, this was not so when it came to *The Sleeping Beauty*; most of us felt a heavy weight of responsibility in presenting this masterpiece of the great Petipa. As I was waiting in my rôle as Catalabutte before the ballet began, I looked around, hardly able to believe that this was the very stage on which Madame Brianza, the original Aurora, had danced. She was one of a number of ballerinas from France and Italy, including Madame Taglioni, making their way to this beautiful northern city from Europe to contribute to the fusion of the French and Italian techniques within a Russian framework. My thoughts turned then to Nicholas Sergeyev, who had been a *régisseur* of the ballet at the Maryinsky Theatre and had scurried around backstage as part of the staff, never dreaming that the small English company that he was to know after he left Russia in 1917 would finally come to his old stamping ground in 1961. He had managed to bring with him from St Petersburg the invaluable notation books, using which he produced *The Sleeping Beauty* for us in Islington in 1939. How remarkable that *Giselle*, *Coppélia*, *Le Lac des Cygnes* and *Casse Noisette*, as well as *The Sleeping Beauty*, should all find their way to our company through this one man. What a debt of gratitude we owe him!

I was delighted when Margot invited me to accompany her to the famous Theatre Street, which contained the dancing school of the Maryinsky Theatre. There we were shown around by the archivist, an elderly lady to whom we took an immediate liking. While looking at the pictures of the original production of *The Sleeping Beauty*, we were both impressed by how close it seemed to our version produced at the Sadler's Wells Theatre in 1938. Among the scores of photographs, programmes and general memorabilia, there were many referring to Madame Karsavina; when we came to them, Margot would turn to me showing great delight and leaving no doubt that she and Karsavina were great friends, who saw much of each other in England.

The archivist then asked Margot if she would sign a book for her, and asked her assistant, who was accompanying her, to fetch a pen from her office. This may have been a ruse to be free of her colleague, whose partial function, as in every department in the Soviet Union, was to ensure that no fraternising took place. Barely had the woman left the room when Margot was bombarded with questions about Karsavina, whom the archivist had last seen in St Petersburg in 1917. She had had no idea that the great ballerina was in London, nor indeed that she was safe and alive. Karsavina had been the old lady's favourite artist because of her beauty and charm and the thoughtful way in which she dealt with everyone at the Maryinsky Theatre; 'She was always a great lady', we were told. The assistant came swiftly back to say she had found no trace of the pen, at which point Margot opened her bag and proceeded to sign the book with her own pen, thus delighting the archivist and her assistant. Before we left, Margot cleverly managed to mention the names of a number of former Maryinsky dancers then living in London, so strengthening further this reassuring link with the past.

We had on one occasion a special matinée at 11.30 a.m. to celebrate the successful output of steelworkers, many of whom were invited members of the audience. I smiled to myself when I pictured their opposite numbers in Sheffield being rewarded by a performance of *Swan Lake* at the Royal Opera House for their prodigious output of cutlery for Messrs Mappin and Webb!

In the triple bill that we presented on the tour, the big success was *The Rake's Progress*. I tried to suppress the thought that maybe the audience saw Hogarth's London as reflecting the decadence of the West, hoping rather that they were appreciating its beauty as they looked at Rex Whistler's backcloth of one of the city's eighteenth-century streets. The main praise, though, was for its music and for the composer, Gavin Gordon, to whom the audiences at the Maryinsky gave great acclaim. They thought it strange that he had only written one score for the Royal Ballet. They were even more surprised to learn that he was, in fact, a musical comedy actor: at the time of the first production of *The Rake* he was playing in a musical comedy at the Savoy Theatre, *The Jolly Roger*, in the role of a pirate king. In Russia he would have been encouraged to compose further scores for the ballet and duly installed in his dacha. There is no doubt that his music is a perfect complement to Ninette de Valois's ballet, giving an appropriate theme for each consecutive turn in the plot, and it was very gratifying that our Russian audiences gave it such praise.

We had two ladies to dress us at the Maryinsky, called Anya and Maria. At our first meeting we could tell that they were weighing us up. I am sure there was little thought of our being friends – after all, we were from the much-despised capitalist West – but they proved to be excellent dressers and soon a mutual respect grew between us. There was a smile or two and when we had to demonstrate how our many costumes worked, they got to know our various idiosyncrasies and later our names. Although we had no common language, we all managed to understand one another. Fred used to come and sit in our dressing room, and with his quick ear for languages and with what Russian he had learnt from Sophie Fedorovitch and Marie Rambert, he made great strides. It was the year of the cha-cha in the West; we all loved it but it was completely unknown in Russia – until, that is, Fred came along. By the end of the week he was cha-chaing with Maria, who would hold out her hands to him when he arrived before the performance and invite him to dance; in no time they would be beating out its rhythm right down the corridor. When our season in St Petersburg was nearing its close, we were all such great friends that they showed that they were very sad to think that we would soon be parted; on the last night we were all hugging the two of them and they could hardly see to do up our costumes for their tears. We gave them presents from our store of things brought from home; they in return gave us each a brightly-coloured wooden spoon and, in doing so, had a friendly and trustworthy interpreter explain that the spoons were to catch our tears as they fell.

A ballet that again very much appealed to the audiences at the Maryinsky was Ashton's *La Fille mal gardée*. It had long been popular in Russia in various versions, and pictures abounded of Karsavina, Pavlova and many legendary ballerinas who had enjoyed success in this work. Ashton had drawn heavily on the conversations he had had with Madame Karsavina about the productions in which she had danced. As always, she had been generous in her help, managing to recapture long passages of mime sequences for many of the Royal Ballet productions of the classics. For my own part, I remember how wonderful she was in teaching me Hilarion in *Giselle*, so much so that I felt I could never do the rôle justice; when I said this to her, she replied, 'My dear, always remember, tell story'.

For his part, all that Fred gleaned he skilfully wove into his ballet, which he also cast perfectly; Nadia Nerina danced Lise joyously, giving each variation vivacity and charm with her effortless technique, while David Blair as Colas made an ideal partner for her. He had made his mark previously in the Sadler's Wells Theatre Ballet, particularly in the ballets of John Cranko, the very talented South African choreographer. In the rôle of the slightly stupid but endearing Alain, son of a rich farmer, was Alexander Grant who, from the moment he arrived by boat from New Zealand immediately after the war, had become a firm favourite with the public and had risen to new heights in this part. He was a talented, enchanting dancer, prone to injury although never missing a performance; one would see him hobble through the stage door, perform a few of his own particular brand of warm-up exercises, and then go on stage and practically dance everybody off it! He seemed to move with every fibre of his body, and never more so than in *La Fille mal gardée*.

We had hoped to travel to Moscow from Leningrad by train, but the authorities would not hear of it. The general reason noised abroad was that it was not desirable for us to have a close view of the countryside, but I put it down to the bureaucratic stamp of the Soviet régime – where once a thing had been arranged, it remained as such, however uncongenial to the situation. We, who had a more romantic view of things, longed to arrive in Moscow shunted into the station as Anna Karenina had been, or as had Garbo in her guise in the film, steam pouring out from beneath the train to engulf the travellers. No such luck. It was Aeroflot once more, with its own distinctive smell and spartan in-flight refreshment to correct any such extravagant imaginings.

Our hotel in Moscow was totally unlike the charming Astoria in Leningrad; it was a huge, impersonal, concrete building, a poor man's skyscraper with a twinkling red star lit on its pinnacle. This hotel pattern was repeated all over the city and featured in every brochure of Moscow. Our rooms were stark and cell-like with not a vestige of chenille, but as compensation we had a good view of the river. Taped music accompanied our rides in the lifts; one tune in particular, which we got to know well, was dedicated, we were informed, to the Red Star – not one we felt disposed to wish upon!

We were fortunate in regard to the financial arrangements that had been made for us in London before this tour, drawing only a portion of our pay in roubles because any surplus could not be changed back into hard currency or taken out of the country. By contrast, a large company of Canadian ice-skaters staying in our hotel had received their entire pay for theatre and television performances in roubles; we found them wandering round the gift shop, forced to load up with art books, records of Russian opera and rather dubious fur hats, which, to a Canadian, was like taking inferior coals to Newcastle. We had one extra television appearance not allowed for in our schedule, for which we were paid in roubles. Those of us at my table in the restaurant, where the service was no speedier than it had been in Leningrad, spent the lot on huge bowls of caviar, which, in this enforced extravagance, we gluttonously devoured.

The Bolshoi Theatre was as huge as its name implies and resplendent in red and gold. The atmosphere was totally different from that in the Maryinsky, to which we had all lost our hearts, and we never grew close to our dressers as we had with Anya and Maria. In Moscow generally there was a feeling of much stricter and more closely guarded security, and Michael gave the chandeliers a miss. Although the city lacked the beauty of Leningrad, it was very impressive; I particularly liked the Kremlin where, after surveying the great gold onions, one walked through the gilded rooms and chapels as if in the most ornate production of *Boris Godunov* and felt a chill at the mention of Ivan the Terrible. It was all gloriously theatrical. At the end of our first morning of sightseeing, we had a rich bonus when we saw none less than Mr Kruschev emerging from one of the great heavy doors of the Kremlin and popping, as we supposed, out to lunch.

We were invited to attend an open-air performance given by a section of the Bolshoi Ballet company in Gorky Park. It was a bright and sunny day and a festive atmosphere prevailed among the immense audience, many of whom were eating ice cream, which came for us, as did the caviar, high on the dietary agenda. The stage was large and the programme consisted mainly of divertissements, including Madame Maya Plisetskaya dancing Pavlova's 'Dying Swan' for which she was famous and in which, on this occasion, there was sufficient resuscitation to allow for an encore. Then there were the Polovtsian Dances from *Prince Igor*, given their true national vigour and colour. However, as the group formed up for the well-known finale, something went amiss and all its members collapsed like a pack of cards; as the curtain fell on this disarray, one had a glimpse of dancers bursting into fits of giggles. We loved them for it; it had happened to us all and from that moment on we felt close to our Russian counterparts.

When I entered Gorky Park, I saw to my astonishment the statue of the Soviet Workers that Michael and I had encountered at the Paris Exhibition in 1937, when the hammer and sickle seemed to be menacing the German pavilion directly opposite the Russian. It was immediately recognisable in its native home and served to bring back memories of our pre-war visit to Paris. That visit was recalled again when a former ballerina of the Bolshoi Company thanked me for letting her watch the class that I was giving for the male members of our company, and mentioned a resemblance in my style of doing so to that of Alexandre Volinine, with whom she had also studied, as had Michael and I. I am afraid that I was not sporting the black velvet court style of dress – however, I seemed to have created the same effect!

I was very moved by a visit we made to a home for retired theatricals in Moscow; I had not thought of that sort of thing existing in Soviet Russia. With help from interpreters, we had conversations with some of the residents and I was surprised and interested when an elderly gentleman, who spoke a little English, said that he had once visited London and had danced in a variety show at the Hippodrome, Leicester Square, producing a photograph of himself in costume as he spoke. He and his fellow residents were of another era, but we all got along together famously. When we were leaving, a one-time singer was so carried away by the occasion that, in a strident soprano, she accompanied our departure with a passionate rendering of 'La Marseillaise'. Wrong nationality but right intention!

A bizarre note was also struck one day in the hotel restaurant; while we were seated and resigned to the interminable wait for our lunch, we saw the double doors of the large foyer open and a group of officials, led by the hotel manager, usher a VIP towards the reception desk. He was a tall, dusky figure in Eastern robes with a high, feathered head-dress; it took us only a minute to recognise the character, well-known to us on the TV newsreels as the popular tipster at all the race courses at home – Prince

Monolulu, famous for his rallying cry, 'I gotta horse'. As he made his dignified way to the desk in the foyer, which we could see from the restaurant, one of our stage crew could not resist ringing out with the Prince's signature call. The important visitor turned in surprise and utter disbelief; but by the time we had left our table and gathered round him, genuinely pleased to see a figure from home, he seemed equally pleased to see us. We never discovered what his visit was all about, but he was evidently delighted with his reception in Moscow and said to us in confidential tones, 'They do know how to welcome you here'.

He was not the only one. We heard during our stay that a big film gala was shortly to be held in the city, with such luminaries as Elizabeth Taylor included in the list of visitors to it. On our way to the Bolshoi Theatre in our bus each night we would pass the site on which the special cinema that was to house the gala was being built. We thought that there was not a hope that it would be ready in time, because all we could see was a heap of scaffolding that masked unfinished walls; there was no sign of a roof, and the opening night was looming up at the end of that week. But this was Communist Russia, with not a single restrictive practice, and so work went on by day and by night under a flood of arc lamps. As the hour of the opening approached, it still seemed to us that it would take a miracle to get things ready, but in fact they managed it; we heard that the seats arrived just in time to be pushed under the audience's sit-upons as they entered. There had been a great deal of excitement in the city, with huge billboards and pictures of the stars who were to appear, and crowds of Muscovites milled around them admiring the sophistication of these icons from the West, enjoying, without any sense of rancour, this free street show. It was all very good-natured and everybody later was to find Miss Taylor especially exciting, and deservedly so. The gala was a great success and we were sad to have missed it, but we were giving our all at the Bolshoi at the same time. It was, however, good to see what, in those days of a strict Communist régime, a touch of showbiz could do.

On our last night there was a wonderful moment as Ninette de Valois led her young company forward to receive the applause of the audience on a stage banked by the traditional baskets of flowers to celebrate the occasion. The Minister of Culture, Madame Furtseva, had shown her appreciation by joining the company on stage for the final calls, and there was a typical gesture from Ashton, who as the curtain fell presented her with a red rose that he had craftily plucked from the floral display.

We assembled next day at the airport for the journey home with mixed feelings and many memories. For my part I had found the whole experience interesting and rewarding on many levels. Being who we were and doing what we did, we had been able to make closer contact with the Russians whom we met than might otherwise have been the case; there were common bonds and shared interests that gave us the personal knowledge that, in spite of the régime that governed their lives, they were in so many ways people like ourselves.

I spent the first weekend following our return to England in my cottage by the Thames. I took the ferry across to Bray and had a delicious and typically English meal at my local, *The Hind's Head*. It felt good to be home.

The next time I went down, I saw Margot over the hedge in her mother's garden, and I noticed in the background a young man whom, strangely, she did not introduce. The following day in London this young man turned up at my class, which I was still giving the company; I was told that he was called Roman Jasman. Before class he had apparently been shown into the principal dancers' dressing room to change but, on being told that it was out of order for him to be there, was duly transferred to the *corps de ballet*'s dressing room. The position was soon reversed, for in no time at all the whole world was to know that this R. Jasman was in fact the famous Russian dancer Rudolf Nureyev, who had jumped across the barriers at the airport in Paris and escaped to the West.

Margot, who had for many years organised an annual charity matinée in aid of the Royal Academy of Dancing, of which she was President, asked Rudolf to be in the forthcoming one at the Drury Lane Theatre. Ashton choreographed a solo for him and he danced the Black Swan *pas de deux* with Rosella Hightower, the American ballerina with whom he had already appeared in France with the Marquis de Cuevas Ballet company. It is no exaggeration to say that he was an immediate success, and the stage door was besieged by practically everyone who had attended the performance. When Ninette de Valois asked him to appear with the Royal Ballet and to dance with Fonteyn in *Giselle*, the die was cast.

For Nureyev's first six months in the company I was working with a ballet company in Washington, having been given leave of absence to do so by Ninette de Valois. When I returned I felt, from the atmosphere that prevailed, that Nureyev's arrival had created something of a revolution. A number of the ground rules seemed to have been swept aside; the new star was temperamental, to say the least, and I thought that his intense bad temper could have been modified had he been given less latitude. He must have heard beforehand of the strict discipline of the company and its policy of ensemble performance, one that also obtained with the Opera Company as it did at Stratford with the Royal Shakespeare Company. But suddenly the Royal Ballet seemed out of balance. This was perhaps understandable, since Nureyev's name was on everyone's lips; the press no longer featured pictures of ballerinas tying up their ballet shoes à la Degas, but instead gave full coverage to the megastar's latest tantrums. His appearance, too, was very much that of the sixties, with long hair worn in the Mick Jagger fashion and dress in accordance with the dictates of Carnaby Street, which must for him have been in startling contrast to the style displayed in the Moscow department store, Gum. But in spite of this ultra-extravagant behaviour, there was so much to applaud, particularly his generosity with advice and help to any dancer who was having trouble with the execution of a difficult step; he would give instruction with great patience and exactness. My goodness, he was a handful, but his coming together with the great artist, Margot Fonteyn, was truly wonderful. They packed the Royal Opera House.

When they first appeared together in America during our 1963 tour even Garbo wanted to meet Nureyev; this was duly arranged by our friends, Tug Barton and John McHugh.

One day, after a fairly stormy stage-call at the Metropolitan Opera House, Rudolf was hungrily roaring for a steak. Margot anxiously asked me to go over to Bill's restaurant bar opposite the stage door and warn Sis Kanowitz, the much-loved owner, that she was bringing him over for a meal, and to 'wise-up' Sis, who had not met him before, that Rudolf might be rather fractious. But Margot had forgotten that Sis was used to handling the toughest clientèle in New York and, if necessary, of settling their hash. As we entered the bar, Sis greeted Margot with a kiss; before Margot could introduce Rudolf, Sis firmly rested her welcoming hand under his chin, as she was wont to do, and in honey tones said, 'So, you're the little new boy', leading him by the chin to a table where immediately a delicious steak was served. Sis joined them, talking gently to both as she did to all of us when we were nervously preparing for a first night. She was a remarkable woman. Frederick Ashton, Alexander Grant and I would often stay on after lunchtime when the rest of the customers had gone, and during this lull the favourite members of her staff would come and have a word with us; one of these was her cook, always referred to as 'my wonderful Millie'. Sis would serve us drinks during our conversations; there was, for these, never a sign of a bill.

Oh, how we loved New York and indeed the whole United States during those halcyon days of the American tours, when we seemed to be surrounded by so many genuinely loveable people. Sis used to refer to her particular group of Royal Ballet friends as 'my English family'; well, I felt that I had an enormous American family myself.

Nureyev was pursued by an excited and feverish group of fans from state to state and the clamour of the adoration for this great artist was justly deserved, for he was indeed unique. The first time that he and Fonteyn appeared in *Swan Lake* at the Metropolitan Opera House, I recall how, during the third act, his Black Swan solo received salvoes of applause and he had to take call after call in acknowledgement. Margot had to follow this; she left the wings to begin her solo in the middle of the stage, walking on without accompaniment in measured steps, slowly and unruffled, taking up her first position. There was a stillness, and then applause broke out before she had started her variation. It was as though the audience were reassuring her of their love, in no way diminished by the advent of her great partner. At the end of the whole *pas de deux*, Rudolf led her forward and, recognising as he did the true attributes of the *prima ballerina assoluta*, presented her to the audience as if he, too, was sharing their admiration for her. That moment demonstrated what was, I think, the secret of that great partnership; my respect for Rudolf doubled when I saw this true graciousness of spirit.

Chapter 18

The main event of 1965 was Kenneth MacMillan's *Romeo and Juliet* with Fonteyn dancing Juliet to Nureyev's Romeo. To hear later that MacMillan had accepted an offer to become Director of a company in Berlin and was leaving us was something of a blow. We had been fortunate, thanks to Ninette de Valois' foresight in the early fifties, in having a number of first-class resident choreographers in the team: Frederick Ashton, John Cranko (who had subsequently left to develop a distinguished company in Stuttgart), and then Kenneth MacMillan, together with notable guests such as Massine, Balanchine, Roland Petit and Andrée Howard.

I remember a Sunday night at Sadler's Wells Theatre back in the early fifties when Ninette de Valois gave an opportunity for aspiring choreographers to try their hand, and out of that performance had come Kenneth MacMillan, whose obvious genius no one could deny. We hoped that occasions such as this would become an established project, but unfortunately the enterprise was short-lived. Of course, the company was in the safe hands of Ashton, but without a backing group of talent I felt we might lose the choreographic stakes. I also maintained that members of the company should themselves be given an opportunity to show what choreographic talent they might possess. I had heard mutterings to that effect and so knew that people would be willing to take a chance to demonstrate what they could do.

An important factor in the situation was that in 1963 Ninette de Valois, having reached the age of sixty-five, had retired as she had planned. Inevitably, the mainstay of all our enterprises would no longer be present in her original capacity, although the company looked up to her in continuing allegiance and there were obviously times when we called upon her unique and unparalleled experience.

However, an opportunity to promote a choreographic group came from an unexpected source. Through Moyra Fraser I had become a friend of Laurier Lister, the producer of the revue *Airs on a Shoestring* in which Moyra had starred with Max Adrian at the Royal Court Theatre. Laurier had in due course become the Director of the Yvonne Arnaud Theatre in Guildford, and one day while we were discussing the ever-present need to raise funds for that theatre, I offered to produce a gala there to that end. I managed to get together a good performance, beautifully danced by members of our company. I was greatly helped in this by Lord Nugent, who had a house near Guildford and was on the Board of the Yvonne Arnaud Theatre. I had known him previously, and he and his wife had long been devotees of the ballet. The gala was a success and was followed, to Laurier's delight, by a second one before the Christmas of 1965.

When I think about it, I wonder at my temerity, since I had never produced anything in the theatre in my life; but at the second performance I wanted to experiment and see if I could have at least one item newly choreographed by someone in the company. At the back of my mind was an insistent desire to help in the nurturing of fresh talent in this important aspect. In planning the new piece, I asked Alexander Grant to participate; he was a fine artist, musical, with a true sense of theatre and willing to 'have a go'. He decided to choreograph a hornpipe using three dancers in the company: Wayne Sleep, Kenneth Mason and Lambert Cox. We went to our principal conductor, Jack Lanchbery, for advice; he was not only enthusiastic about the idea but said he would compose the music for the piece. All went well and the evening was again a success.

My campaign gathering momentum, I volunteered a third gala. Laurier was very pleased at this, imagining it would be for the next Christmas, and was somewhat taken aback when I told him I wanted do it in three or four months' time. We arranged the date for 2 April 1967. When I returned home after this meeting, I realised where my temerity had led me. How did I know that Ashton, now the Director, would allow me to gather enough young choreographers in time to put on the show? I went next day to see him in his office, and to my delight he said 'Yes'. There is one thing that never changed with Fred: when he said 'Yes' he meant it, and when he said 'No' he meant it too. However, I was told to see the Ballet Master, Jack Hart, and tell him of Fred's decision.

I could see from the start that Jack Hart disapproved and, looking at me with his most avuncular expression he said, 'Well, I think it's a good idea, but now is not the right time for it'. I replied that I thought it was just the right time and that anyway Fred had given me his permission to go ahead. The Ballet Master went on with his paperwork as I left the room, and I went straight away to the dancers whom I knew to be ready to try their hand; David Drew, Geoffrey Cauley and Alexander Grant were game to be included, and altogether I collected eight volunteers. I telephoned my old friend, John Field, who was then in charge of the Second Company. In spite of the fact that they were playing in Newcastle, he assured me that a section could be included in our programme, and offered to help in any way he could in rehearsing them. They would come down from Newcastle in time for the performance in Guildford.

How on earth our gallant dancers managed to rehearse and to get the show ready I shall never know, as they were not allowed a moment of company time to do so. Yet it was the most wonderful combined operation that I ever remember; principals, soloists, *corps de ballet* pitched in and rehearsed in every available corner of the Upper Section of the Royal Ballet School in Baron's Court. We all became a sort of secret society, beavering away, becoming more feverish as 2 April drew closer. On our nights free from performance at Covent Garden and when the company rehearsal rooms at Baron's Court were empty, we took over, and I would run from room to room to see that all was progressing well. Although I had to bear the brunt of his displeasure, I felt sorry for the poor caretaker, Stanley, who was at heart a dear man and should have closed the premises much earlier to start his cleaning operations.

Then the blow fell. I was sent for by the Ballet Master, who said in his most unsympathetic tone, 'I hear you are expecting to give a performance in public of this choreographic stuff you've been doing. I don't think we can allow that. You must remember this is the Royal Ballet. Anyway, when is it?' I told him, 'On Sunday' – this was the previous Wednesday. He was appalled and said angrily that he had to see Fred immediately and tell him about it. 'He already knows', I replied. 'I've given him his tickets and some to Ninette de Valois as well.' He gasped at this and went to see Fred, who countered his wrath and kindly said that he would cancel a rehearsal for Friday and come to see a run-through. Thank goodness Thursday was not a performance night for us; that evening everyone worked as though possessed.

Hilda Gaunt, our rehearsal pianist, who had distinguished herself during the war when she and Constant Lambert had played for us in the absence of an orchestra, had supported the Choreographic Group from the word 'go' and had given her time and help musically, her professional acumen and, most of all, her enthusiasm. She had high hopes for the moving *pas de deux* that Geoffrey Cauley had choreographed for two girls, one of whom was Georgina Parkinson, an important company principal. When some of the company staff heard about this, they put their foot down and forbade her to appear, saying that she had enough work to do without being involved in any Choreographic Group. This was much to Georgina's regret and, naturally, to Geoffrey's chagrin. There were only a few days left, and replacing Georgina would be almost impossible. However, there was one person, one of our leading ballerinas, who had always joined in all the company's extramural activities and, in fact, as a very young dancer had taken part in the famous Sunday night performance at Sadler's Wells Theatre when Kenneth MacMillan made his choreographic début: this was Anya Linden. I telephoned her, explaining our dilemma, and she said she would come to watch a rehearsal of the piece. This she did, liked it very much and said that she was willing to appear in it. Being such an experienced dancer, she managed to learn the work very quickly and Geoffrey was overjoyed.

The whole run-through went well, the dancers working for all they were worth. Fred was delighted and gave us his blessing, insisting that we had the Friday afternoon to polish up the performance; this would not have been possible on the Saturday, when we were appearing twice at the Opera House. Early on the Sunday morning, 2 April 1967, we arrived at the Yvonne Arnaud Theatre, our dancers and stage staff with their stage director; they would later be joined by the resident theatre staff who were also involved. We were nervous and apprehensive as to the outcome of the whole project, but the spirit and determination of the dancers was beyond belief; convinced about what they were attempting, they worked all day with a fervour that promised success. But our troubles were not yet over. David Drew's ballet included back-projection slides to complement the modern score and, unfortunately, on the first run-through these slides were dropped and smashed beyond repair. There was a spare set at home and David's father, who had come to watch the proceedings, was despatched to fetch them in his car. John Field's dancers arrived from Newcastle just in time for a run-through of their ballet but, what with some unavoidable delays and hiccups, it was necessary to delay the start for half an hour. However, Laurier Lister turned up trumps and opened the bar early so that the audience and our friends from town, led by Ninette de Valois, Margot and Fred, could have a welcome drink after their journey.

Our performance was a triumph. There was no doubt that the Royal Ballet Choreographic Group was launched and had justified all the efforts of the dancers, the generosity of Laurier Lister in arranging for us to use his theatre and the encouragement of Frederick Ashton.

The Group gave its second performance, the last one at the Yvonne Arnaud Theatre, in the autumn of 1967. I have always believed in artists performing as much as possible and I planned to organise three shows a year, in spring, summer and autumn, to give good opportunities for the choreographers to have their work evaluated. This I did for the twenty-five years in which I organised the Group. In order to achieve my aim I needed to keep a fairly low profile in the general run of things and, at times, to resort to guerrilla tactics, but, throughout, my main support came from all the dancers of the company, both principals and *corps de ballet*, with their loyalty, diligence and enthusiasm. They also understood the importance of maintaining this activity to encourage the choreographic talent that is the main bloodstream of any ballet company. I did get a certain amount of flak from the young members of the Group when leading artists were involved in new work, but I felt that by linking the two it gave invaluable experience to those beginning to make their way in this field. Such had, after all, been the case throughout the years with Diaghilev, Massine and Ashton (who had cut his choreographic teeth on such artists as Karsavina, Lopokova and Markova).

I had realised from the start that I needed a base nearer to the Opera House to facilitate conditions for the artists taking part, though I always acknowledge the fact that Laurier Lister, with his understanding and encouragement, had made the whole thing possible. At the outset the funds for the enterprise were not on an extravagant scale. Sir John Tooley, the General Administrator of the Royal Opera House, had kindly allowed me £100 for costumes and out-of-pocket expenses for each performance. As I left his office after having been offered this he said, with a twinkle in his eye, '... and I shall expect some change!' – which is what he got the first time round. It was the only occasion on which I ever kept an account book; I have it to this day, showing that I spent sixty-eight pounds seven shillings and fourpence. One of the principal items was the material for Geoffrey Cauley's ballet *Impressions*, at a cost of three pounds; this was for butter muslin, more commonly associated in the past with the larder on hot summer days when, fringed with beads, it covered milk and lemonade jugs. In this stage environment it made the two girls look delightful.

I was greatly helped by the generosity of Hilda Gaunt, who refused to accept a fee for her piano accompaniment; it was her contribution to the Choreographic Group, convinced as she always was of its importance. Nevertheless, I am afraid that with the second performance at the Yvonne Arnaud Theatre, which was more elaborate than the first, I got into debt. This worried me but not for long, as a way to clear it presented itself almost immediately. This happened because the very successful group run by Peter Brinson called Ballet For All, which was due to appear at the theatre in Shell Mex House for the Friends of Covent Garden, was cancelled at the last moment. When I heard this I straight away offered to replace it with the performance done in Guildford the week before, subject to my finding the Shell Theatre suitable for our use. I took the company stage director, David Moggridge, to inspect it. We found the stage rather hard, but David said that he could borrow a serviceable linoleum and stage cloth, plus some additional lighting from the Opera House, and we would be in business. Kensington Davison, the Director of the Friends of Covent Garden and known to us as Ken, was delighted and only too pleased to defray any additional costs. This was the beginning of an association between the Friends and the Royal Ballet Choreographic Group that has lasted to the present day.

In the event, we had the audience at the Shell Mex Theatre that was intended for Ballet For All. Among them was Nevill Coghill, the scholar of medieval literature, who was also about to produce a musical based on Chaucer's *Canterbury Tales*. He was so impressed by David Drew's ballet – the slides remaining intact this time – that he engaged David to choreograph his show. So there we were at the very outset with a West End choreographer for a musical that ran for six years at the Phoenix Theatre.

We gave only the one performance at the Shell Theatre, for, grateful as I was for what that had done for us, I did not think it the ideal permanent home. Now that the Group was launched, I scouted around and found a venue that was suitable, the Collegiate Theatre in Gordon Street, affiliated to London University as was Lord Annan, its first full-time vice-chancellor, who was also on the board of the Royal Opera House and the Royal Ballet School. He readily agreed to our using the theatre and set about making us welcome there.

Success then came very rapidly in those early days. Each year the Friends gave a Christmas party in the Opera House, during which there would be some form of entertainment on the stage. This had variously taken the form of the one-act Stravinsky stage work *The Soldier's Tale*, produced by John Copley and starring Geraint Evans – with a new young actor, Derek Jacobi – or a cabaret. However, for the forthcoming Christmas they were without specific plans for the entertainment and I thought, 'In for a penny, in for a pound. Why don't I suggest one myself? Perhaps an all-star performance of *Façade*, a ballet that has not been in the repertoire for some time.' Ken Davison thought it an excellent idea and one that would fit the bill perfectly.

I went immediately to Ashton to ask not only his permission but whether he would take part in it himself, dancing his famous Tango. After a few minutes of demurring, he agreed. I asked him whom he would like as his partner, and without hesitation he said, 'Moira Shearer'. That delighted everyone, as it was a while since we had seen her dancing on the stage at Covent Garden, where she was always a great favourite. Fred stipulated that he would do only the Tango and would like Alexander Grant to dance the energetic finale. But, after the volume of applause that greeted him and Moira in the Tango on the night, he was on like a shot in the finale. The following day I met him on the way to see the physiotherapist and I took the full brunt of his displeasure at being in agony after such unwonted physical exertion. The Friends, however, were much delighted by the success of this all-star performance, and for me it was the beginning of many years of producing the Friends' Christmas cabaret.

At this time I went to see another member of the Opera Board and Director of the Royal College of Music, Sir Keith Faulkner, to ask him if I could take a group of our young choreographers to meet his young composers. He readily agreed and invited us to listen to the new scores that had been written. During our visit, Geoffrey Cauley, who was part of the young Choreographic Group, was much taken by a composition inspired by Walter de la Mare's poem *The Listeners* that had been written by a student, Douglas Young, and he chose it for the music to accompany the ballet he had choreographed for the Royal Ballet School's annual performance at the Opera House.

That was a happy outcome of our joining forces in this way, and when I later decided to combine music and ballet for a programme to be given at St Paul's Cathedral at Christmas in 1969, I included this work, which had proved a great success. For the rest, eight members of my group choreographed to their favourite carol, each work contributing to an aspect of the Christmas story. This event had come about largely through the fact that one of the students at the senior school was Richard Collins, son of the then Dean of St Paul's. He introduced me to his father, who was happy for me to produce my *Carols and Ballets* in the cathedral. The choirmaster at St Paul's willingly co-operated and brought in the choir from the Royal Ballet School to sing with the cathedral choir. The organ played for all the carols and the orchestra from the school also contributed.

By the time we gave the performance, Dean Collins had been succeeded by the Very Reverend Martin Gloucester Sullivan, a New Zealander, who gave me great support and was delighted to watch the performance in the company of Ninette de Valois, Frederick Ashton and Marie Rambert. It was a perishingly cold December night, but warmth pervaded the proceedings through the wonderful spectacle of the dancers, members of the Choreographic Group augmented by young dancers of the Royal Ballet, Vyvyan Lorrayne, Vergie Derman and Deanne Bergsma. Knowing that I was a bit stumped for costumes, Ninette de Valois had generously allowed me to use some from *Job*, so those in the cast who were not draped in butter muslin were wearing dresses designed by John Piper for her ballet. The pink shades covering the candlelights in the choir gave a fine background effect for the dancers and for the readings given by two boys from the school in pulpits facing each other across the nave. In the cathedral the atmosphere of beauty and the feeling of simplicity under the shelter of the great dome were extremely moving, right up to the finale when the dancers, in joyous celebration, came down the nave to 'Tomorrow shall

be my Dancing Day'. It was wonderful the next day, a Sunday, to wake up
to the morning's papers carrying on the front page a picture of the event
and capturing, even in the black and white of those days, the beauty of
the spectacle, its simplicity combined with the majesty of the cathedral.

Chapter 19

In the latter half of the sixties I seemed to be taking on a new persona within the framework of the company. The performances by the Choreographic Group gave me an opportunity to nurture the talents of my colleagues in that field, and I felt that I was in the theatre in the fullest sense. I was doing what I had dreamt about from my earliest years, when I had hoped that my life would be in show business, taking up the curtain and getting on with the job of production. Other circumstances also added to my more varied activities; during the summer break, Rudolf Nureyev started to organise performances by major artists and himself, known as *Nureyev and Friends*.

For these extramural events Ashton gave him permission to include *Marguerite and Armand*, the ballet that Ashton had choreographed for Fonteyn and Nureyev and that had brought these two artists together in a dramatic evocation of the Dumas story, giving it a new magic. The music chosen for it was by Liszt, a composer who had always served Ashton well. I recall the young Fonteyn and Helpmann in *Apparitions*, with designs by Cecil Beaton as with *Marguerite and Armand* later. There were the occasional know-alls who were apt to be dismissive about a reworking of the old theme being used merely as a vehicle for the two stars, but Fred countered this by saying, 'Well, what's wrong with a vehicle?' It was a short ballet, but the rapturous applause that always greeted these two dancers when it was performed was anything but short. The rôle of Armand's father was wonderfully taken by Michael Somes, and when upbraiding Marguerite in the garden scene, his firmness accentuated the frailty and heartbreak of her renunciation of Armand. Fred brought about the fusion of the talents of Margot, Rudolf and Michael with an instinctive feeling for their special interpretative qualities and by his brilliant inventiveness in the choreography.

Nureyev was about to produce a new version of *The Sleeping Beauty* at La Scala, Milan, with costumes and designs by Nicholas Georgiadis. This performance was somewhat delayed – not unusual for La Scala – so Rudolf was asked to fill the gap with his *Nureyev and Friends*. Unfortunately no one in the Royal Opera House was willing to mount the ballet, and Michael Somes even declined to appear. Margot was very upset at all this and to my amazement asked me if I would put it on. And so I did. That was the beginning of my *Marguerite and Armand* period. In fact I mounted this work twice in Milan and subsequently in Rio de Janeiro, Buenos Aires, New York, Washington, Manila, Paris, Vienna and London at the Coliseum. So there!

For the first trip to Milan the Royal Opera House allowed me to take the costumes but no scenery. Margot said that she hated the thought of dancing against a background of black curtains, which seemed to be the only viable alternative; but then I remembered the dark blue ones we had all those years ago at the Ballet Club, and I was fortunate in finding some like them backstage at La Scala. I looped them up in the way that Sophie Fedorovitch had done so effectively in Fred's ballet *Les Masques*, but still the scenes at the elderly duke's house and in the casino looked desperately dull. Then I also discovered backstage some immense and imposing gilt candelabra; having obtained permission to use them, I managed to place them effectively to give the stage the required opulence. It was only after the first night when Nicholas Georgiadis came backstage that I found that the said candelabra were part of his new and lavish design for his production of *The Sleeping Beauty*, which was still under wraps. However, he forgave me because he had had some misgivings as to whether they would prove too overbearing for his ballroom scene, but, having seen them on stage that night, he was relieved to know that they would be very suitable.

Because of the missing Somes, it fell to me to play Armand's father. I already knew the piece well, having taken the part of a duke, the elderly admirer of Marguerite, in the original production, but I was only too aware of what a poor substitute I was. However, Georgiadis, a great film buff, said I gave a Lionel Barrymore performance – not, after all, a bad family to follow! Anyway, it all went well and beyond my wildest dreams – or should I say nightmares, because I experienced the most extreme nervousness I had every known: my baptism of fire as a producer, and at La Scala to boot. Rudolf was delighted and asked me to join his party at dinner after the performance.

During 1968 we danced for the first time at the new Lincoln Center in uptown Manhattan, leaving the dear old 'Met' down at 39th Street, which, to our sorrow, was being demolished nineteen years after our memorable opening there and after a period of so many memories connected with it. The opening ballet at the Lincoln Center was to be Ashton's *Cinderella*, in which the leading rôle would be taken by Svetlana Beriosova, who had joined our section of the company after many years as principal with the Sadler's Wells Theatre Ballet.

At the same time, a great friend of Margot's, Dalal Achcar, was planning to take *Marguerite and Armand* to Rio de Janeiro and Buenos Aires to

9. Bilby in *A Mirror for Witches*

10. With Nadia Nerina in *Noctambules*

11. Thomas in *La Fille mal gardée,* with Alexander Grant

12. *Marguerite and Armand*, with Margot Fonteyn

13. HRH Princess Margaret at a Friends of Covent Garden Christmas party with, left to right, Anthony Dowson, Michael Batchelor, Stephen Beagley, Ross McGibbon

14. The Tsar's Aide de Camp in *Anastasia*

15. Dame Margot Fonteyn's Sixtieth Birthday Gala. Sir Robert Helpmann, Michael Somes, Fonteyn, Sir Frederick Ashton

16. Celebrating the fiftieth anniversary of the re-opening of the Royal Opera House after World War II. Back row, left to right, Gerd Larsen, Oenene Talbot, Jean Bedells, Margaret Roseby, Julia Farron, Barbara Fewster, Leslie Edwards, Pamela May; front row, Dame Beryl Grey, Dame Ninette de Valois, Pauline Wadsworth.

be performed by Fonteyn and Nureyev with her ballet company. This was made possible by the fact that Margot was not dancing at the beginning of the New York season. I was roped into putting it on for Dalal at both dates; so, after dancing in my rôle as Thomas the Farmer in *La Fille mal gardée* at Covent Garden on the last Thursday night performance before the company left for America, I had to fly off to Rio on the Friday in time to audition the Brazilian boys of Dalal's company and teach them their movements in *Marguerite and Armand* over the weekend, before flying on to Buenos Aires to do the same for the Argentinian boys for their performance later that week. I was also asked to play Hilarion in *Giselle* with the local ballet in the famous Buenos Aires theatre, the Colon, returning to Rio on Saturday night in time to 'polish' the Dalal Company, then continuing on to New York on the Sunday night.

Before I left London I had to call in at the school in Baron's Court to collect the orchestral scores to take to Brazil and to say goodbye to the staff. Looking up from his desk in the office, John Hart, rather short on valedictions, made it clear that I had better make sure I arrived in New York on time for the rehearsal of *Cinderella*, in which I now played the Father.

Safely in Rio, I was met by Dalal, her husband and Marcia de Barbarà, a close friend who featured in the general scheme of Dalal's company. I was rushed immediately to the theatre where the dancers were waiting for the audition. After this I went straight to a rehearsal lasting well into the evening, following which I was taken to Dalal's apartment, where I was staying overnight. By that time I felt punch-drunk, but off we went to dinner and my first sight of Rio, with which I was further intoxicated to the point of not knowing what day it was. The next morning I helped the ballet mistress with a second rehearsal, to be continued the following week when I returned from Argentina.

All went well with the schedule in Buenos Aires, except that it was decided that *Marguerite and Armand* should be televised in a straight run-through on my last day there. But, as one would expect in a land of *mañana*, we over-ran and I missed the plane back to Rio on the Saturday; this necessitated taking the Sunday flight to New York, which had a stopover of only one hour in Rio, if I was to fulfil my obligations in time to be at Cinderella's ball! In the event, Dalal's ballet mistress plus a secretary met me at the airport in Rio and took notes about details of the production that had been worrying them and then off I flew again, arriving in New York on the final stage of this whirlwind tour. I made my way to the unfamiliar hotel that had been booked near the Lincoln Center. My first sight of its dingy foyer did not reassure me, but I was dead tired; in no mood to complicate matters, I dragged my luggage up to my room, which reassured me even less.

The rehearsal next day was not until late afternoon, so I telephoned my old friends, Tug and John, who told me that they had tried to reach me, but that no one in the company knew where I was staying. When I gave the name of the hotel, there was a cry of horror at the other end and Tug said firmly, 'You will pack your luggage, settle up, get a cab and come straight round to us.' I arrived at number 48 East 73rd Street, where my two dear friends invited me to stay. I was then somewhat shaken to hear that there had been a murder at my hotel the week before I arrived. But the happy outcome was that, not only on this occasion in 1968, but on every subsequent tour in New York, I stayed with them until some twenty years later when John died and Tug left the spacious house and took an apartment in Sutton Place on the East River.

Life at 48 East 73rd Street was marvellous and luxurious. I confess I soon got used to the luxury and accustomed to the world figures, film stars and New York socialites who had a way of dropping in. My hosts had already established that they would give a lunch party for a large number of the company (some twenty-five of us) on the Monday, our free day, and among the other guests I was delighted to meet Adèle Astaire, the sister of Fred. She had appeared with him in West End musicals in the pre-Ginger Rogers days and had introduced the music and words of George and Ira Gershwin to London audiences in the famous *Lady Be Good* in the twenties.

One day Adèle asked Ashton and me to lunch in a smart New York restaurant where another guest was Anita Loos, famous for her book *Gentlemen Prefer Blondes*. She was as bright as a button, tiny and with black kiss-curls framing her face in the fashion of the twenties. She talked about her early days in Hollywood when she was a successful writer of subtitles for silent films. These comprised not only dialogue but also a description of the locations: 'Way down West, where men are men and girls are glad of it'. This would take up the whole screen and interweave the action of the film, which might star such as Valentino, Mary Pickford, Chaplin or Buster Keaton, while suitable piano music would provide the atmosphere, comic or tragic as the case might be. It was fascinating to meet and talk to someone so famously a part of the history of the cinema and very much a star in her own right.

Tug and John also had a weekend home on Staten Island with very easy access by the ferry, which one could catch after the show on Sunday night before taking a cab to their house on the far side of the island, overlooking the Atlantic. It was a big, rambling house with a terraced garden and swimming pool, a delightful place to spend our free Monday, returning to work on Tuesday morning. I missed the old 'Met' very much, but the new theatre was a spacious one and with very comfortable dressing rooms, one of which I shared with Michael Somes for many years, in fact until he left the company.

These were halcyon days. By now the Sixties were drawing to an end; the Beatles had held sway and Flower Power had come and gone, withered in the winds of change. One could look back on the time as a golden one in the world of the Royal Ballet. Rudolf Nureyev was a key figure in this period, particularly because of his re-introduction of Act III of *La Bayadère*, which was led by the superb dancing of Fonteyn and Nureyev himself. He also rehearsed the young ballerinas Deanne Bergsma, Monica Mason, Vyvyan Lorrayne and Vergie Derman in their solos. Michael Somes and John Hart were joined by such fine artists as Desmond Doyle, Ronald Hynd, Alexander Grant, Brian Shaw, and a very special character dancer, Wayne Sleep.

The sixties were also important for the company because Ashton was developing the exciting partnership of Antoinette Sibley and Anthony Dowell; like Margot Fonteyn and Michael Somes before them, they showed the same matching style and sensitivity. It was a period, too, of outstanding ballets both by Ashton and by MacMillan, great favourites such as *La Fille mal gardée*, *The Dream*, *Marguerite and Armand*, *Romeo and Juliet* and *The Invitation*. I shall never forget the first night of *La Fille mal gardée*, with Madame Rambert jumping to her feet from the front row of the stalls in ecstasies of delight at seeing her protégé, Frederick Ashton, having such a success with the Royal Ballet in the great Opera House. This underlined the essentially professional give-and-take between the two great figures of British ballet, Marie Rambert and Ninette de Valois.

Very important in the 50s and 60s were the performances of John Cranko's *Pineapple Poll*, *The Lady and the Fool*, *Antigone* and *Bonne Bouche*. Cranko was a choreographer of great distinction, showing that ballet can show wit and humour as well as richness of character, and extending the boundaries to include the delightful irreverence of pastiche.

For me personally a great moment in the sixties was when Peter Wright joined our company to produce with Ashton a new *Sleeping Beauty*. This was no easy proposition, because people naturally harked back to the production that had re-opened the Royal Opera House in 1946 and had conquered New York three years later, remaining a star attraction in our subsequent American tours. On the other hand, it was a stimulating challenge successfully taken up. Peter Wright showed all the promising signs of his later productions of the classics, and Frederick Ashton choreographed new variations and a wonderful *pas de deux* for the awakening scene. This was beautifully executed by Antoinette Sibley and Anthony Dowell, who led the company with great success both at Covent Garden and at the Lincoln Center in New York.

In this production I said farewell to Catalabutte and played the King. I did very well by my costume, being in full armour covered by a cloak lined with lambswool. I came on followed by two dancers from the School who were leading two small goats; in the wings waiting for my entry, I had to fight off the goats to prevent them from nibbling away at the lambswool lining. But this small occupational hazard apart, I thoroughly enjoyed Peter Wright's production, which was full of rich invention, adding interest to the company's repertoire of that time.

At the latter end of the sixties and on one of our American tours, David Webster came over to New York and made the announcement that Frederick Ashton would be retiring in 1970, the same year that he himself would retire as General Administrator. This came as a tremendous shock to us all; Fred would have served for only seven years as Director, after Ninette de Valois' thirty-two-year span following her founding of the company in 1931. David Webster also announced that Fred's successor would be Kenneth MacMillan and that he would take office in two years' time. As a result of this there was a long interregnum, inevitably putting a strain on both the outgoing and incoming Directors, and it was difficult to see the rationale behind the plan. 'The King is Dead, Long Live the King' has great virtue in its political context because no time is allowed for uncertainty or indecision, and no breeding ground is available for the various factions and intrigues that have full scope in the interregnum. How much better it might have been to have followed the example of Ninette de Valois, who retired unobtrusively, as she wished, handing over to her successor without any period of delay.

As the time drew near for Fred's departure as our Director, the company decided to work on the plan for his farewell gala. This would be organised by John Hart and Michael Somes, John to deal with the general *mise-en-scène* and Michael to rehearse the dancers. I was very pleased that both asked me to give a helping hand. The programme matter was to be a complete secret only to be revealed on the night and, to keep the secret intact, a number for each item was allotted in lieu of a title and appeared as such on the noticeboard with reference to the various rehearsals involved.

John and Michael decided very rightly that they would ask Fred's old friend and colleague, Billy Chappell, to write a narration to be read out by Robert Helpmann throughout the show, which began with a large picture of Fred projected on a white background, accompanied by with music from his ballets. However, I suggested increasing the number of slides, to which John agreed.

Knowing that pictures of celebrities when children always bring forth gasps of delight, I went to see Fred's sister, Edith Russell-Roberts, who found me a very early photograph of a small lad clinging to a very formal dining-room chair. Edith told me that her mother said that Fred had disliked being put up on the chair for the purpose of the photograph because he felt he was going to fall off it, saying with a childish lisp, 'Itth tho thlipperly'. Fred told me after the gala that he had to fight to keep back a tear – he was always one to blub – when this picture came up.

Next I tried Dover College, his old school, as I thought a group picture might be fun. I spoke to the headmaster who said, to my surprise, that he did not have such a one; he was friendly but not very forthcoming, possibly because Fred had often made it known that he and Dover College were not always on the best of terms.

Madame Rambert lent me a little-known early picture of him in his days of dancing with the Ballet Rambert, and one way and another I managed to collect an amusing and interesting group. I was greatly helped in setting it up by the man responsible for all the slides used in the productions at the Opera House, whom I had met through my work with the Choreographic Group and the Friends' Christmas show.

On another note entirely, this collection brought about one of the all-too-frequent summonses to the office, and the bill of £600 for the slides was presented to me, together with a severe wigging for such extravagance. But I displayed righteous indignation, citing the intention of the Opera Company to fly in many international opera stars for David Webster's gala, which was to follow Fred's, pointing out that their air fares and suites at first-class hotels would make my bill shrink into total insignificance by comparison. The point was reluctantly taken.

One of the items planned for the gala was the gallop from *Apparitions*, that wonderful dash around the stage to Constant Lambert's orchestral arrangement of Liszt's piano music. We had not performed this ballet for many seasons and there was not a sign of Cecil Beaton's beautiful costumes for it in the wardrobe; no one appeared to know where they had got to. It was suggested that the costumes from *La Valse* would do instead, but I thought otherwise and decided to enlist the help of the redoubtable wardrobe mistress, Joyce Wells. Her fury knew no bounds when I told her of the disappearance; she always guarded the company's wardrobe zealously, especially anything worn by Margot, whom she greatly admired, and in no time at all she had initiated a search worthy of MI5. Having interrogated everyone in the entire organisation, she finally tracked down the *Apparitions* costumes packed up in a theatrical basket and deposited in a warehouse in Drury Lane. So we won the day.

The gala was a great success and a suitable tribute to Ashton's fame and position as Director; it was a well-planned programme, not too long, and ran smoothly, very much to Jack Hart's credit. After the show we all attended a party at the Café Royal and Princess Margaret was there to add to the farewells. As Fred would have wished, it was fun, going on into the early hours. As I walked from the restaurant to search for a taxi home, I suddenly had mixed feelings: of relief at the success of the performance, of pleasure at the glow of affection so deeply manifested at the party, but of dissatisfaction that Fred's régime had been relatively short and had not extended to at least ten years.

However, Kenneth MacMillan was a family member of the company and I had known him since he first joined it. We had become close friends and I felt that in his case I could adopt a more avuncular tone than would have been appropriate in previous régimes. We shared a sense of humour, something that I always put in the forefront of any association; we would delight in many in-jokes and there were times of pure fun, especially during our first American tours. I remember our tentative swims in the surfers' ocean at Santa Monica, where I took a snap of him draped from head to toe in huge lengths of seaweed, and the larks we had when we appeared in Alfred Rodrigues's cabaret for our Christmas party in Chicago. But I had also noticed his extreme sensitivity, quick to take hurt at the slightest rebuff. In those days there was no shortage of sharp edges to be encountered and endured in the company, and I knew when a downcast look was a signal to me to find a quiet corner where Ken could unburden himself. But the fun side predominates in my memory, and I had no doubts about his rightful claim of accession as our new Director.

Just before he took over officially, there was a request for Margot and Rudolf to repeat their *Marguerite and Armand* in a mixed bill at La Scala, Milan. There was also the usual fuss as to who would produce it; once again Michael Somes had declined, and it fell as before on my shoulders to undertake the task, which, with the blessing of the administration, I did. So off I went to Italy on 3 September 1970, that date bringing back many memories of the start of World War II and our returning from Liverpool to London wondering what our fate would be, the company supposedly disbanded for the duration. Now here I was in Milan, about to work with these two great artists, so far beyond my wildest dreams of that day in 1939.

When I arrived at my hotel I found a message asking me to meet Margot and Rudolf at a nearby restaurant for lunch. I had an unexpected shock when I saw Rudolf entering the restaurant wearing an Italian version of an Anthony Eden black homburg hat and a long black formal overcoat, which he discarded to reveal a beautifully tailored black suit, complete with white shirt and dark tie. He had been through the Carnaby Street period with its style that he took to extremes, so this was indeed a sea change into something certainly rich and from the smart shops in the centre of Milan. In 1947 I had been with Margot during her 'New Look' period and now I was seeing Rudolf through his. He looked great, but his Anthony Eden style was short-lived and did not outlast his return from Milan.

After our performances of *Marguerite and Armand* I returned to London and to the excitements of the new régime. I was in time for a meeting called by Kenneth MacMillan and held in the Covent Garden rehearsal room; it was one that no member of the company would have missed at any cost. Kenneth outlined his intended policies and future plans for us. I was naturally pleased when he mentioned me in connection with the Choreographic Group, saying that he would see to it that it continued and that it would receive his close interest.

In general, however, in spite of the election promises made by the administration during the two years prior to Kenneth's accession, things did not seem to be turning out as we had hoped. Our faith in the future had then been fostered by the understanding that John Field was a candidate for the assistant directorship and was offered to us as someone to remove many of the obstacles that had impeded the natural progress of our evolution as a company. For these two years, during which he was successfully steering the Second Company, he had been represented to us at Covent Garden as a potential guardian angel. In the event, when MacMillan took over, John Field was missing from the Cabinet, an instant victim of the new régime, and the election promises were dismissed. Indeed it seemed, in the words of the new Director's namesake, the then Prime Minister Harold Macmillan, that the winds of change were blowing over us.

We were mystified, particularly since John had always been a favourite with the Board under Sir David Webster, who had appreciated his success with the Second Company (a title now firmly banished) and the large public he had attracted on their account. During the times when we in the resident Covent Garden company were on the long coast-to-coast tours in the States every two years, Field's company always had great success when they replaced us at the Opera House for a season. Ninette de Valois praised their work highly, so much so that, on our return from the

States, we of the senior company had felt somewhat overshadowed by John Field's younger team back home. John Hart and Michael Somes, two of the original triumvirate, were in fact more than disgruntled.

The turn that events took demonstrated that, alas, Field himself was never popular with the upper echelon of the original First Company at the Opera House. To most of us these U-turns were totally inexplicable. Confused? Well, who wouldn't be?

On a personal note, John Field had told me during the interregnum that he wished me to become Ballet Master to the Opera Company, a position previously held by Harold Turner. Fortunately, this did come about in spite of the shake-up, and gave me a third string to my bow in addition to my being a principal in the main company and Director of the Choreographic Group. Shortly after, we heard that Field was to be replaced by Peter Wright, who was leaving Stuttgart. I was delighted with this move, as I had so enjoyed working with him on his production with Ashton of *The Sleeping Beauty*. I also enjoyed joining in with his classical classes, even though on stage I was confining my dancing to character roles.

The last year of Fred's régime had provided much emotion, with his ballets featured in most of the programmes at the Opera House, and the company and audience behaving as though it was the last time we would ever see them. With all this adoration and acclaim, it must have been very difficult for MacMillan waiting in the wings. At every performance of an Ashton work, the audience came to expect the culmination of the final calls, and one could be forgiven for saying that on these occasions there was a section of those present who had come to see Fred's performance in the calls as much as his ballets. As the weeks went by, the finales gathered fresh momentum and choreographic ingenuity among the laurel leaves and floral tributes that were showered upon him. There were times when he seemed to out-Pavlova Pavlova!

Chapter 20

I started my new job as ballet master to the Royal Opera company by making my way down the Commercial Road for the rehearsal of *Cavalleria Rusticana* and *Pagliacci* in the rooms used by the Opera in an old cinema, the Troxy. I enjoyed renewing my work with singers, recalling my days at Sadler's Wells Theatre before the war. Already in office was a truly excellent ballet mistress, Romayne Grigorova, who had danced with the Royal Ballet and in many musicals; she had a very thorough knowledge of all the opera ballets and of practically every movement of the whole cast in each production. She welcomed me with great kindness as her opposite number, and once more the Opera Company had a ballet mistress and master, as was traditional.

The Troxy belonged to that age of huge cinemas in the thirties when an audience would queue for hours to see their favourite screen idols. 'Queuing in all parts' was often the cry of the commissionaire as one approached. Alas, hard times came to parts of the bomb-damaged East End after the war, and the Troxy stood sad and empty until it was spotted by a distinguished conductor on his way to Tilbury Docks to embark on an engagement abroad. He later told David Webster about it, who snapped it up as somewhere for the Opera to rehearse. It became not only a rehearsal room but the location for the Opera School. The auditorium with the seats removed provided a spacious area for rehearsal, and the producers with their assistants and the theatrical and musical staff sat in a line under the proscenium arch of the stage where the screen had once been.

The well-known twinning of '*Cav*' and '*Pag*' that I began working with was a wonderful production by Franco Zeffirelli. Although there was no ballet in this, he used two young male students from the Royal Ballet School who worked throughout with the principal singers. Then Equity insisted on our using only union members so the students had to go. Thank goodness the Royal Ballet let us have two boys who were actually in the company and therefore Equity members; but this ruling forbidding students from the School was a great shame. Many a principal will tell you that, when they appeared in the Opera during their time as students, they learnt a great deal from this first experience of dancing on the Opera House stage, storing up important knowledge of stagecraft and working with the opera stars and producers. Many of the girls are still grateful to Romayne Grigorova for helping them with their make-up and hairstyles, and I personally have always thought that potential choreographers would gain a great deal by working in these opera productions. The early days at the Opera House with Sir Thomas Beecham were notable for the fact that Ninette de Valois was often the ballerina, while at the same time Ashton and Chappell and other future pillars of the British ballet were in the ensemble. It was a rich nurturing ground and an important source of supplementary income for the dancers – five shillings a performance, to be precise.

The first brand new production I worked with was *Eugene Onegin*, produced by Peter Hall. I had a great but pleasurable culture shock when, addressing us at the first company rehearsal, he said, 'I don't want to hear anyone call me "Mister Hall". I'm Peter'. I realised then that I was in the world of the big theatre, and for this reason I loved working with him. It was not my first time around with this wonderful opera and I was delighted that Geoffrey Cauley was engaged to be the choreographer – one up for the Choreographic Group. He too was marvellous to work with; his contribution to *Onegin* was excellent and met very much with Peter's approval. A joy for me was Ileana Cotrubas, the prima donna; she expressed great admiration for dancers and told me she longed to see Fonteyn perform – a wish we were able to grant, after which their admiration and friendship became mutual. Cotrubas and Yvonne Minton were perfect as Tatyana and Olga; even so, I was still loyal to my youthful memories of Joan Cross and Edith Coates in our very simple production all those years ago in the thirties at the Wells. Gazing at the rich costumes and décor by Julia Trevelyan Oman at the Opera House only made me admire Miss Baylis even more for having frequently staged an opera of this magnitude with such meagre resources. I could never forget polonaising round the stage with my jangling orders and medals, worn to augment my simple costume.

Later I enjoyed working on John Copley's production of *Faust*, although I would have liked him to have ended the opera with its famous music danced by the Royal Ballet, to parallel the performance that Michael Somes and I had seen in Paris in 1937 when they used the resident company directed by Serge Lifar. Whenever I see the waltz in Act I, it brings back memories of the time when I danced it at the Old Vic, where it had provided the occasion for one of Miss Baylis' legendary stories, touched on earlier, about her concern for the state of the fiddles after a member of the cast had landed in the orchestra pit.

During a rehearsal of John Copley's *La Bohème*, I spoke to Ninette de Valois who was watching it from the stalls. 'Who is the choreographer of this opera?' she demanded to know. I replied that there wasn't one, but I realised that she must have been referring to the witty jig danced by the leading male singer and his friend, which John himself had arranged. I explained this to her and added that he had started life as a dancer and trained at the Ballet School. She immediately attacked me (verbally) and said 'I told you that there was a choreographer!' When I related this to John, he was delighted to hear that Ninette de Valois regarded him as one of the choreographers to emerge from her school.

I felt great pleasure and pride in the fact that the Choreographic Group had supplied the choreography for various operas. One example was Michael Corder for *Khovanshchina*, in which he featured two young dancers who had recently joined the company – Sharon (later to be known as Elizabeth) McGorian and Linda Moran. They covered themselves in glory, winning the approval of the guest star from the Bolshoi, Evgeny Nesterenko, who thought they were in fact two leading dancers from the Royal Ballet. He was further most impressed by Michael Corder's choreography. Derek Deane, Ashley Page and Wayne Eagling also contributed to the list of those from the Group working within this operatic context. When she heard that the young David Bintley was choreographing the final scene, the Bacchanale, in *Samson and Delilah*, Ninette de Valois made a point of coming to a stage-call and told him that *Samson* was the first opera ballet she ever danced in. Once again one was aware of the great interest she had in all of these activities, an attitude that sadly is not always shared by other senior members of the ballet administration.

A particular favourite of mine was Handel's *Semele* and especially the great aria 'Where'er you walk', and I remember a rehearsal that included it, the singers being Robert Tear and the Australian soprano, Yvonne Kenny. The producer was John Copley, and Eleanor Fazan was responsible for the choreography. While Romayne and I were watching from the stalls we heard that the whole opera might be cancelled because of a strike by the Musicians' Union; alas, this rumour was very soon confirmed, much to our regret.

John Schlesinger knew what he was about when he cast Deanne Bergsma as Stella in *Les Contes d'Hoffmann*. This wonderful dancer, so favoured by Ashton, only had to walk down the staircase at the end of the opera saying 'Hoffmann' twice and then, in a sumptuous costume by Maria Björnson, glide off the stage and reappear at the curtain calls to make such an impression that one heard people praising her as they left the theatre. The movement of this production was arranged by Eleanor Fazan, highly regarded by distinguished directors and especially by John Schlesinger. I had admired her long before we met, because of the pleasure of seeing the witty revue she directed called *Share My Lettuce*, starring Maggie Smith and Kenneth Williams, and written by Bamber Gascoigne.

I grew very fond of the opera chorus, and made some close friends among them who were always willing to be in my Christmas cabaret for the Friends of Covent Garden. They were good sports and fell in with some of the harebrained schemes I thought up; special among them was Gwynneth Price, who even put on point shoes to perform ably in a number called 'Nobody loves a fairy when she's forty', with four members of the Royal Ballet *corps de ballet*.

Romayne and I were given seats for the first nights of the operas on which we had worked with the dancers. However, we always attended on subsequent nights to check that the quality and correctness of their performance was maintained. Often the ballet would be on towards the end of the opera concerned, in which case I loved to go in front and sit down quietly on one of the commodious sofas in the corners of the grand tier behind the partitions of the boxes and listen, out of sight of the audience, to the orchestra and singers. Looking up at the staircase leading to the next tier and at the pattern of the distinctive red-striped walls, I would think how lucky I was to work in this wonderful House. Stella Chitty, the stage director of the Opera Company, sometimes came up from backstage to check the lighting and staging from the back of the tier, and on her way would give me a smile of acknowledgement. She always looked elegant even when rehearsing and supervising every stage call of the Opera company – not always an easy matter given the large numbers involved – and at the final dress rehearsal she would step forward through the rich folds of that great red curtain, look at the conductor over the footlights and announce, 'Ready, Maestro'. She was always very kind to the guest dancers from the Ballet Company, reassuring them if she felt that they were at all nervous.

On most nights I shared my sofa with a couple of St John's Ambulance nurses, always comfortingly armed with their small attaché cases containing medical first-aid to cope with any emergency during the performances – fainting, missing the last step coming down from the Crush Bar, or perhaps being overcome by the lengthy rigours of *The Ring*. Old friends among the programme girls would slip past to powder their noses whilst the performance was in progress, and we would have a cheery whisper. My old friend the Fireman would give a nod during his rounds of inspection, while the familiar faces of the waiters and waitresses passed with drinks on trays which they placed near the doors of the boxes, ready to serve during the interval. I loved the warmth of the togetherness of this beloved theatre; I hope that this atmosphere may return to the new and enlarged building of the Opera House.

Finally, Romayne would join me to watch our dancers from the back of the tier. I grew very fond of them; they remained good-natured throughout all their trials. They often were asked to work on impossible surfaces: dancing on sloping rakes designed by people unaware of the strain that they inflicted on a dancer's calves, or moving in and out of black velvet drapes over glass to give the effect of pools. They might warm up on chilly days for the sometimes lengthy ballets, and then, as they gathered in the wings to perform, hear an order from an imperious maestro to delay their entry because he wished to repeat a chorus ensemble. Worse still, they might spend the entire day waiting about only to be given the announcement that the ballet would be cut on that occasion to make way for a reprise from the chorus.

It was a great experience for me to work with Sam Wanamaker, who was directing the opera *The Ice Break* by Sir Michael Tippett. Sam was friendly and thoughtful – qualities needed when dealing with a complex theme and musical score reflecting racial conflict between white and black. I was alone in charge of these rehearsals at the Troxy because Romayne had to be at the Opera House to supervise changes to the choreography of the production of *Aida*, the result of the Italian conductor's whim in wanting to import the version used at La Scala, Milan, replacing the superb choreography of Peter Wright. For *Ice Break* we had an extremely clever and pleasant choreographer, Walter Raines, himself black, as were half the cast. He had previously worked with John Cranko's company in Stuttgart.

After I had finished taking class one day, one of these dancers broke the news to me that Kenneth MacMillan had decided to retire as Director of the Royal Ballet and that he was to be replaced by Norman Morrice, former diretor of Ballet Rambert. I was staggered to hear the news and in that way before a formal announcement had been made. I did not discover until later that my informant had been told by a well-known critic, also well in the know, who leaked the news. When I had more time to think about it, it seemed strange that Fred had reigned for seven years and so, to date, had Kenneth. It was almost biblical in its numeration.

I was to meet Sam Wanamaker some years later when Wendy Toye and I were on a committee to organise a gala at the Albert Hall to help raise funds for the new Globe Theatre. He attended most of the meetings, full of enthusiasm about the project, always in good heart, having in between times travelled far and wide to raise funds for the whole enterprise and, as we learned later, in spite of increasing pain from his fatal illness. One remembers him with the deepest admiration and affection. It is now thanks to his vision and dedication that the Globe Theatre has returned to the South Bank.

Chapter 21

Robert Helpmann was always busy with one thing or another, mostly choreographing for the Australian Ballet and producing plays. He also had a great success in Australian films, receiving nationwide praise for his performances in *The Mango Tree* and *Patrick*. Although his connections with the Royal Ballet became fewer, he did appear occasionally as Dr Coppelius or as the Red King in *Checkmate*. When he came over here, as he did frequently, he never failed to phone me, and we would meet in his flat and catch up on whatever was new in the theatre world, laughingly recalling the fun and high jinks we had enjoyed during our long association. At the beginning of our 1977–8 season, he asked me round to Eaton Square and told me about a tour of various towns in Australia that he was planning to direct, to be called *Stars of World Ballet* and to comprise leading dancers of international repute. It sounded exciting, and for the next few months when he was in London I would discuss ideas with him. Suddenly, I found that I was having my say as to how the production should go. This was a subtle change; I was giving answers to his questions and he, in turn, was anxious to hear my views.

One day he asked me to join him as his assistant on this Australian tour, provided he could get permission from the Royal Ballet for me to miss whatever performances coincided with its duration. I was delighted at the invitation; I had never been to Australia and welcomed the opportunity and all that it entailed. Bobby, being who he was, managed to fix matters and all was well. The company would be touring the United States during July 1978 when my trip down under began; I was to remain with them in America until we had completed our time in Chicago and then leave from there for Australia.

When I arrived in Sydney, Bobby met me at the airport, where we then waited to greet Merle Park and David Wall, who were coming from London, as they too had not been on that leg of the American tour. By this time Bobby had assembled an all-star cast: Margot Fonteyn, David Wall and Merle Park from the Royal Ballet, Peter Breuer from the Düsseldorf Opera Ballet, Ann Marie De Angelo from Robert Joffrey's Ballet company, Maina Gielgud, Cynthia Gregory, John Meehan, Ivan Nagy, Fernando Bujones and Danilo Radojevic from American Ballet Theatre, Birgit Keil and Vladimir Klos from

Stuttgart, Marina Kondratieva and Maris Liepa from the Bolshoi, and Yoko Morishita and Tetsutaro Shimizu from the Matsuyama Ballet Company in Tokyo. It was a cast and a half! Years later an Australian dancer who was in the Opera Ballet at Covent Garden told me that *Stars of World Ballet* was a legend in Australia, a fitting tribute to its originator.

Ashton had given Bobby permission to use the opening and closing sequences of *Birthday Offering* to be danced by the entire cast, which gave a coherence to the whole performance, avoiding the impression that it was a series of divertissements. In the finale everyone wore the costume that he or she had appeared in for the individual dances; this both gave a special touch to the whole and contrasted with the uniform blue and white ones designed by Desmond Healey, the well-known Australian, in the opening. Margot did not appear in this ensemble but entered from the back of the stage, bursting through the dancers to take her position in the centre to perform the famous solo from *Raymonda*. It was always greatly acclaimed, and I felt it set the seal on the success of each performance. It was a real *coup de théâtre* on Bobby's part. Between the divertissements that comprised Acts I and III, as it were, there was a complete ballet with its own set and costumes, called *The Lesson*, choreographed by a well-known Danish dancer, Flemming Flindt. He himself took the rôle of a teacher and was partnered by Vivi Flindt; it was one of our number from the Royal Ballet who played the young girl coming for her lesson in ballet.

I was left alone in the galaxy during part of the tour when Bobby was busy producing a play in Sydney. I managed to keep the stars in orbit with much help from the wonderful production team led by Carole McPhee. We danced at the Princes Theatre in Sydney, but our rehearsals had to take place at the Opera House, where the room allocated turned out to be far too small for our needs. Dame Joan Sutherland, who was rehearsing alone in a very large room, heard about our accommodation problem and very sportingly came to our aid by swapping her room for ours. No wonder she is so well liked!

Sydney was followed by Melbourne or, to be precise, the nearby St Kilda, where they had an art-deco theatre called the Palais. It was freezing cold with no central heating in the theatre, the spartan conditions possibly a legacy from the early days of Empire, but apart from this we all liked Melbourne. When we had returned to our hotel after a performance, we would later go to the park opposite and watch the ubiquitous possums.

After Melbourne came Brisbane, followed by Adelaide, not far from

Mount Gambier where Bobby was born. There was not enough time for a visit to his home, but he told me all about his youthful trips to the city for lessons with the local dancing teachers. I found Adelaide to have a great deal of charm; the wrought-iron tracery on the balconies of buildings and houses was reminiscent of New Orleans. There were many individual aspects that were pleasing to the eye as I went about the business of finding suitable rooms, both for classes and rehearsals, the dancers liking to practise as much as possible and particularly at the slightest sign of trouble with any step. Yoko and Tetsutaro were both relentless in this regard and would wait anxiously until I found them a rehearsal room. Nevertheless, I grew very fond of them both.

To relieve the tedious repetition of dancing the same rôle night after night for the six weeks of the tour, operation 'all change' was put into effect, giving rise to some interesting variations of partnering; we all enjoyed seeing Margot with Liepa in a very turgid Russian *pas de deux*, and this element of change provided a useful extra stimulus all round. Unfortunately, there was one unlooked-for alteration; David Wall was plagued by an old injury and had to leave us and return to England. We naturally missed him very much, but his place was taken by a worthy successor, Wayne Eagling, who soon became very popular with the company and someone with whom I enjoyed working.

A well-known Australian, Michael Edgley, presented the tour in company with Bobby. The Edgley family were great figures in the Australian theatre and art world; Michael's mother and father had been dancers and when I eventually met his mother, Edna, during the Royal Ballet's later tour of Australia, she told me about her dancing with her husband in England in 1939. She mentioned that they were appearing at the Empire Theatre, Liverpool, the week before war was declared. The Vic–Wells Ballet had been in the same city at the Royal Court Theatre, so we and the Edgleys were in close proximity at the outbreak of war. (We returned to London, and the Edgleys, as far as I know, went straight back to Australia.) As we talked together in Brisbane, it seemed remarkable that thirty-nine years later their son had brought us together in the very successful *Stars of World Ballet*. In the same vein, working alongside Carole McPhee was also to renew a friendship, for when she came from her native Australia to work in London, she would stay with Mrs Hookham, Margot's mother, in her house by Bray Lock next to my small cottage. Extremely efficient, she proved a tower of strength on the tour.

The musical director was Ray Cook. Born in Adelaide, he came to London in 1960, and from then on there was hardly a musical he did not conduct. One of the best known was the National Theatre's first production of *Guys and Dolls* starring Julia Mackenzie, a great friend with whom he worked many times. He also had a very close professional association with Stephen Sondheim, but his début with regard to ballet was with *Stars of World Ballet*. What a plunge into the deep end, having to deal with a group of international dancers, the various tempi and the wide range of scores from classical composers! He succeeded magnificently and was a most charming and modest man besides.

William Akers was production director and also lit the set in a masterly fashion. He, too, was a man of the theatre and a true professional, like the rest of the production unit.

We ended the tour in Perth, the beautiful city by the sea in the westernmost part of this continent. I had to leave from there before the last performances to re-join the Royal Ballet for a season in Greece. The Australian company gave me an affectionate farewell at the airport. Margot presented me with a gift from them all. There was champagne – and then, for me, a lengthy wait for the plane to Greece. But, thanks to the kind arrangement made by an important gentleman who had come to greet Margot at the airport when we arrived, I was able to use the VIP lounge, the comfort of which somewhat allayed my feelings of sadness at leaving those friendly faces. Working with them all had been wonderful; it was only a matter of days before they completed the tour, so I had had the lion's share and had enjoyed it greatly.

My visit to Greece reminded me of an earlier visit when we performed at the open air theatre of the Herodes Atticus. We could not rehearse at the open-air theatre during the day, as the heat was too intense, so our first stage-call was held in the evening of the following day. We opened with *Romeo and Juliet*, which for me was the one ballet that looked appropriate in the expanse of the theatre with its background of massive rocks. The Greek extras, actors and actresses whom we used, with their expressive gestures and faces, gave an extra classic dimension to the production. Their long experience of working in this timeless theatre with the starlit sky above the tiers of the amphitheatre helped to put the ballet into this new perspective.

The fact that the heat of the day made rehearsals impossible was to our advantage, since we were able to take trips outside Athens and to the nearby coast. In addition, I was delighted to be invited one evening to a supper party given by King Constantine and his young Queen. As we arrived, we walked past the guards wearing their distinctive pale beige summer uniforms and into the grounds, to see the immaculate table settings in the garden nearest the palace. Though I was sorry not to be able to see the inside of the palace, the whole scene before us made up for it. We were told that a member of the royal family would head each table; at mine was Princess Irene, the King's sister, whose English was perfect – in fact, so much so that a young man in the company, well-known for his *naïveté*, mistook her for one of the ladies from the British Embassy and turned to her saying, 'How do you like the Greeks?' Without a flicker of surprise the Princess replied, 'Oh, I've grown to like them very much'. The King and Queen had Margot and Rudolf at their table and Robert Kennedy, who had turned up once or twice on our continental tours and on those in the States. He was always very friendly and jokey, and Rudolf, with his simple Russian background, was much taken by the fact that there was this close interest shown towards the ballet company by the brother of the President of the United States. When later we read of Robert Kennedy's assassination at the Ambassadors Hotel, which we had liked so much on our first visit to Los Angeles, I thought with sadness of that splendid night in Athens and of his presence among us all.

I left Greece with regret and a great regard for the country. When I returned some years later, the political situation had changed; the King and Queen had left the country and settled in London. However, I did have the pleasure of meeting the King once again when he was a dinner guest of Margot and Tito in their flat in Thurloe Place, and this was a happy occasion on which to recall that famous evening.

In 1977 there was a fresh development in the *Marguerite and Armand* saga. Margot's arrival in London from Panama was followed by a telephone call to me, as happened when Bobby arrived from Australia. After the usual enquiries as to what I had been doing, Margot led up to what I knew was going to herald another *Marguerite and Armand* sortie. This time she wanted me to help her plan a gala in Manila for President Marcos' birthday, to meet a request from Madame Marcos. This would be a 'money no object' exercise, for which Nureyev had agreed to take part in the supporting divertissement in addition to appearing as Armand.

I felt that for such an event we should use the full stage sets designed by Cecil Beaton, to be borrowed from the Opera House, instead of the velvet drapes which I had improvised before. But the problem here was the enormous weight of the metal scaffold poles used to represent a circular cage imprisoning Marguerite. It all looked light and easy to move, but in reality made very heavy work for the stage hands when they had to set it up and then later remove it. Knowing of the prevalence of bamboo in the Philippines, I thought that I could possibly use this material, painted to look like the metal of the original structure. I took photographs of the latter with me, and in the event found that the bamboo was very pliable; it was possible to use it to simulate the curves of the cage and create a dome-like effect. By mixing various paints – green and black with touches of gilt for the highlights – we achieved the appearance of iron, after applying layer upon layer of paint to the bamboo. This, of course, was all done with the help and expertise of the staff of the Cultural Centre, the large theatre in Manila in which we were appearing.

The flight to the Philippines was a long one, but I was fortunate in being able to travel in first-class comfort, thanks largely to the fact that Margot had entrusted the President's birthday present to me, a large framed antique print of Manila. The crew of the plane asked me to give it to them to store in the luggage hold, which did not please me at all. When I disclosed that it was a present to the President from Dame Margot, I was allowed to keep it with me in the cabin, where I was given a seat in the front row with a place in front of me to rest the package.

The President's wife, always referred to as the First Lady, had the equivalent of ladies-in-waiting who were called the Blue Ladies, and one of them was always put in charge of each guest on official visits. When I arrived at the airport, there was my Blue Lady with a large, heavily scented and exotic lei, which was placed round my neck. I was told that, dispensing with the hotel that had previously been booked for me, the First Lady had decreed that I should stay along with Margot and Tito at the presidential guest house. I had a marvellous suite on the first floor, while Margot's and Tito's rooms were below at ground level to facilitate access for Tito's wheelchair (he had been the victim of an assassination attempt in 1964 and was subsequently confined to a wheelchair). It was a beautiful building and luxuriously furnished.

Margot told me later that we had been invited to a buffet lunch the following day, a Sunday. In the meantime I had met Dr Lucrecia Kasilag, the head of the Cultural Centre where we were to perform. She had arranged a meeting for me with the stage staff on that Sunday afternoon at 2.30, in order that they could look at the photographs of the *Marguerite and Armand* set and discuss the question of the bamboo and how we should go about creating a new version of the metal original.

Margot, Tito and I left for our luncheon date, which was an early affair, allowing me plenty of time to get to my rehearsal – or so I thought. When we arrived, we were told that the First Lady was expected at the luncheon; when she appeared, Margot introduced me and Madame Marcos gave me a few words of welcome, spoken in beautiful English. Then the announcement was made to the guests that the First Lady was going to prepare a special soufflé for us. If Escoffier had come back from the grave, there could not have been such incredulous joy. Nectar was forecast for us all, but when I looked at my watch I realised that, with all the ceremonial preamble, time had passed and I would very soon have to leave or I would be late for my rehearsal. So I told Margot, who then looked thoroughly perturbed, saying, 'But you can't leave now; everyone will be appalled at the slight to the First Lady'. 'But it's not a slight,' I said. 'If she wants a gala for the President, it's essential that I attend this rehearsal on time, so I'm afraid I shall have to ask her to excuse me.' This I did with all the English diplomacy I could muster. Anyway, she took it very graciously and gave a command for a car to take me to the Cultural Centre.

When I arrived there, all the crew had gathered and were delighted that I was on time. I knew right away that they were a good bunch, and our friendly association started from that moment. Naturally, I was dressed for the reception, and there was an immediate shaking of heads when I started mixing the paints. The leader of the crew took me aside and asked me to remove my jacket. His mates then brought some polythene and fashioned a suit of overalls for me, fastening the material together with staples. I must have looked pretty odd, but we all had a good laugh at my appearance and then proceeded to do a fine day's work in preparation for the gala. Although I was soufflé-less, the pot of coffee brewed up in the prop room and a very substantial local bun were nectar enough.

Madame Marcos liked to surround herself with important figures in the arts, especially performers, hence her great liking for Margot. The American pianist, Van Cliburn, was another artist she admired; he had played in many of her galas in aid of various causes, and was staying in Manila during the time we were there. I realised early on that the First Lady also liked to include her visitors in official ceremonies; one such particularly significant occasion was held to announce the President's repeal of the curfew law, which up to that point had limited the freedom of movement late at night. The President was in the chair and Tito, Margot and I were given centre-court seats. Margot insisted that I wore the *baronne*, a coat-like shirt, a fashion adopted by the President himself and by most of the male members of his entourage. I had acquired a simple cotton version that I preferred to the more elaborate ones, and was pleased to sit in front of the President in my best *baronne*. This later prompted a comment from him, and he went on to mention the fact that the first cotton material came to Manila from England. I felt justly proud.

His wife saw to it that we were lavishly entertained, and she took us herself to sumptuous restaurants and even nightclubs, where she would join in the fun to the point of performing with me one of her favourite songs. Apart from all this though, we had to get down to the serious business of rehearsals, which meant that there was a great deal for Margot to do. Fortunately, she had brought Buenaventura Modina, Tito's faithful Panamanian valet, who was such a help in looking after him while Margot was at the theatre. There were occasions, though, when she would have to leave a rehearsal in answer to a call from Tito, who wanted her to help him through an important meeting with a business associate. Since his paralysis, his voice was so soft that at times only Margot could understand what he was saying, and at such a juncture she could clarify matters about the business in hand. This entailed her having to change out of her practise clothes and rush away, rejoining us as soon as was possible. Her priorities never faltered.

The gala proved a great success. The bamboo set won the day; nobody realised that it was not metal, and the stagehands could move it off in a trice. Afterwards, the First Lady gave a large party, which we enjoyed enormously. Staying on a day or two more in Manila, we all relaxed and were taken on a visit to the house where the First Lady was born, before we dispersed to various points of the compass.

Interestingly, Rudolf had not been impressed by the lifestyle of Madame Marcos and her world. On his way to Manila he had stopped off for a few days in Thailand, where he was fascinated by the river life of the boat people. They seemed, he thought, to make a world of their own in spite of their poverty, and the complete quality of their life owed nothing to worldly possessions. It was ironic that he should feel this at a time when he himself had success, riches and general acclaim. Maybe the plight of the boat people put him off the Versailles-like atmosphere of the Marcos' palace, the immediate contrast being too stark for comfort.

We heard that the First Lady videoed every performance given at the Cultural Centre, no matter who appeared in them, and when the President invited Margot, Tito, Van Cliburn and me to dinner with him and his wife in their private apartments, we were shown the recording she had made of *Marguerite and Armand*. I have often wondered what happened to all those tapes after the mob broke in at the fall of the Marcos régime. Perhaps they suffered the same fate as the quantities of shoes and other personal effects that accompanied her eminence. I have wondered, too, what became of the large dark-wooden chests that were presented to us at the end of our stay, with 'Ferdinand Marcos' inscribed on the lids and a promise that they would be delivered to our homes. I never saw mine again, which was a disappointment as I had pictured it looking rather handsome as a coffee table in my cottage, as well as providing a good conversation piece when the moment was appropriate.

I went back to Manila in 1980 to organise yet another gala, this time to honour the First Lady, and financed by Pepsi-Cola. Margot and I worked together on lists of artists whom we wished to perform in it, aiming at the tops. When later I received details of the proposed arrangements for the event, I was not entirely happy about them and told the Pepsi-Cola office in London about my doubts. As a result of this they sent me to their head office in New York for a week to straighten things out. Once there, I had to wait until the end of my stay before the powers-that-be in Pepsi found time to see me. They were very reassuring and civil, yet I still remained uneasy; by then it was too late for me to make any radical change in the plans, even if they had allowed me to do so.

However, my week in New York was otherwise very enjoyable. I managed to contact Mikhail Baryshnikov, as Margot had hoped he would be able to perform in the gala. He had recently become Director of American Ballet Theatre, which was then starting its autumn season. I accepted their invitation to join the whole company on a picnic in the country in upstate New York, and to my great delight my old friend Nora Kaye was among the guests. We had a wonderful day, talking of old times and of the plans for the gala in Manila, promising, too, to see more of each other in the future. Sadly, it was not to be, for Nora died not long afterwards.

When I returned to London I did my best to reassure Margot and even myself about how things stood, but the answers I received to the subsequent questions I put about the promotion did nothing to allay my doubts. I then realised that the real trouble was in Manila, and I took a week's leave from the Royal Ballet to fly there. When I arrived, my worst fears were confirmed; the blow came immediately when I went to the Pepsi-Cola office to be told that the gala was in no way connected with that branch. They then telephoned New York, who also denied having any knowledge of it.

Margot was by then in Panama and was naturally distressed when I told her this. She said she would ask Roger Meyers, an Australian friend, who had gone into the management side of ballet, to join me in Manila and give a second opinion. I was relieved and pleased, for not only did I like Roger, but he had performed some of the same rôles as I when he had danced in Australia. It was good to have his support, and once he had arrived it did not take long for him to share my forebodings; we were getting bad vibes from all sides and were conscious of an undercurrent of unrest, a foretaste of the political upheaval that was imminent. The gala was a non-starter, but Roger and I managed to settle the business as satisfactorily as was possible given the circumstances. Margot sent me a cable from Panama saying that all the dancers who would have been involved were very understanding when they learnt about the cancellation. Roger left for Australia and I left for London. That was the last adventure of my *Marguerite and Armand* period.

Chapter 22

In addition to going on foreign jaunts with *Marguerite and Armand*, joining Helpmann's stars in Australia and teaching in Canada, touring with the Royal Ballet continued for me almost as a routine. Our regular trips to the States were always a joy, enabling me to see old and much-loved friends such as Theodora Christon, Dorothy Hammerstein, Tug and John and their coterie. These were all in New York, where in between rehearsals there would be visits to Sis Kanowitz's bar and restaurant on 39th Street for a meal and a long chat afterwards. By now we were dancing up-town at the Lincoln Center in the new Metropolitan Opera House, often at the same time as the New York City Ballet who performed at the adjacent State Theater. This meant that I was able to see a lot of my old friend, Robert Irving, who had left the Royal Opera House to become the conductor for George Balanchine's New York City Ballet. We met in the theatre, or in his nearby apartment, or in the friendly hubbub of O'Neil's Balloon restaurant opposite the Lincoln Center. On our free Mondays I kept up with the new musicals, adding *My Fair Lady*, *Mame* and *Damn Yankees* to a splendid list that had begun with Cole Porter's *Kiss Me Kate*.

Ronnie and Harriet Bodley became my close friends through the years, and each time we visited Boston they gave a large party at Chailey Manor in Newburyport, arranging for buses to bring the whole company out to their home. They would also spend part of their year in England, where Ronnie had family connections; his sister Ava had married Lord Waverley, formerly Sir John Anderson. Famous for his wartime air-raid shelters (known to everyone as Anderson shelters), he was Chairman of the Board of Governors of the Royal Ballet, and the company named one of their new rehearsal studios at the school at Baron's Court 'The Waverley Studio'.

By this time in the seventies, our US tours were starting in the spring; so when we reached Chicago, Santa's bells were not clanging outside Marshall Field's Department Store but we were taking our swimming trunks down to the lakeshore. It was in this city that our old colleagues Richard and Christine Ellis had settled down, having left us to do so after the second coast-to-coast American tour. They had established a flourishing dancing school, where the company was invited to take advantage of the classrooms for rehearsals during our stay.

In 1975, however, our touring reached out to the Eastern Hemisphere when we visited South Korea and Japan. On our first trip to Seoul, which we found very staid and rather uneventful socially, there was not even a theatre for us to perform in. We would board a bus outside our hotel and drive along leafy roads to the university high above the city to dance in the College Theatre – not ideal, but in those days any theatre was better than none and we were glad to have this one, where we played to a packed and enthusiastic house. All the theatre staff proved delightful to work with, and we met with equally friendly personnel at the hotel, though this was far from being a four-star one. The men in the company took advantage of the local tailors, who had their abodes alongside the small restaurants in the winding back streets, to have their shirts copied and made up from the range of fine materials available.

We were generously entertained by Doctor Kim Sang Man at his beautiful and historic ancestral home, very Korean in style and mounted on stilts, and we were given lunch in its surrounding gardens. I was of an age to remember the pre-war newsreels full of the events during the Japanese invasion of Korea but in 1975 the aggression was between South Korea and the Communist North. We were taken on a sightseeing tour, going close to the frontier that separated the two rival sections of the country. Near this part of the border there was a funfair where the traditional Aunt Sally, to be knocked down by balls thrown at it, took the form of a grimly painted wooden effigy representing a North Korean.

On subsequent visits to Seoul, we danced at a splendid new theatre in which we were able to present Kenneth MacMillan's full-length *Manon*. I remember Margot's joining us on one such visit to Korea – by this time she did not take part in all the tours – and her arrival coincided with her fifty-ninth birthday. She was rather put out by seeing banner headlines in the newspapers welcoming the sixty-year-old ballerina and was not amused when it was explained that in Korea you always gave your age according to your next birthday. However, it all ended with our having a good laugh.

On the last of my four visits to Seoul I was disillusioned at the difference in the attitude of the Koreans, who seemed to have changed out of all recognition. Perhaps this obtained only in the capital, but over the years since 1975 tourists had brought them new-found wealth. High-rise buildings and new hotels were springing up, particularly for the coming Olympics; all this had radically altered the older and more traditional way of life that we had encountered on our first visit. However, the fact that Seoul was hosting the Olympic Games that year was of great interest for me, as Kitty Godfrey, the distinguished tennis player related to me by marriage and in her ninetieth year, was invited to visit them. I was very fond of Kitty; she was a delightful person, full of humour. With her continuing interest in the young players, and her knowledge of them, she reminded me of Ninette de Valois with her encouragement of young dancers and her total and discerning awareness of the contemporary scene.

In one of the new hotels in the city, the Lotte, we were asked to attend a reception to meet HRH the Duke of Gloucester, who was in Korea to honour the 'Gallant Gloucesters', and their memorable rearguard action during the Korean War. Michael Somes, who seemed to know every last move in the campaign, laid into any of the young dancers who failed to respond to his eulogies of this famous regiment.

I had always longed to visit Japan since those far-off days when Non, Naggie's niece and sister to Bon, had heard on the Mighty Wurlitzer at the super cinema in Kingston a selection from *Madam Butterfly*, which she would then play on the piano in the front room. I fell in love with the melodies, conjuring up romantic ideas of this distant country. I finally made it for myself in 1975 and it was everything I had hoped for.

The company stayed at a huge hotel, the New Otani, and travelled to our theatre, The Bunka, by tube. I liked the hotel and would wander through its various reception rooms. On venturing down to the basement I was fascinated by a collection of small rooms in each of which a bride was being made ready for her wedding, her delicate face painted with tiny brushes before the exquisite head-dress was put on. Feeling that I was an intruder, I hurried away before I might be ordered to do so.

With Monica Mason and Alexander Grant I went to a theatre outside Tokyo where revues with an all-female cast take place, and a very spectacular performance it was – rows of girls kicking away in the chorus line wearing waxed, plumed head-dresses in the best Rockettes tradition. When it came to the dramatic sketches, these talented Japanese artists acquitted themselves well and very realistically. I particularly remember one scene in which Marie Antoinette was bidding farewell to her lover, played by a sturdy girl doing justice to the memory of Tyrone Power, who made such an impression in the film version of the story when he played opposite Norma Shearer. The show was all very *comme il faut*, and is justly famous and considered comparable to the dramas of the all-male Kabuki.

I felt very worried, however, about dancing in Hiroshima. It was difficult for people of my age in the company who remembered so vividly the day when the voice of the BBC news announcer told of the dropping of the first atomic bomb. We shared, it seemed, a universal guilt for the dreadful carnage and suffering that was imposed on the people of Hiroshima, although inevitably accepting the fact that it was necessary to stop the further suffering that would have been caused by the continuation of the war in the East. This was a new dimension of warfare that the world had never experienced, and its dire consequences were to continue long after the event.

On the day we arrived in Hiroshima, the whole company paid a visit to the scene of this destruction. Skeletons of buildings that had survived the blast had been deliberately preserved within a site that was dominated by an iron framework of a giant dome and had part of a river running through it. This was a reminder of what the whole city must have looked like after the holocaust. We were appalled by everything, but particularly moved by the hundreds and thousands of prayers written, as is the custom in the East, on pieces of paper, then twisted and hung by strings attached to the ruins, prayers for those who had died either then, or later as victims of the fallout.

On the day we left the city, Alexander Grant and I decided to take a taxi to this memorial site and to be there at the same time of day that the bomb had been dropped, at eight o'clock in the morning, in the hope of being there with relatively few people about and before the tourists arrived. We just had time to do this before leaving for the next city on our tour. All was quiet there, and the only people present with us were some middle-aged Japanese ladies with large straw hats who, like gardeners, were sweeping the paths around the rose beds. These roses had been given by many countries throughout the world, and it was reassuring to see them in bloom; we had been told that it had been thought that the soil on the site would be for ever sterile.

From Hiroshima we continued on our tour, which was full of interest and enjoyment, leaving me with an assortment of impressions: the crammed bustle of Tokyo, the beauties of Kyoto, the temples – and flowers everywhere, especially the peonies in Kaikan. But most important of all was the success of the company. The dancers and the ballets were greeted with an interest and admiration that was muted but sincere, and especially popular was *La Fille mal gardée*. This always called for a rehearsal with a local horse to draw the carriage taking Lise and the widow Simone to the picnic; but in Kobe the mare that was designated for the job showed no interest in taking part and refused to leave her young foal. So I suggested that, as Farmer Thomas, I should lead on stage both the mare and her foal across the front cloth. This seemed to satisfy the mare, and there was a buzz of delight from the audience as we made our way across, stopping halfway to present the habitual carrot.

Japan delighted me as much as I had anticipated. I loved the lines of schoolchildren we encountered, so delightfully dressed in their school uniform, often of a naval style with sailor hats, all blue and white or yellow and white. When we were carrying our issue of Royal Ballet bags with our sponsors' names also printed on them, these tiny mites could, to our surprise, read and understand who we were, and would point to us and say laughingly, 'Ah so, Loyal Ballet'.

Mr Tadatsugu Sasaki of the Japanese Performing Arts Foundation, who was presenting us, always generously entertained the company in his home when we were in Tokyo. As we entered the house we would remove our shoes as is the custom, and don slippers in which to shuffle about comfortably. Sometimes one had difficulty in recognising one's own pair among the huge pile inside his front door, especially if being among the first to leave. On one occasion on returning to the hotel after a very enjoyable party there, I realised that, instead of wearing my well-used shoes from Marks and Sparks, I had taken a particularly polished and expensive Bally pair. I immediately telephoned Peter Brownlee, our General Manager, and reported the error, expecting that I would shortly hear from the rightful owner. But not doing so, I wore the elegant ones for the rest of our stay in the city. It was not until our departure, when we were waiting in the airport lounge during a long delay to our plane, and where I had put my feet up on a convenient bench, that my neighbour let out a cry that I was wearing his shoes. It was my long-time friend and colleague, Michael Somes. He had them off me in a trice. My soft-shoe shuffle became the joke of the tour and was even reported in the *Evening Standard* by Mr Sydney Edwards, no less, the representative of the press on this occasion.

In 1983 we visited the People's Republic of China, starting with Beijing, renamed from Peking – which for me still carryied with it the childhood associations of the pantomime, *Aladdin*, at the Kingston Empire, the comic laundry men, and the ballet of the jewels that materialised at the rub of Aladdin's lamp. All this light-hearted irrelevance went through my mind as we left the airport on the night of our arrival in China, our bus taking us through dark, quiet streets leading to the city of Beijing. There was not the sudden burst of neon or the myriad lights of tall apartment blocks that usually greets one on arrival at today's great capital cities, but I felt nevertheless excited at this start of a new adventure and at the opportunity of performing in China.

On arriving at our modest hotel, we were handed pocket money for our entire stay by a representative of the Chinese Performing Arts Agency. As this was in lieu of salaries, it was clear that the visit would not admit of extravagance; the tone had indeed been set when we had been advised to eat before we took off on our charter flight to Beijing, since the in-flight refreshment would be limited. But there were many compensating factors in store for us. Our first day in the city was free, and we went sightseeing at the Summer Palace, where we were given lunch organised by our hosts. In the evening we attended a buffet supper given by the Chinese Performing Arts Agency.

There were optional classes at the Beijing-based Central Ballet Company, attended by all the dancers taking the principal rôles in *The Sleeping Beauty*, which would open our season in China. The standard of classical ballet dancing was very high in this country, owing to the close alliance with the Soviet Union at that time; excellent training was to be found in their schools, and its results were evident in their companies. We had to be at the top of our form to prove our own worth. As a gesture of friendship we had invited members of the local ballet schools to the general dress rehearsal of *The Sleeping Beauty* – in fact our whole visit was a mixture of performing and, in whatever way we could, creating an atmosphere of friendly interest among the Chinese.

The first night went extremely well. The Chinese orchestra under our conductor were wonderful; we could hear them practising our scores every minute we were in the theatre, their energies being directed to casting aside that dark period of life under the régime of the Gang of Four, when most of the musicians were sent to work on the land or in factories and had their instruments confiscated if they had not managed, as some had, to bury them to avoid this fate. The Cultural Revolution (a misnomer if ever there was one) had denied many their rightful place in the performing arts. As we sat in our dressing rooms making up for this first night's performance, we could hear its music, which clearly vibrated for them with memories of happier years. When later they encountered other scores from our repertoire, we could tell again that every note they played came from the heart. We also felt a great warmth from the demonstrative audience; as we were easily recognisable with our Western faces, many members of the public would come up afterwards and express their pleasure in our performance.

Sightseeing had further wonders in store: the Forbidden City captured all our imaginations, as did our later excursion to the Great Wall. I shall never forget the excitement I felt as our bus approached it and we suddenly had our first view of this monumental fortification. It was extremely hot weather and we only managed to explore a limited amount; the going was rough and the surface of the ground slippery, and we were thankful that we had been advised to wear rubber-soled shoes. In spite of our limited trek, however, the impressions it created are indelible, a final and unexpectedly exotic touch being added by the sight of a number of camels grouped together close to the Wall.

We left Beijing for Shanghai. For me, visiting this city was another new experience, yet it was a place that was full of associations of people whom I had known for years. First and foremost among these was Margot Fonteyn who, as a young girl, had accompanied her mother and father, who had gone to Shanghai to work as an engineer. Whilst there, Margot became friends with a girl of her own age, June Brae, both of them attending the local ballet school in which June's mother played the piano to accompany the classes. The school was run by George Goncharov, one of many White Russian refugees from the Revolution. To augment his resources, he also appeared in cabaret with another dancer, Vera Volkova. Both these people continued to feature in Margot's later life, Vera becoming a great friend and mentor and establishing a successful school in London in West Street opposite the Ivy restaurant. George later taught at the Royal Ballet School at White Lodge in Richmond Park and also gave classes to the company, as did Vera. June Brae came to the notice of Ninette de Valois in the early thirties when she danced at the Coliseum in a musical, *The Golden Toy*, choreographed by de Valois. Through this association she later became a member of the Vic–Wells Ballet. She was a principal in several Ashton ballets and was famous for creating the role of the Black Queen in de Valois' *Checkmate*.

The hotel in Shanghai was newly built, but in the grounds of a house that looked like a mock-Tudor in Esher. The only people I saw going into it were the maids from the hotel, and I presumed it was where they were accommodated; I was delighted when one of them asked me if I would like to see inside it, and I readily accepted. With its beams and minstrels' gallery, the whole interior looked like a scene from the Whitehall farces of the thirties with Tom Walls and Ralph Lynn. When I described all this later to Charles Gordon, Pamela May's husband, who had also lived in Shanghai as a young boy, he thought it might originally have been a golf club, and I visualised his father and Margot's teeing off from the first hole and joining the lady wife for a dry sherry after the game. This between-the-wars atmosphere was repeated for me many times in Shanghai, which by 1983 was somewhat shabby, with faded awnings above the once-flourishing restaurants, and the fine houses and embassies of the earlier fashionable district seeming in need of renovation. I thought also of Noël Coward, who wrote *Private Lives* during a stay in Shanghai. I did my best to find the hotel in which Coward stayed, but as they were almost all called the Hotel of Heavenly Peace and all claimed the distinction of housing the playwright, I never discovered which one it really was.

One evening before the performance I walked with Monica Mason along the Bund, the great riverfront of the city, which was crowded with Chinese sauntering along. A group of them came up and spoke to us and we found ourselves in the middle of young people speaking excellent English and asking about life in London. It was extraordinary how knowledgeable they were, and they explained that they had learnt to speak our language by listening to the BBC World Service, which was of course strictly not allowed. They were aware that we belonged to the visiting Royal Ballet and asked us about the English theatre and David Hare's last play, for example, and some of their questions we were hard pressed to answer. They were also conversant with films, books and art galleries, and one sensed that they were hungry for knowledge about life in the West. They were indeed very pleasant to meet and to talk to.

In Shanghai the theatre seemed to be more important to people than it appeared to be in other cities in China, and leaving the stage door after a performance it was almost as if we were back in Covent Garden. Fans asked about the company and the repertoire in an almost colloquial way, and we got to know the regulars. I felt that this was a reflection of the interest in ballet that went back to the early days of Volkova and Goncharov, when Margot's mother was searching for a suitable ballet school for her young daughter, newly arrived in Shanghai.

Margot often talked about a tea house in the centre of the city situated on a small island and approached by a narrow pedestrian bridge of many zigzag spars. This had been a favourite with her mother; so, armed with an old picture postcard of it, I set out to discover its whereabouts. It seems strange that I had no qualms whatever about doing so in this crowded city. On the first tram I got on, I showed my postcard to the driver, who gave me a nod of recognition as to my destination. The tram was packed, with standing room only, and the ticket collector motioned me to move down inside. Soon I had to pass down the money for my ticket; not too conversant with the currency, I took a handful of money out of my pocket and this was duly passed down the car to the conductor, who took the amount required and returned the change, together with my ticket, via the line of passengers. All this took place with honest good nature. Everyone was anxious to indicate where I was to get off, waving me goodbye as I left the tram.

I found the tea house without difficulty, crossed the zigzag bridge and entered. It was very full and I had to share a table with a number of elderly Chinese men, obviously regular patrons, engrossed in a game of draughts. However, they broke off their game to engage me in conversation; again their English was excellent, the reason for which was soon explained by the fact that, as young men, they had worked in various English clubs and establishments in the twenties. They had affectionate memories of those days and were clearly anglophiles.

In addition to feeling close to so many old friends in remembering their time in this city, I felt an affinity with the people of the Shanghai of the day, and I think we all sensed this. Indeed, the men in the company organised a football match, playing against the waiters and other staff of the hotel. I realised, too, how hard the waiters worked; having served us during the day at our hotel, they worked in the refreshment bars at the theatre in the evening. I discovered this when they gave me evidence that they had watched the performance in between the intervals. When I came down to breakfast one morning, they gave me a splendid imitation of my Master of Ceremonies act with my long ceremonial staff; I loved this, and on subsequent mornings I would stalk into the dining room à la Catalabutte, which sent us all into fits of giggles.

All too soon we moved on from Shanghai, going by train to Canton, now called Guangzhou, where we were to perform for four days before crossing the frontier into Hong Kong. I felt happy to think that everything pointed to our having made a favourable impression on our hosts in the People's Republic of China, and a very friendly one at that.

Everything in Hong Kong, where we had an eight-day stay, was in startling contrast to life in mainland China. There was a plethora of luxurious hotels (ours facing the sea being one of them), shopping centres, restaurants and magnificent views everywhere. Hong Kong was also the home of the parents of a member of the company, Ravenna Tucker; they had a house across the bay, where we spent a memorable free day sailing to it in a clipper-style yacht. There is a picture of all the men after they had climbed up the tall rigging and were spreadeagled across the spars. If you look carefully you can see Michael Somes at the top of the formation; when the younger chaps had climbed up, Michael, with his usual dogged determination, surpassed them all by reaching the pinnacle.

While in Hong Kong we met Anton Dolin, who was producing and teaching there. I had always had great respect for this dancer since those early days when he came with us on the first tour undertaken by the Vic–Wells Ballet in 1935, and it was a pleasure to meet him in the hustle and bustle of this international port and to recall our memorable trip on the Manchester Ship Canal!

Chapter 23

By the time I made my second visit to Australia, Anthony Dowell had become our fifth Director and was joining us on this tour. I had known and admired this extremely popular and brilliant dancer throughout his career, and had in fact taught him at the School when I stood in for a short time for Harijs Plucis at White Lodge. In addition to admiring the technical excellence of his solo dancing, I regarded his partnership with Antoinette Sibley as marking a very high point in the life of the Royal Ballet – this in relation both to the classical ballets and to the works of Ashton, whose inventive choreography provided the perfect foil for these two artists.

On this second visit, it was particularly interesting for me to see the progress that had been made in Melbourne in the provision for the arts and entertainment. The days of going out to St Kilda to the Palais were over, for there was now a new theatre in the city, the principal home of the Australian Ballet and a fine venue for all visiting performers. In Brisbane it was the year of the Expo, and our then Prime Minister, Mrs Thatcher, arrived to celebrate British Day while we were there. A group of us went along to see her make her speech to mark that occasion, and we were all pleased at the tremendous impression she made. She attended our performance that evening and the reception held afterwards. Paul Findlay, the Opera Director from Covent Garden, who was visiting us on tour, introduced me to her. I talked about our recent visit to Russia when the young male dancers in the company had had a great success with a folk-dancing programme that they had learned at the school at White Lodge. They had formed a group calling themselves the Bow Street Rappers and toured the streets of Moscow giving out large and well-illustrated posters of the Royal Ballet, which were eagerly sought by the Muscovites. Mrs Thatcher was delighted to hear about this and told me about her visit to Moscow, when she had seen the Bolshoi performing *Swan Lake*. She was very complimentary about our production of this ballet, which she had seen that evening. She commended the Russians on their disciplined style, which she admired, but she felt that our version of this classic had more soul. She showed a fine discrimination!

Brisbane was the last date on this tour and then we were on holiday. Under the new arrangements with regard to the company's travel, the dancers could use their return tickets when they wished, incorporating a holiday within the country in which the tour had been made, if they had ideas of doing so. Through David Drew's enquiries, we learnt of a travel company that organised trips by sea to the Barrier Reef, a place I had always wanted to explore. David rounded up a small party of us: Anthony Dowell, Rosalind Eyre, Jay Jolley, Derek Rencher, Brian Shaw and Christopher Newton, to join him and his wife, the actress June Ritchie. We duly flew from Brisbane to a port called Townsville, where we spent the night before embarking on *The Coral Princess*, the boat that had been put at our disposal with its crew of three – the captain, first mate and engineer – plus two women, Sophia and Joanne, sturdy and capable, and a chef. With slight misgivings, we found out that our craft was a reconditioned wartime vessel; our doubts were somewhat allayed when we saw a picture of her in the ship's lounge, obviously doing yeoman service in her original guise before being fitted out in later years as a small cruise ship.

After embarking, and anticipating the adventurous pleasure of this holiday trip, we met the crew, sat on deck drinking Buck's Fizz and eating smoked oysters, and were soon under way. At the end of the day we weighed anchor at a nearby island and had a swim while a magnificent sunset blazed deep red and reflected on the water. Afterwards at dinner the captain apologised for the delay in serving the main course, and then announced that the chef had been taken ill suddenly and that Sophia and Joanne were taking over. In fact they did so for the rest of the trip, and the chef, who had been shipped back to Townsville, was never seen again.

That incident signalled the overture to a chain of disasters that were to beset *The Coral Princess*. Suffice it to say we never did see the great coral reef; the nearest we got to it at the end of our week's voyage was Dunk Island, appropriately named, where we arrived one windswept and rainy morning to discover that we had apparently missed the smaller boat that was to take us on to the reef. However, we did at least get ashore on the island, which some of the more enterprising among our number explored in the pouring rain. David, June and I decided to make for the nearest shelter in a hotel, where we found that Paul Findlay and his family were staying. They invited us in for hot coffee and we waited for the rest of the party to join us, after which we all made our dripping progress back to *The Coral Princess*, on which the rum ration was handed out *sans* delay.

The boat limped back in the worst of storms and rough seas, losing in the process one of her propellers and suffering engine trouble such as to make her scarcely seaworthy. We made it back on this last lap of the round trip from Dunk Island only as a result of the fine seamanship of the captain and the skill of his engineer. It must be said here that, while the rest of us were all huddled together in the ship's lounge, Rosalind was up on the bridge indulging her love of adventure and fondness for rough waters.

It was with much relief this time round that we boarded our plane for home, to complete our holiday in calmer waters. Brian Shaw, for one, made straight for his cottage in Alfriston near Beachy Head, and I returned to the simple tranquillity of Bray Lock, where I indulged in some home thoughts from after being abroad.

Chapter 24

Since 1957 when Margot had persuaded me to buy the cottage that leaned against the barn next to her mother's house, it had become an enjoyable part of my leisure life and I did manage to get to it fairly often. In my early days there, transport was more flexible, particularly for those of us without a car, and it was possible to go by train to Taplow, my local station, before Dr Beeching saw fit to close it and other similarly small stations on Sundays. The district adjoining Taplow is called Amerden and features in the names of Mrs Hookham's weekend house, Amerden Bank, and of my cottage, Amerden Priory Cottage. Amerden Priory was once a religious house, subsequently occupied by my friends, Ralph and Peggy Southward.

If Margot was at Amerden Bank and Tug and John were staying in London, they would make the trip for lunch with Mrs Hookham and pop in to see me next door. Margot was especially happy when Tito was over from Panama and could be with her there. As one might expect, there was a galaxy of stars and other notables, all happy to enjoy a friendly lunch and Mrs Hookham's excellent cooking, and, having seen my small house over the hedge, they would sometimes wander in to see me. It seemed natural to be sitting in my living room with figures from the world of entertainment and be chatting with Trevor Howard over a glass of whisky or enjoying the infectious humour of Richard Wattis, whom Shelagh Fraser, Moyra's sister, had brought down.

A day I shall long remember with acute embarrassment is the one on which Dorothy Hammerstein came down to see me with one of her New York friends. I had put a chicken casserole in the oven for dinner later that evening before going in to have a drink with Mrs Hookham. We talked for a while over this, Dorothy stitching away at her petit point, and then returned to the waiting casserole. It was not until I came to serve it that I realised it was very far from being cooked. I had put it in the oven inadvertently at too low a temperature. Fortunately for us all, Dorothy's friend, assessing the situation and eschewing formality, said 'Look, we're all grown up here and this is just not cooked'. So out came my emergency tin of ham. A far cry from the Oak Room in New York.

In later years, Pamela May and her husband, Charles Gordon, adapted a wing of Amerden Bank for their weekend retreat. By this time, Pamela was teaching at the Royal Ballet Upper School as well as appearing as a guest artist at the Opera House. Her husband was a capable and know-ledgeable gardener, and it was not long before his skills became evident. When it was decided to fence off the ground surrounding our joint properties, leaving only a private road as our right of access, Charles planted an orchard of pear, greengage, apple and plum trees, which greatly enhanced the whole area and gave us additional privacy.

Within this community of friends there were two young girls: Lavinia, the daughter of Margot's brother, Felix Hookham, and his wife Phoebe, and my old friend Harold Turner's daughter, Solveig, so called by reason of her Norwegian mother, Gerd Larsen, who was a principal of the Royal Ballet. I had known Harold over many years from the days of the Ballet Rambert and as a fellow member of the tap-dancing classes at Max Rivers's studio in Wardour Street, and I had looked forward to having him as a neighbour. He had bought the nearby cottage overlooking the river, and we all welcomed him down for his first weekend there. Sadly, it was to be his last. He died on the Monday following this visit, while rehearsing at the Opera House. This was a tragic blow for Gerd and Solveig, and it seemed likely that they would forego coming down to the cottage. However, with a practicality that we all admired, Gerd took driving lessons immediately in order to facilitate the journey down. Solveig and Lavinia became great friends and, both being animal lovers, took a great interest in the local riding school.

Jean Gilbert, the pianist who played the César Franck music for *Symphonic Variations*, became a very close friend of Margot and a frequent visitor to Amerden Bank. I was able to repay a little of the kindness shown to me by Rita and Aylmer Macdonald, the directors of the Wilderness Ballet Camp in Ontario, when they came down to see me while on a visit to England. Rita, a dedicated anglophile, loved the surrounding countryside and lingered long by Bray Lock. She gloried in all the wild flowers growing in profusion along the lane past our houses and chided me for not being enthusiastic enough about them. They would all be in bloom for the glorious Fourth of June, when Moyra Fraser visited her two boys who were at Eton and then brought them and their friends to my cottage to cook a delicious lunch for them and relax between events. My absence on these occasions was due, as was so often the case, to commitments at Covent Garden.

One of the nicest things about having the cottage was the fact that there I could entertain my brothers: William, with his wife and his son Martyn, and Fred with his wife and his daughter Mary. This made up for my being away earlier on in my career for many family occasions. Having a place of my own, I could contribute my share of family continuity and in addition have the opportunity of introducing my close friends. This was all part of the congenial atmosphere that prevailed among us, the essential ingredient being that wonderful thing called fun.

On the family side, Bon had from the first taken a great liking to the cottage, and always enjoyed seeing Margot and her mother, who were both so kind and friendly to her. Alas, she died in 1982, which seemed at the time to finally to cut off all my connections with 'Melrose', the house in Teddington and scene of my childhood. However, as Bon's nephew, John, and his wife and children then moved into the house, that early phase did in fact continue, as we have remained in touch with one another ever since. Another sadness was the recent death of my friend living at Amerden Priory, Ralph Southward, who had become Sir Ralph and was prominent among the team of Her Majesty's physicians. He and his wife Peggy had four sons, Robin, David, Nigel and Ian, and Nigel has followed his father as physician to the Royal Household.

Chapter 25

From its earliest days as the Vic–Wells Ballet, the company would be asked to dance at fund-raising galas. The first of these was in aid of what was known as the Building Fund, which was to help Miss Baylis in her endeavours to improve and expand the Sadler's Wells Theatre. Others followed, with programmes consisting of contributions from the existing ballet companies plus one or two notable guest artists from abroad, such as Serge Lifar, Mary Wigman or Harald Kreutzberg.

Forty years on and I found myself involved in various galas, the first being on behalf of a charitable organisation formed in 1970 for handi-capped children, called 'Kids'. My producer was David Ritchie, closely involved with the Coliseum Theatre where the performance was to be held. He was to provide the operatic talent and I the balletic, this in the form of an excerpt from *La Fille mal gardée* and the solo from Ashton's *The Wise Virgins*, to be danced by Margot Fonteyn, wearing the long, flowing dress designed by Rex Whistler. She had not performed this for a very long time and, giving the occasion the importance she knew it deserved, was meticulous in her rehearsals of this rôle; this particularly impressed David. I asked Anthony Dowell to be our commentator. He readily agreed and was delighted to be joined in the task by the Countess of Harewood, the two of them sitting on each side of the proscenium arch.

As the evening was in aid of children, I felt that children should be represented on stage. I obtained permission for the boys in the cast of *Oliver!*, then running in the West End, to sing 'Food, Glorious Food' as our opening number, which got us off to a good rousing start. All in all, it was a tremendous cast, with Margot at the head of a list of great dancers and Rita Hunter leading an equally good team of singers.

In the next gala in which I was involved, my co-producer was Michael Rennison, well known at the Royal Opera House. This time I featured the little girls from the musical *Annie*; the show had two alternating casts and it was a great bonus that I was able to use both to fill the Coliseum's huge stage, where they scrubbed away on the floor and won all our hearts.

A particular favourite for me was a pantomime gala at the Theatre Royal, Drury Lane, involving all sections of show business and a cast of matching diversity that included John Gielgud, Elton John, Maureen Lipman ... the list went on and on. This was produced in rattling good style by Pamela, Lady Harlech, and the audience was captivated once again by the young; this time it was a group from the Royal Ballet School, the very young Junior Associates performing the chickens' dance from *La Fille mal gardée*. They stole the show.

In 1979 the Royal Ballet gave a gala to honour Margot Fonteyn's sixtieth birthday. For her devoted friends, as for the public in general, she would always be 'younger than springtime'. If she was to appear in the programme herself, however, it was difficult to decide what form her contribution should take, as it was also hard to visualise an evening that could adequately celebrate such an anniversary. In the event, the main core of the programme consisted of ballets and divertissements that had always been Margot's favourites. Then it was announced that she herself would dance in a solo specially choreographed by Ashton, in which she would recall moments from her many rôles, from her earliest days in the Vic–Wells Ballet to the time when she reached the pinnacle of her achievements in the Royal Ballet. Ashton managed to give the essence of the many characters that were associated with her rôles – a step, a gesture, a certain inflection here and there – and he brought these together in a skilfully contrived entity, all the ingredients of which the audience recognised with delight.

In the midst of this I could not help thinking how happy Ninette de Valois must be, remembering that earliest moment when she first noticed in Ursula Moreton's class a little girl whom she mistakenly took to be Chinese, and then her later insistence that Margot should take the rôle of Aurora in the first production of *The Sleeping Beauty*, a rôle in which she subsequently conquered New York in 1949. There would be the memory of the great partnerships with Robert Helpmann, Michael Somes and, later, Rudolf Nureyev, completing the triumvirate and rekindling Margot's world fame when she was in her forties and on the brink of retirement.

Ashton's solo for her was danced to Elgar's haunting *Salut d'Amour*, and her costume was a simple pink dress designed by William Chappell, a great friend who she said had been the first person to make her feel really part of the company.

The climax of the whole evening was when the first of her great partnerships was relived and Margot and Robert Helpmann danced the Tango from *Façade*. This was greeted with tumultuous applause, and as the audience left the theatre there was a consciousness in everyone of how much this great artist had given to so many people throughout her long, shining career.

Chapter 26

The Friends of Covent Garden was founded by Sir David Webster in 1962, with Kensington Davison, later to become Lord Broughshane, as its Director. It was to prove comparable to the Friends of the Royal Academy and to contribute greatly to the activities of the Royal Opera House. To me its help was invaluable, particularly with funding the activities of the Choreographic Group at the different venues that followed its launching at the Yvonne Arnaud Theatre in Guildford. We had a period of performances at the Collegiate Theatre in Bloomsbury, made possible by Lord Annan, and then a brief interlude at the New London Theatre, thanks to one of the Royal Ballet School's great benefactors, Sir Joseph Lockwood.

We were then allowed on Sunday nights to use the small theatre belonging to LAMDA, the theatrical academy in Earl's Court. The construction of its auditorium, the lighting and the sight-lines were ideal for the young choreographers and enabled them to learn about the mechanics of theatre and every aspect of production. This was valuable in that it compensated for their not having worked in the commercial theatre as had Massine, Balanchine and Ashton. The limited seating, however, was inadequate to accommodate an audience of the Friends, who nevertheless paid for performances seen by such as Ninette de Valois, Frederick Ashton, Kenneth MacMillan, Sir John Tooley and members of the Covent Garden administration.

I had long felt that the first efforts of the would-be choreographers should be kept strictly private and not viewed by the critics, not because I feared a harsh verdict or even an over-enthusiastic one, but because we aimed to create an atmosphere of study and experiment in preparation for the time when the aspirants became fully fledged. This time at LAMDA was a fertile one, particularly for the young members of the Royal Ballet company who were to make their mark as choreographers, such as Derek Deane, Wayne Eagling, Matthew Hawkins, Ashley Page and Michael Corder. We received invaluable help from the director of the LAMDA theatre, Steven Hocking, and have much to be grateful for when we look back on this association and others that led up to it. The present achievements of the early members of the Choreographic Group have more than fulfilled our expectations and have, I hope, well justified the support given by the Friends.

To repay them for this in part, when I became responsible for producing the Christmas party-cum-cabaret, I kept the audience strictly to the Friends. This annual event with its revue format became what people most loved to see, and it filled the house to the point at which it was a case of 'returns only', the Friends' office keeping a list of strict priorities to deal with this eventuality. This popularity was not surprising, since the show drew upon the talents of the Royal Ballet Companies and the Royal Opera, but before long I was able to extend the cast to every section in the Opera House. There was the wig department, for example, led by Ronald Freeman and Juan Lierado; the hat department and their boss, Jenny Adey; and the men and women of the wardrobe, who one year combined in a Busby Berkeley routine manoeuvring the racks of clothes carried on wheels in a pastiche of the complex patterns that were the hallmark of the film choreographer, all this to a spirited Harry Warren accompaniment. One triumphant opening number was a song and dance performed by a dozen stagehands to the tune of 'You're Never Fully Dressed Without a Smile'. They had rehearsed this for weeks at the Dance Centre, and on the night were so darned good that they even convinced Burt Shevelove, the American director and writer, that they were professionals.

The staff of the Crush Bar also contributed the opening number on one occasion, enabling the delighted audience to see the people who had served them drinks through the years – something, in fact, that they were all doing up to the last minute before making their entrance on stage to give their musical comedy routine. Lyrics for this were specially written by Ken Davison and Keith Gray, the stage manager of the Ballet Company.

Sergeant Martin, the doyen of all commissionaires and known to generations of Opera House patrons, made an appearance at these performances, his unsuspected talents ranging from playing the nanny of Wayne Sleep's Shirley Temple to a turgid scene in which he was disguised as an old-fashioned Brünnhilde from a Wagnerian opera, again accompanied by Sleep. Knowing, as everyone did, his stern face and eagle eye when on professional duty, it was a translation to be wondered at!

Apart from contributing to the success of the show on stage, all these departments gave me unstintingly of their time and help in the business of putting the whole thing on. Peter Greenwell and Nina Walker made all the musical arrangements, which was no small task, and performed as pianists themselves, augmented by a rhythm section. I had invaluable help from a posse of stage managers from the Opera and both Ballet Companies, and props and costumes were made available as needed. All this was a *sine qua non* and made it possible to give the cabaret a panache and style commensurate with the size of the Opera House, while yet retaining some of the intimacy of revue.

Early on, the Patron of the Friends, the Prince of Wales, joined in the fun and sang 'For I am a Pirate King' from *The Pirates of Penzance*, fitted out in suitable costume by Michael Brown, the wardrobe master. His Royal Highness was supported by a chorus line of lady pirates played by members of the Ballet Company with a backing group of principal male singers from the Opera. He expertly tripped the light fantastic with Karen Paisey, a principal dancer with the Royal Ballet.

In 1982 Princess Margaret opened the show by giving a welcoming speech from the stage. The red tabs were down and eight principal male dancers led by Derek Deane (later Director of the English National Ballet) proceeded in movements to the music of Offenbach to open the great red and gold curtains. The Princess was revealed standing in a flower-decked arbour from which she spoke, ending with the words 'And now I must fly', which she did, going straight up inside the arbour and ending in the flies. I borrowed this effect from John Copley's production of *Semele*; in that case the apparatus came down from above, while in this one it went up, and the Princess did indeed fly. I have to thank John for providing the *deus ex machina*, which proved very effective – for as the Princess went up, she brought the house down!

The occasion when Princess Diana danced with Wayne Sleep in the 1985 Christmas show has been recorded on film and is well known to the public; but this was not her baptism of fire at the Opera House, since she had appeared in the Friends' cabaret before this time. Wayne Eagling had thought up the idea of Prince Charles' playing Romeo to Princess Diana's Juliet. The Prince came on stage wearing the cloak that belonged to Kenneth MacMillan's production and moved stealthily around to the music of Prokofiev. We had extended the stage over the orchestra pit so that it was possible to place a ladder on it against the Royal Box, on which Romeo climbed up to his Juliet, who leaned out of it and, with a perfect imitation of the Wall's Ice Cream commercial popular at the time, demanded 'Just one Cornetto...'.

Besides welcoming our Royal guests, we were joined from time to time by artists from other branches of entertainment. Elisabeth Welch sang one of her famous numbers, dancing off the stage partnered by Donald MacLeary of the Royal Ballet to the final line of the lyric, 'Come on, big boy, ten cents a dance'. Moyra Fraser gave us 'One Wet, Whit Sunday' from the revue in which she starred, *Airs on a Shoestring*, and she also joined Rose Hill and a member of the Opera Company, Gwynneth Price, in *Joyful Noise*, a number by Donald Swann about three lady choristers in a performance at the Albert Hall. This was from a Laurier Lister revue, *Penny Plain*, at the St Martin's Theatre, where it was sung by Joyce Grenfell, Moyra Fraser and Rose Hill. Rose was also a distinguished opera singer and had appeared at Sadler's Wells Theatre in *La Traviata* and *The Bartered Bride*. Many tributes were paid to her by opera singers in the audience of the Friends when she sang her 'Stone, Tone Deaf' about a supposedly famous diva who 'can't tell a B from an F'. Only a true singer could make so convincing a pretence of being off-key.

Richard Baker, the well-known announcer and TV personality, sang about 'Little Miss Bouncer' who 'loved an announcer, down at the BBC', made famous by Flotsam and Jetsam on radio in the years before the war. Stephanie Lawrence, who had been associated with shows such as *Evita* and *Blood Brothers*, did a number with Brian Shaw, who wore a very realistic mask and was dressed as Miss Piggy. Caroline O'Connor, an understudy in *Cabaret* at the time but later to be the much-celebrated Mabel in Jerry Herman's *Mack and Mabel*, sang for us.

Moira Shearer was the highlight of the show one year, doing a mock striptease in the manner of Gipsy Rose Lee; but instead of peeling off her gloves she made her exit through the gap in the curtain, casting behind her as she went a pair of red shoes as a token of her famous film. Later in the same programme she gave a literally sparkling, sequinned *Come Dancing* number with Michael Coleman. Everyone in the Opera House welcomed her back, and the young members of the Royal Ballet in this production were delighted to be working with her, for she had become something of a legend for them.

A figure from way back in the days before the war when we were appearing at the Arts Theatre, Cambridge, and by this time a famous TV personality, was Arthur Marshall. As a great friend of Ken Davison, he was allowed to come to the rehearsals, for which he would arrive regularly and punctually and subsequently became an enthusiastic member of the audience. He chortled away as merrily as he did on *Call My Bluff*, and sent me letters afterwards pointing out his favourite items.

Margot Fonteyn, as one would expect, always showed great loyalty in appearing many times in the cabaret. One notable occasion was when with Merle Park she mimed to a record of the soundtrack of *Gentlemen Prefer Blondes*, and Marilyn Monroe's and Jane Russell's voices accompanied movements splendidly arranged for the two ballerinas by Derek Deane.

Aspects of life at the Opera House also provided material for the shows. Stephanie Lawrence again did splendidly in a version of Noël Coward's 'Twentieth Century Blues' with an additional lyric by Keith Gray that lamented the disappearance of James Street, off Floral Street, which had been reduced to a mere passageway in the extended building complex of the Opera House. In 1985 Philip Gould, the young Australian star of *42nd Street* at Drury Lane, had an opening number 'Waiting in the Queue', inspired by the crowd of Friends going to the general rehearsals for opera and ballet productions and waiting outside to be ushered in under the aforementioned eagle eye of Sergeant Martin. In the early days the seating was allotted on a first-come-first-served basis, which could at times give rise to heated competition; a call to order would then be forthcoming in the martial tones of Ken Davison. All this Philip incorporated in his song; as in a later number, Gershwin's 'Stairway to Paradise', he was accompanied by Ray Cook, who had conducted the orchestra for Helpmann's tour of Australia in 1979 when Ray and I had become friends.

Like the rest of the artists who appeared that year, Philip was not aware that the Princess of Wales would also be appearing in the show. While he was watching in the wings after his opening number he was amazed to find himself standing next to the Princess, who had left the Royal Box earlier than anticipated. I had told her that I would escort her backstage when it was time for her to change and get ready, and so I was surprised to see that she had already found her own way from the box and through the pass-door leading to the stage. She explained that she was too nervous to continue watching the show as a member of the audience and wanted to be backstage with all of us. I understood perfectly how she must have felt. What lay ahead for her was her partnership with Wayne Sleep in 'Up-Town Girl'; as everybody now knows, it did not go down too badly!

Chapter 27

It was very gratifying for me to see that the activities of the Choreographic Group had extended to both the Upper and Lower divisions of the Royal Ballet School. Each put on an annual performance after which awards were given that commemorated distinguished members of the company. Princess Margaret, the President of the School, always attended these occasions at White Lodge. I was on the panel of judges for both groups and I never ceased to be impressed by their work – that of the younger ones particularly, who were full of invention allied to a strong sense of fun.

The choreography of Jonathan Burrows inspired by a Wilfred Owen poem was, on the other hand, full of poignancy and showed a remarkable insight for so young a person into a particular aspect of the 1914–18 War – a mustard gas attack and the suffering that ensued. At another occasion, I joined Kenneth MacMillan in judging the entries for the Ursula Moreton Award at the Upper School; it was won by David Bintley, again inspired by Wilfred Owen's poetry. He showed the great promise then that was later to result in his following Peter Wright as Director of the Birmingham Royal Ballet.

That good choreographers should emerge from the framework of her school and companies was part of their Founder's aspirations, and it was good to feel that all this activity justified the support that those who believed in it had given the Choreographic Group since its inception. Sadly, this belief did not extend to all parts of the general administration. By the mid-eighties the lack of co-operation from that direction was such that it became virtually impossible, in spite of the continuing dedication of the dancers, to put on the full programmes that had earlier been associated with the Group.

Thanks to the Friends and to the unswerving loyalty of Ken Davison, the old Collegiate Theatre, now renamed the Bloomsbury Theatre, was again made available to us for performances on Sunday evenings. When Anthony Dowell succeeded Kenneth MacMillan as Director, he came to one of them. As I watched him from a seat a row or two behind, I noticed he was visibly unamused; every vertebra in his back seemed to bend with disbelief at what he was watching. Apart from the performance being inadequate, the rains were coming down outside and the theatre was full of umbrellas and soaking wet mackintoshes. I was nevertheless pleased to see Lord Bonham Carter, whom I had known for many years, turn-ing up and taking an interest in the work of the Group. I relieved him of his dripping umbrella and showed him to his seat. As he left at the end of the performance, he said only two words to me, 'My umbrella', and was gone.

There was a board meeting the following day, Monday, and on Tuesday Anthony Dowell told me as gently as possible that I had come in for a great deal of unfavourable comment at the meeting. Some weeks later, as I was thinking it time to consult him about the arrangements for the next Ashton Award at the Upper School, Dowell said that he had decided to relieve me of all the harassment (sic) I had endured in the past, and that he was replacing me with a new director. This was Norman Morrice who, in the event, had even less success than I did, because of the same problem – the lack of co-operation with the Royal Ballet. But that is another story.

My being relieved of my post as director is linked with an event earlier in the eighties when Sir Joseph Lockwood had invited me to be a Gov-ernor of the Royal Ballet. I accepted this invitation and looked forward to the opportunity of studying the inner workings of the company. Needing to familiarise myself with the type of subject under discus-sion and the general range of the proceedings, I asked to see the min-utes of some previous meetings. In reading them I was gratified to see the degree of appreciation given to the Choreographic Group, and amused that the remarks in this context were followed by a record of the assurance that I would be helped in every way possible. I recalled John Wayne's phrase, 'That'll be the day'.

During the three years of my tenure as a Governor, I worried about the lack of decisiveness in settling some of the problems that confronted the board, who did not all pay sufficient attention to the invaluable profes-sional experience of those among their members, such as Ninette de Valois and Alicia Markova. There seemed to be a lack of liaison between the Governors and the company as well as the Friends, who had stepped in time and time again with financial support, particularly for our tours. Ken Davison had even opened up a branch of American Friends to further the cause, while on the home front Sir Joseph Lockwood, who had done wonders in raising funds for the School and the Benevolent Fund, offered to put some part of the huge financial success of his company, EMI, at our disposal; he had been the one to put the Beatles under an exclusive re-cording contract. The Governors on the whole did not seem at all keen on this idea, and I was appalled by their lack of enthusiasm for what would have amounted to a very considerable offer of help. In the following years, the city of Liverpool became the beneficiary that we might have been, and these funds were used to establish a centre of excellence there for training for the theatrical profession.

However, in spite of all this, my term of office meant a great deal to me. I enjoyed it and I wish that I could have contributed more, as I might have done had it been longer lasting. After my three years, it was decided to adopt a policy to exclude from the governing board any artists still in the company. I would have been entitled to remain among its number had I still been the director of the Choreographic Group, but as that position had been taken from me there was nothing for it but to suffer what is now colourfully called a 'double whammy'.

The whirligig of time can bring its rewards as well as its revenges; for, thinking about this chain of events some years later, it struck me as odd that on that wet and unfortunate Sunday at the Bloomsbury Theatre none of the aficionados among the audience had appreciated the two ballets choreographed by William Tuckett. William later became a very successful contributor to the Royal Ballet's repertoire, admired both by Ninette de Valois and by Anthony Dowell himself, whose vertebrae by that time must have straightened up.

However, the eighties and nineties gave me opportunities to prove that there was life in the old dog yet. One such was provided by Peter Wright, who had always featured as a friend, and whose work as a producer of the great classics I had greatly admired. Now he was about to embark on a new production of *Casse Noisette*, or *The Nutcracker* as they now insist on calling it, and Peter actually created a character, 'The Captain', in it for me. What was wonderful was that I also danced in part of the ensemble as I had done in the early thirties at Sadler's Wells Theatre, an *Incroyable* who partnered one of *Les Merveilleuses*, as the guests were called – I remembered the charm of Ursula Moreton as the Hostess, welcoming everyone to the Christmas party. This time round, much to the amusement of the assembled company, I found I could still manage the nifty footwork of a rather difficult and rapid *pas de bourrée*. I enjoyed every minute of that first act.

This was a production that Peter did for the Royal Ballet at the Opera House, to be followed by another memorable version for the Birmingham Company at the Hippodrome. All my associations with Peter have been happy, and I was especially pleased when, even after my retirement, he asked me to go to Birmingham to play my rôle as Basil Nevinson, the amateur cellist, in *Enigma Variations*.

Turning back a year or so, I was also happy to receive a telephone call from Kenneth MacMillan, who asked me if I would play a supporting rôle in his new production of *The Prince of the Pagodas*. John Cranko had choreographed this three-act ballet in the fifties, to music by Benjamin Britten; in it I had played the part of the Emperor, with Svetlana Beriosova and Julia Farron as my two daughters. In Kenneth's new version Anthony Dowell became the Emperor, with Darcey Bussell and Fiona Chadwick as his daughters. I enjoyed myself hugely playing a court official, with an eye-catching costume designed by Nicholas Georgiadis and worn under a voluminous cloak.

As I have already mentioned, I was always a great admirer of John Cranko and I was pleased to be once more in a work associated with him. His amusing *Bonne Bouche* and *Pineapple Poll* packed the house when they were first produced and *Poll*, his delightful pastiche of Gilbert and Sullivan, remains a favourite to this day. One of his ballets that I much regret having gone out of the repertory is *Antigone*, a work that offered many fine rôles, taken originally by Beriosova, Michael Somes, Julia Farron and Desmond Doyle, and with a remarkable score by the Greek composer, Mikis Theodorakis. John was greatly missed when he left us to go to Germany, but we all admired the way in which he created his famous Stuttgart Company.

I added to the list of parts I had played in *Swan Lake* when Anthony Dowell's version of the classic was performed at Covent Garden in 1983. I had started in 1934 with the Vic–Wells as a huntsman in Acts I and II, dancing the Mazurka and the Spanish Dance in Act III. I had later played Benno, the Prince's friend, who in the Maryinsky version assisted the Prince in the onerous task of partnering the Swan Queen in Act II. In Helpmann's production at the Royal Opera House I was the Tutor, and joined in the Peasants' Dance at the end of Act I. Later in this version, I added Von Rothbart to the list. Anthony cast me as yet another Master of Ceremonies and I appeared in the ballroom scene in Act III; with that, the Catalabutte wheel seemed to have come full circle.

Towards the end of the eighties there was a revival of Ashton's *Ondine*. It had been many years since it had been seen with Margot Fonteyn dancing the role created for her. In this new production I played my original part as the watery old Cardinal, dripping seaweed from my hat.

But the highlight of this decade for me was to have the privilege of working with Ninette de Valois when she lovingly reproduced Nicholas Sergeyev's *The Sleeping Beauty*, with Lesley Collier dancing Aurora. Robert Irving, on leave from New York City Ballet, came over to conduct the first performances and to renew a happy collaboration.

Lesley, whose interpretation was sensitive, musical and full of charm, also danced the rôle at the Lincoln Center in New York at a memorable gala attended by the Prince of Wales. Ninette de Valois had gone over there especially to rehearse it, but found conditions very different from those that had obtained at the old 'Met', particularly as far as rehearsal time was concerned. Whereas we had had a week allotted for this, it was now off the plane and into the performance, with only the minimum time before it to supervise changes needed when covering the much larger stage at the Lincoln Center. However, there were two previous evening performances of *The Sleeping Beauty* before the gala (which was in aid of the English Speaking Union and the American Friends of Covent Garden), so we had had time to play ourselves in, as it were. There was also a matinée to precede the gala.

London that year had experienced rough times with IRA bombing; New York was naturally very much on alert and security conscious, it being a matter of pride to show that the city could be host to public figures with impunity. The avenues leading to the theatre were crowded with armed police, and we were told not to leave the theatre between the matinée and evening performances. We therefore stayed put, but made our way to the roof of the theatre building to view the vast throng of blue-uniformed police giving the appearance that the new 'Met' was awash in a sea of azure, or more prosaically of NYPD blue.

Before the curtain went up, the audience welcomed the Prince of Wales, who had recently become engaged to Lady Diana Spencer, as he took his place in his box in the middle of the dress circle. When the performance began, I felt the somewhat taut mood of the audience possibly sensing some disruption – and with good reason, for shortly afterwards ugly and abusive cries came from a small group of IRA members who had managed to infiltrate the audience. They were quickly rounded up and taken through the pass-door backstage, where they were held in the office used for this tour by the Royal Ballet.

After these alarms and excursions, the rest of the evening went well, and at the end of the performance His Royal Highness, accompanied by the then President's wife, Nancy Reagan, came on stage to meet the dancers, presented by Sir John Tooley, the Director of the Royal Opera House. When it came to my turn – I was at the end of the line of principals – he told the Prince about my many years of service, which in fact covered all but one of the fifty that were then being celebrated to mark the anniversary of the founding of the Vic–Wells Ballet. After asking me about the early years in the company, Prince Charles told me of his fiancée's love of dancing, demonstrating, as he did so, her way of standing in the fifth position. Then, as if reassuring me of my continuing professional longevity, he jokingly gave an impression of me, still on stage but leaning heavily on my redoutable Catalabutte staff for support.

By this time we had been joined by Mrs Reagan, and after I had been presented to her I heard her say to Prince Charles, 'I think we could leave now'; but he quickly demurred, as before leaving he wanted to talk to members of the *corps de ballet*, who were standing at the back of the stage. After my presentation I was free to go back to my dressing room; on my way I passed one of the American dressers who, not wishing to miss the opportunity of seeing the Prince come on stage, had watched my lengthy conversation with him. Her enthusiasm for this royal visit was typical of that of everyone that evening, and to me she added a delightful, 'Gee, I didn't know you were so big with the Prince'.

During the American season of which this time in New York had been part, Robert Helpmann's *Hamlet* was presented for the first time since our initial visit to the old 'Met' in 1949. Forty-two years on it was beautifully performed, with Antoinette Sibley as a moving Ophelia, while the role of Hamlet was shared by young dancers including David Wall, Wayne Eagling and Michael Batchelor. Michael died tragically so young; he loved this ballet when he first encountered it, and was complimented on his performance by Helpmann when he saw it during the short run in London before the US tour.

On my return home I visited Bobby and told him what a success this ballet had had. I said that it was sad that the critics had not responded to it in the same way on our first visit to the States. As I mentioned in an earlier chapter, this was at least partly because *Hamlet* had then always followed the full-length *Swan Lake*, which the management had mistakenly taken to be Act II only, as had previously been the case before we came. They therefore added *Hamlet* so that the public would not think they were being short-changed. By the late hour at the end of our programme, the critics had already left the theatre to write their account of *Swan Lake*. This time round, *Hamlet* was part of a triple bill, and audience and critics alike were able to appreciate the brilliant twenty-minute scenario against the background of Leslie Hurry's powerfully designed set. With choreography that was the essence of clarity and precision, it was possible to follow, as if through the eyes of the dying Hamlet, the complex action of the events that had led to that moment and to recognise each of the dramatis personae. It is an engaging paradox that Bobby succeeded in creating the atmosphere of Shakespeare's longest play in so swift a traffic of the stage.

Chapter 28

In the summer of 1988, after returning from our Australian tour and the abortive trip to the Great Barrier Reef that followed, I came back from my cottage to London and had only been in the house for a short time when I turned on the radio to hear the announcement on the news of the death of Frederick Ashton. The telephone rang immediately afterwards; it was Alexander Grant, kind enough to tell me of this in case I had not so far heard it. He had been staying as a houseguest with Fred in Suffolk and told me how they had all been sharing the pleasure of a holiday, on the last evening of which there had been a party. With his voice breaking, Alex said that Fred had been found in his bed next morning, having died in his sleep. This was naturally a terrible shock, but Fred had been rather frail for some time, and we were all thankful that his end had been so peaceful.

I went up to Yaxley, where he was to be buried in the little churchyard opposite the charming cottage in which he had earlier lived before buying his house, Chandos Lodge, in Eye. It was here that his mother, too, had been buried. I joined Alex, Brian Shaw and Michael Somes in giving out the service sheets and, having done so, we made a small line by the church door. Ninette de Valois arrived and gave each of us a kiss of sympathy, which, I felt, was with a sense of sharing in our grief and our closeness to Fred.

After the service we drove to Chandos Lodge. The house was full of memories for me: all those bargains I had bid for at the Caledonian market in Islington every Friday, pay day, when we were dancing at Sadler's Wells. I recalled Fred's habit, as we approached the market, of giving me his expensive watch to put in the safekeeping of my pocket. I suppose I looked the less likely to own such an extravagant bauble, particularly as I was made to do the menial job of bartering. There were settees, Victorian chairs that were later richly upholstered, gilt mirrors, vases embossed with his favourite motif of corn on the cob, and many odd pieces that I remembered having been knocked down to me for a song. Some of the trophies came from Maples in the Tottenham Court Road, acquired when we were rehearsing at the nearby Chenies Street rehearsal rooms.

These were all happy reminders to soften the sadness of the occasion that day. A small group of close friends were present, including the American dancer and choreographer, John Taras, who had flown over from the States; he is dearly loved in our profession and this gesture was typical of his loyal friendship. Later, hundreds more were able to pay their tribute to Fred at the memorial service held for him in Westminster Abbey.

Chapter 29

It was also in 1988 that Mrs Hookham died. She had moved from Amerden Bank to a pleasant and friendly home not too far away, where I would go to visit her with her son, Felix, and his wife, Phoebe. She had a large portrait of Margot in her room, which Margot herself later donated to the staff to thank them for having tended her mother so well and so kindly, and they in turn were grateful to have this permanent reminder of someone whom they all had met and greatly admired.

The sadness that year continued for Margot when Fred died, and to this was added the knowledge that she was suffering from cancer, although she kept the fact a secret from everyone. There was also an increased worry over Tito, whose condition was requiring more medical treatment and further medication. She battled on nevertheless, and saw to it that Tito's lifestyle did not in any way fall below the high standard that she had always helped to maintain on his behalf.

I became aware of the seriousness of the situation when I realised that her illness warranted visits by her brother and sister-in-law to Panama. At this stage she went for treatment at a hospital in Houston, Texas, and on her visits back to England she would also go for treatment at a hospital near Slough. However, she managed to combine these visits with week-ends at Amerden Bank, staying with Felix and Phoebe, who would invite me over to dinner. There was never any mention of her illness, only amusing anecdotes about the antics of her chickens on the farm in Panama, and conversation, unusual for her, about the organisation of the cattle at her ranch, La Quinta Pata. She discussed the intricate matters of cattle breeding down to the last heifer with the same precision that she might have applied to the running of a ballet company.

On these visits, she would find time to go to the Royal Ballet studios to coach the young principal dancers. When I heard Phoebe bringing the car round from the garage, I would come out of my cottage to wave good-bye. She was walking now with a stick, and to counter any reaction on my part she would wave and smile and say, 'I'm incapacitated', as though this was a perfectly ordinary state of affairs.

After dinner one weekend, I was sitting talking with Margot, Felix and Phoebe when the 'phone rang. Phoebe answered. It was Rudolf calling Margot, who motioned us not to leave the room as she took the call. While she spoke to him I thought of all the times I had watched these two great artists weaving magic before a packed audience. Margot laughed as she was talking, and it was wonderful to see her so relaxed. At that time Rudolf was Director of the Ballet company at the Paris Opéra and was clearly relating some dramatic event there that amused Margot. I always felt that he was a man generous of heart and that he was helping Margot in many ways at this difficult time. It later transpired that this was indeed what had happened.

Tito died on 22 November 1989. It was moving to see newspaper pictures of his funeral in Panama with Margot there, slight, sad and seeming so alone.

In 1990 a gala was organised to honour Margot for all the wonderful years that she had given to the Royal Ballet. It was also to be given in the hope that it would help to allay some of the financial burden that she was facing in having had to meet medical expenses, first for Tito and then for herself. For my part, however, I always felt that she did not like anything so formal as a gala occasion to be associated with her personal difficulties in this context.

It turned out, nevertheless, to be a wonderful event and an opportunity for the public to show their deep admiration for Margot. Kenneth MacMillan's *Romeo and Juliet* was performed in the presence of Princess Margaret, President of the Royal Ballet, her son Viscount Linley and the Princess of Wales. They sat in the Grand Tier, leaving the Royal Box to Margot. Sylvie Guillem danced Juliet to Jonathan Cope's Romeo, with Rudolf Nureyev playing Mercutio for the first time. As a prelude to this, Placido Domingo came in front of the curtain to sing a serenade, directing it to Margot, who was a good friend and someone whom he had always admired as an artist; this was his very personal tribute to her.

While I was getting ready for the performance and making up for my rôle as Prince of Verona, some of the young dancers in the company came to my room to tell me that they had filled a book with messages to Margot and, being unable to decide who should present it to her, asked me if I would do so on their behalf. When at the end of the performance she left her box and came backstage to take calls with the company, I told the young dancers that, after the calls were over, they should give me the book and gather round, when I would present it to her. When I had done so, Margot was, as always, wonderful in her generous response to the occasion. After thanking the dancers, she spoke without sentimentality to them of the loyalty, hard work and dedication that their profession demanded of them, but added her personal conviction that it was worth it, that it was great to be a dancer and that they should, above all, enjoy it. She said all this with her habitual directness and concentration on the people to whom she was speaking, and I was sure that her words would always be remembered.

Following this, Margot went up to the crowded Crush Bar to join a party of invited guests. Instead of sitting down at her table, she moved about among her friends, giving everyone a word of thanks for having come. Later I realised that she had been in a great deal of pain, but of this she gave no sign. As she came down the staircase leading into the foyer before leaving the theatre, her innate grace remained, in spite of her frailty, as memorable as ever.

In the years preceding this and after she had left the Royal Ballet as a permanent member of the company, Margot's professional commitments had taken her to many parts of the world. She had worked with Rudolf and his Friends Group, with the Australian Ballet, and with Ben Stevenson's company in Houston, Texas, and had performed as a guest artist on numerous occasions. As well as this, she was President of the Royal Academy of Dancing, a position that she took very seriously, as she did that of Chancellor of Durham University. The duties that they involved had brought her back frequently to England from her permanent home in Panama, and this pattern continued after Tito's death.

Now she returned to England once more but became no longer well enough to stay with her brother and sister-in-law, remaining instead at the hospital in Slough. I would go over to see her there with Felix and Phoebe, and it was clear by that time that she was fighting to get strong enough to be able to return to Panama, to be united finally with Tito, who was buried there.

She did, in fact, succeed in doing this. Before she left, I asked Margot if I could call and see her alone during the last week of her stay. She agreed, and I arrived at the hospital in the afternoon at 2.30, as she had arranged. As I entered her room she smiled and said, 'I knew you'd be on time', and I replied, 'Well, not all of us are always late!' We talked away about the old days, remembering affectionately incidents of our life in the company and the laughs we had had on so many hundreds of occasions. Then, in what seemed like no time at all, the nurse came in to give Margot her treatment and we just said 'Goodbye'. She died in Panama City on 21 February 1991. She is buried beside Tito in the Arias family plot in Panama.

My last memories of Margot are all centred round the little cottage she persuaded me to buy next to her mother's. In the end we returned to being neighbours.

Chapter 30

The latter half of the eighties was not exactly the happiest time of my life. A few of my colleagues made it clear that I was no longer *persona grata*, which naturally gave me a feeling of insecurity. Although I realised, or at least hoped, that this was not the view of the majority, even a small minority can be extremely and effectively disconcerting. Of course, I had been with the company a very long time, but there were many traditions, notably among the Danish and Russian companies, of keeping their established dancers to play leading character rôles over a long period of time. However, I still appeared regularly playing my rôles such as Thomas in *La Fille mal gardée* and Catalabutte in *The Sleeping Beauty*, and I loved being the Captain in Peter Wright's *Nutcracker*, especially when watching the young dancers from the Royal Ballet School as they gave evidence of a growing awareness of stagecraft while developing their rôles in this ballet.

But as the decade approached its end, it seemed that, for me, a line was going to be drawn under all this. I was told that the management had fixed the date for my retirement to be 1990. I was in the process of coming to terms with this decision, which was a reasonable one and in the nature of things, when I was told that Anthony Dowell had decided that, after such a long association with the Royal Ballet, I should be awarded an extra two years with it. This was a gracious gesture and naturally very good news for me, particularly since this extension of time meant that I would be making one more tour with the company in the States.

Then, in that perverse way in which one tends to qualify the terms of one's good fortune, I knew that I would feel a huge wave of sadness that would engulf me with the remembrance of things past on our American tours. This coming visit would not be the first that we had made without Margot in the company, but it would be the first following her death, and I knew that every second of my stay in New York would remind me of her.

But then the day came when I was actually there and, in a way that I had not thought possible, the memories and associations were so full of past happiness that I felt close to Margot at every turn, and the sadness that I had anticipated was dispelled. It was marvellous to see our mutual friend, Tug, again, and we prevailed upon him to attend a performance at the Lincoln Center. At dinner afterwards with Theodora Christon, Mary Mathieson and John Cianciolo, we talked over the great times we had had and of the many friends who had helped to make our visits to the US so pleasurable.

I was personally aware of the kindness of the balletomanes who would wait outside the stage door. Very few could remember our first opening night at the old 'Met', but those who did told the younger ones of the splendours of that New York season of 1949, and the appreciation that they voiced gave me a feeling of such gratification as to bring all the past experiences and our achievements there into complete focus.

Leaving my hotel on that first morning in New York, I decided that on this, my final tour, I would walk down to the Plaza, look across to Central Park and remember all the hotels we had stayed in, then catch the bus back to the theatre. When I arrived at the bus stop, a man and a woman were waiting who looked at me as though they knew me. Finally, they said, 'Mister Edwards, we're members of the orchestra at the Lincoln Center and remember you well as a member of the Royal Ballet'. We got on the bus together and I suddenly belonged again. We chatted about the friends we remembered in the company, and when we arrived at the Lincoln Center I was fully attuned once more to performing at this great theatre.

And that is how it remained during my whole stay, helped along by the pleasure of working with old friends among the theatre staff. I looked around the spacious stage-door reception area at the new 'Met' with delight at seeing it again, and inspected the noticeboard to find out the times for rehearsals. On this board there was also a page from the *New York Post* that carried the article I had telephoned from the Royal Opera House after leaving the luncheon given at the Brazilian Embassy following Margot's memorial service in Westminster Abbey. I had been asked to do this by the press office of the Royal Ballet; I was to discuss the programmes of the forthcoming American tour and to fill them in generally about the history of the company. In the event I had talked at some length to a columnist from the *Post*, even going back as far as our narrow escape from Holland at the beginning of the war and our subsequent fortunes both at home and abroad. I was a little apprehensive at the time about how this had gone down, but the resulting article had found favour at the Lincoln Center and appeared to have been a boost to ticket sales, I was very happy to learn. Having been apprehensive, too, about this whole visit to New York, I was now beginning to enjoy it thoroughly, which is just how Margot would have wanted it.

After New York the tour continued, to include two cities new to us all, Austin, Texas, and Miami, Florida. Just before one of the Miami performances, when the five-minute call came, the stage manager announced over the tannoy that the company was requested to assemble immediately on stage. I obeyed with the rest, arriving there to hear Anthony Dowell announce to us all that it was my birthday. Now I have always had an aversion to being the object of this sort of celebration and quail at the thought of having 'Happy Birthday to You' sung to me, but someone had let the cat out of the bag on this occasion. The company had all made a contribution towards buying me a pair of cuff links from Tiffany's, no less, and had also filled the pages of a book with good wishes and messages – some quite long. Although we were about to dance a matinée performance of the full-length *Swan Lake*, a huge cake was wheeled on to the stage on a trolley and Lesley Collier, who was dancing Odette-Odile, came on stage in her costume, gave me a big hug and cut the cake. I asked for the cake to be taken down afterwards to the dressing rooms and shared with the rest of the company. Can you wonder that I have always said what a lucky old boy I have been?

Chapter 31

When I arrived home on 13 August 1991, I found a letter waiting for me from an organisation called the Accademia Internazionale Medicea. Written in Italian, it was an invitation for me to go to Florence to receive an award that is given in commemoration of Lorenzo di Medici, known as Il Magnifico, the fifteenth-century ruler of Florence. I went up to the Opera House in the hope of finding an Italian coach who would give me a complete translation of the letter; it transpired that it was from Doctor Pier Lorenzo Eletti, the Director in charge of the award ceremony, which was to be held in the Palazzo Vecchio in Florence at the beginning of October. All this was totally unexpected and as if another *deus ex machina* had come down to dispel any feeling of anticlimax that I might have felt after my return from the American tour. Following my letter of acceptance, I was sent details of my trip to Florence, where I was to arrive on Friday 4 October, in good time for the ceremony on the following day.

When I duly found myself in Florence, I telephoned two very dear friends, Brenda and Raphaelo Bencini. Brenda was a great friend of Mrs Fraser, the mother of Moyra and Shelagh. Like Moyra, she had been a dancer, and had established a large school of ballet in Florence after having herself performed at La Scala, Milan. Being staunchly English, she invited me to tea, where she told me that she and her husband had been asked to attend the ceremony. It cheered me greatly to know that there would be two old friends among the audience. After tea I made my way back to my hotel, where I was to have dinner with one of the organisers of the proceedings. He told me during the course of the evening that I should be prepared to make a short speech, but that I would have someone next to me to translate as I spoke.

I was free on the morning of the following day, Saturday, and was able to stroll at my leisure round the city. As I passed the Grand Hotel, I remembered vividly the incident when Bobby Helpmann ticked us off for being improperly dressed because we had not got our jackets on; but then that was 1949 BC (Before Carnaby, the street that saw the revolution in men's post-war attire). Florence itself, however, then as now, was magical, and my lunch in a delightful nearby restaurant put me in a suitably expansive mood for the ceremony that lay ahead.

In the evening I was collected by car, taken to the Palazzo and shown where I would sit on the platform. I was to be one of fourteen recipients:

included in this number were Giovanni Agnelli, President of Fiat; Anna Proclemer, the distinguished Italian actress; Cardinale Achille Silvestrini; and Rolf Liebermann, famous in the theatre world and at Bayreuth and Salzburg, whom I had previously met at Covent Garden and the Paris Opéra where he had been general director. In the centre of the platform was a table at which sat the dignitaries who were to present the awards, flanked by two guards of honour wearing uniform very like that of the Swiss Guards in the Vatican and bearing standards of the time of Lorenzo Il Magnifico. We were seated at the side in two rows of seven chairs. As we all took our places, there was no sign of any interpreter.

When my name was called and I stood up and made my way towards the table, I was handed a microphone by an Italian official. I said to him, 'Are you going to translate for me?' His answer was 'No'. So, like all good Englishmen abroad, I thought that if one spoke loudly and clearly enough, everybody would understand what one was trying to say. When I looked around me as I stepped forward to speak, the extreme beauty of the great hall of the Palazzo calmed my nerves, and I found myself able to deliver my short speech with the sincerity that I felt and that accompanied my sense of honour at being given this award. When I got back to my seat, Rolf, who was sitting next to me, whispered, 'Well done', which was most reassuring.

For the party that followed, we had to cross the floodlit Piazza della Signoria in front of the palace, passing the copy of Michelangelo's statue of David, to enter the building opposite, where we all relaxed, talking about the impressive ceremony and enjoying a wonderful dinner – a fitting finale to a truly memorable weekend. The next day I returned home, weighed down by my bas-relief of Il Magnifico in its large and superbly tooled red leather box, but glowing.

Chapter 32

On 15 June 1993 I began my last European tour, which comprised visits to Paris, Palermo, Turin, Istanbul and Frankfurt. In Paris we danced at the Théâtre des Champs-Elysées, where the Vic–Wells Ballet had appeared on its first engagement abroad when the city was *en fête* during the famous exhibition there. By 1993 the Royal Ballet were no strangers to Paris, having been back on several occasions, including a season at the Opéra and several visits to the Théâtre des Champs- Elysées and the Marigny Theatre. My thoughts naturally went back to 1937, when our reception was very muted, in complete contrast to that fifty-six years later when we played to full houses and had notices that were little short of ecstatic. As one review stated, the *petit Benjamin* had grown to become one of the great international companies of the world.

The season opened with a gala in the presence of Her Royal Highness, Princess Margaret, and the auditorium was crowded with elegant Parisians, unlike the few *citoyens* of the first time around. After this performance the full company was asked to a reception at the Hôtel de Ville with the Princess as the guest of honour – again very different from the pre-war opening, when no one, not even Miss de Valois, was asked to the party given 'in our honour' at the British Embassy. That omission had become a legend, yet something of the same stigma remained in respect of the Embassy in 1993, when only a few of the invited guests were included to sit down to the dinner, and the ravenous dancers, who had given performances in three ballets that evening, had to be content with a few canapés set out in an adjacent room. In fact, this gave rise to an angry letter to the *Times* from Lady MacMillan, widow of Sir Kenneth who died in 1992. Nevertheless, it was a memorable evening, and as we strolled through the gardens of the Embassy it seemed to me that the magic of Paris remained undiminished.

I had always wanted to visit Sicily, and from the moment we arrived there I knew I was going to enjoy it. We were due to dance in Palermo at the Teatro di Verdura di Villa Castelnuovo, which was situated in a landscaped garden with trellises covered in clematis. The performances had to start fairly late in the evening to enable us to use the stage lighting to proper effect; an advantage of this was that we had plenty of time during the day, after having rehearsed in the Teatro Politeama in the middle of the city, to enjoy the marvellous beach, a bus ride away.

The young dancers in the company made a great fuss of me, and I would go out most evenings after the show to join them for a delicious Sicilian supper in an open-air restaurant in a street near our hotel. One evening, not wishing to impose myself on them too much, I said that I would stay in the hotel, having had a snack at the canteen backstage at the theatre, and enjoy a book at bedtime. In the process of doing just that, I suddenly thought, 'Why on earth am I here, reading in bed, when I could be with those marvellous young people, kind enough to extend an open invitation to join them for supper?' I jumped out of bed, got dressed and hastily made my way to our accustomed restaurant. As they saw me coming, they gave me a rousing cheer of welcome.

We left Palermo to go north for our short visit to Turin. Here, in our comfortable hotel, we were in the midst of the sophistication of this fine city, which no doubt owed much of its modern prosperity to the fact that it was home to the Fiat Motor Company.

From Turin we flew to Istanbul. Our presence there was of double significance; it was the first time that the company had performed in this city, but by no means the first contact that had been made with Turkey. As early as 1947, the Turkish government had asked Miss de Valois to form a national school of ballet in their country. Since the Russian influence on classical ballet had remained strong in post-war Europe, it was very perceptive of the Turkish government to approach the English in the person of Ninette de Valois, who had that very year opened the Sadler's Wells School in London. When she arrived in Turkey and met the Minister of Education and Fine Arts, it must have been evident, as it had been some years earlier to Lilian Baylis, that here was someone who could deliver the goods. In Istanbul she laid down the roots for this project with the same thoroughness that she applied in pre-war Islington to the foundation of her company. She quickly summed up the physical and mental attributes of the young Turkish dancers, training and developing them as future artists.

As usual, her methods were precise and unfettered, and under the supervision of Joy Newton, a former dancer of the original Vic–Wells Ballet and a ballet mistress of this company for many years, the Turkish National School opened in 1948. It settled finally in Ankara, and after Joy Newton had served four years there, her place was taken by other colleagues, including Travis Kemp and his wife Molly Lake, who had worked for many years with Pavlova and her company, and later Beatrice Appleyard, a leading dancer of the Vic–Wells, and Richard Glasstone, from the Royal Ballet School. Pamela May contributed a great deal both to the school and to the company during her visits to Turkey, and it was she who suggested that a ballet by one of our new and successful choreographers, Ashley Page, would make a valuable modern contribution to their repertoire.

And now in 1993 the Turks were going to see what this redoubtable person, now Dame Ninette de Valois, had created in England over the past fifty years. With a first rate company of their own, they were now in a position to appreciate this to the full. As always, the Royal Ballet showed its sense of occasion and danced superbly. It was rewarding to hear the praise and thanks given to the name of their Founder, and later, in 1995, to mark the 50th anniversary of the Turkish Ballet, the Turkish Ambassador visited Dame Ninette at her home in Barnes to present her with the Turkish Order of Merit. The wheel had come full circle.

From the moment we left the airport on our arrival in 1993 and entered the bustle of Istanbul, with its skyline a glitter of minarets, we were enthusiastically entertained by all those connected with the organisation of our visit. However, as soon as was possible I embarked on a determined path of sightseeing; with a few of the senior members of the company, we hired a motor-boat and sped down the Bosporus, landing every now and again to inspect old palaces and homes by the river belonging to rich pashas. There were visits also to the many markets in the city. A member of our group, Donald MacLeary, had a mind to buy one of the many carpets spread out on the pavements, and was instantly approached by a smiling Turkish vendor, who greeted us with what he took to be the appropriate colloquialism, 'Can I rip you off?'!

I had a great time relaxing by the hotel swimming pool with the young dancers after their classes and rehearsals, and then tucked in with relish to delicious roast lamb in a restaurant in an old monastery garden nearby, or to dishes in the various fish restaurants in the villages by the Bosphorus just outside the city.

I was captivated by the whole atmosphere of Istanbul and by its architecture. The interiors of the mosques had walls covered with tiles of astonishing beauty, the appreciation of which was accompanied by the sounds of the whole city being called to prayer, morning and night, by the voice of the muezzins. There could hardly have been a more exotic and moving setting for any tour.

Chapter 33

I felt my first days of retirement to be somewhat disjointed. I missed the daily routine and the pre-arranged structure of my life, which had remained unbroken since leaving school and indeed was a continuation of the pattern of my school years: terms became the seasons of the theatre and holidays were determined in accordance with the commitments of the company. 'When do you go back to school?' became 'When does your new season start?' As we became more established, so did the routine of the year's work at home and on tour abroad, and this gave an added sense of security and permanence to one's life. By contrast, the prospect of being fancy-free, with all the time in the world at one's disposal, did not appeal to me at all. When I was out front at the Opera House, well-meaning and smiling faces would greet me with 'How are you enjoying your retirement?' My reaction was less congenial, and I would snap out, 'I'm not'.

But it was unfair of me to grouse, because I still had much to enjoy. I attended ballet and opera rehearsals at Covent Garden and became a close admirer of the Rambert Choreographic Group. Tony Dyson, who was on the Board of Directors of the Rambert Dance Company, would take me down to Isleworth to see their performances in the school's excellent and spacious theatre. These had an urgency about them, retaining much of the spirit of Madame Rambert and of her belief in the virtue of giving it all you've got. A friendly atmosphere pervaded the whole enterprise under the direction of Ross McKim.

From its earliest days the Ballet Rambert had included dancers from South Africa, such as Maude Lloyd, Pearl Argyle and Frank Staff. This association has continued; through the generosity of Anya Sainsbury (née Linden) it was possible to bring over dancers from that country to take part in the performances of the Rambert Choreographic Group, which I greatly enjoyed. The finale was always tumultuous and, influenced by the enthusiasm of these black dancers, everyone was swaying to the rhythms beaten out by drums and percussion. We left the theatre filled with the excitement and verve of the large cast, among whom interesting new talent could be discerned.

It also gave me great pleasure to be free to go to Birmingham to see the Birmingham Royal Ballet. When Peter Wright revived Ashton's *Enigma Variations* there and asked me to play my rôle of Basil Nevinson, the amateur cellist, my delight knew no bounds. An additional pleasure was that Michael Somes was directing, and thus I would be working again with my friend of so many years. I attended the final rehearsals with Peter's company, who were dancing this ballet for the first time, and I was reminded of the remark made by Sir Adrian Boult, who conducted the orchestra for the original production; seeing us all on stage in costume was, he said, like seeing his old friends again. This wonderful young Birmingham cast brought to me a similar reminiscence.

On the Sunday before the first night, Michael, his wife, Wendy Ellis, and I went out to lunch near the little town of Broadway, and from there went on to visit the cottage in which Edward Elgar was born. The simplicity of this birthplace moved us greatly, and we felt that seeing it was appropriate to the occasion of the forthcoming first night of *Enigma Variations*.

On the next day, Monday, we had both the dress rehearsal and the first night. All went well and there was a rapturous reception at the end, especially when Michael as director joined the cast for the final calls and brought me forward with him, acknowledging our long friendship. That meant a great deal to me. My whole stay in Birmingham, dancing and performing again, was pure joy, especially when Peter Wright told me that he would like me to give a repeat performance in Bristol in two or three weeks' time.

Soon after I returned to London, Wendy Ellis telephoned me with the news that Michael was ill. None of us was given the full details about his illness, and I travelled subsequently to Bristol not realising the full seriousness of his condition. I was in my room in the hotel, preparing to leave for the matinée, when Ronald Plaisted (BRB ballet master), a long-time friend of Michael and me, rang from the foyer of the hotel to ask if he could come up to see me. It was to tell me that Michael had died. Ronald had felt, kindly, that he should come and tell me rather than that I should hear the news at the theatre.

We performed the matinée after Desmond Kelly, a leading dancer in the company, had made an announcement informing the audience of Michael's death. It seemed strangely fitting that we should all be performing in Bristol, the city to which Michael first came from his native Taunton for special dancing classes; and fitting for me that we had worked together again that short time ago in Birmingham, and in a ballet that he particularly loved.

Chapter 34

It seems now to be a time of refurbishment and rebuilding. The greatly enlarged Royal Opera House has risen as a splendid phoenix in all its majesty, and Sadler's Wells Theatre has been completely rebuilt in Rosebery Avenue, opening on the scheduled day in spite of work still remaining to be done on it. The first night on 12 October 1998 saw the beginning of a short season of the Rambert Dance Company, which was followed by seasons of the Royal Ballet and of the Birmingham Royal Ballet. The new theatre will also make it possible for foreign dance companies, who have not played in London for some time, to perform there and thus enrich the scene for ballet and its audiences.

I could hardly believe it when I was told that a rehearsal room in the new complex, which includes a theatre to commemorate Lilian Baylis, was to be named after me. In my incredulity I thought back to the day in December 1932 when I was sent by Marie Rambert to see 'the de Valois' and, after being ushered into her presence in the only rehearsal room, was accepted by her to appear in *The Enchanted Grove*. This was the room with the famous pillars, features of the architecture that had to be carefully negotiated by the dancers and endured patiently by the choreographers; I particularly recalled Ashton's forbearance in this respect when he was working on *Les Rendezvous*. And now I was to have the considerably larger and unimpeded space of this new room named after me – I had to say it more than twice before I could believe it! However, I would like to think that in my fine room new works will ensue, comparable to the brilliance of those that de Valois and Ashton created.

To celebrate its opening, Lord Sainsbury very kindly gave a lunch party, inviting many of my colleagues, friends and relations. His wife, Anya, made a charming speech; in replying to it I gazed at the abundance of food provided for us all and could not help remembering the early days when the company was without a canteen and the sole refreshment provided was tea, brewed in an urn by the stage doorkeeper, and an accompanying selection of penny and three-ha'penny buns. As I was queuing up at the stage door one day for this much-needed nourishment, I heard Miss Baylis talking to him and doing a spot of market research as to how many of each type of bun he sold. When she learnt that the penny ones went better than the others, she gave the order of the day that the three-ha'penny ones should be cancelled; their extravagance was unwarranted and Miss Baylis knew that, if pennies didn't come from heaven, that went for halfpennies too!

Everyone at the splendidly enjoyable party caught the infectious tone of laughter that belonged to those early days when, in spite of the hard slog and the somewhat primitive conditions in which we worked in the theatre, there was never any shortage of fun or of situations to provoke it. I liked to think that that spirit would happily carry forward into the future in this room and in this new theatre, to be a spur to achievement and a source of encouragement to all the dancers present in it.

As I now approach the end of my autobiography, I am heartened by Ninette de Valois' words to me when she heard that I was attempting to chronicle the events of my life among the members of her company, namely that one can always make room for a personal view, since no one sees the images of the past in the same light. This also stands for my apologia, for I am conscious of the fact that my point of view may differ from that of others who have covered the same ground, and that I may also have left out some incidents of importance in the long period of time with which this book deals. Be that as it may, it has been my motive throughout to make this record of events in my life in order to acknowledge the privilege that I have always felt it to be to have lived it among so many friends to whom my loyalty will remain ever unbroken, and to have been able to be a part of such good company.

Chronology

by John Percival

1916   6 August, born in Teddington (now part of the London Borough of Richmond)

Aged about   5 to 7 studied 'fancy dancing' at Mrs Hepworth Taylor's school in Teddington

From age 11 took part in school plays and Gilbert and Sullivan productions at Hampton Grammar School; also attended weekly ballet classes at Anna Bromova's studio in Gunnersbury, and tap dance classes at Max Rivers' studio in central London

1931   Left school in December and began auditioning for West End shows, without success

1932   June: Accepted by Marie Rambert for entry to her school at Notting Hill; his teachers were Rambert and Antony Tudor

           December: sent by Rambert to audition with Ninette de Valois for performances with the Vic-Wells Ballet

1933   3 January: debut with Vic-Wells (later Sadler's Wells) Ballet in Rupert Doone's *The Enchanted Grove*

           15 January: debut with the Ballet Club (later Ballet Rambert) in the ensemble of Fokine's *Carnaval*

           Danced with Vic-Wells in the mazurka and czardas in *Coppélia* and as a huntsman in *Swan Lake* Act II (these were given also for two galas at the Royal Opera House). Became a full member of the company from 1933-4 season and was in premiere of male pas de six in Frederick Ashton's *Les Rendezvous*. Teachers with Vic-Wells included the virtuoso Stanislav Idzikowski, and later Vera Volkova

           Rustic in *Our Lady's Juggler* by Andrée Howard and Susan Salaman with the Ballet Club

1934   January: in Vic-Wells premieres of *Giselle* and *Casse Noisette*

4 March: a Friend in premiere of Howard's *The Mermaid* at Ballet Club

Also with Ballet Club: Cavalier in Pas de Dix from *Aurora's Wedding* (Petipa) and Gustav in de Valois's *Bar aux Folies-Bergère*

Summer: danced in *The Pageant of Parliament* at Royal Albert Hall (choreography by Margaret Craske and Quinton Todd)

November: in Vic-Wells premiere of *Le Lac des Cygnes* (mazurka and Spanish dance)

1935   6 January: A guest in premiere of Howard's *Cinderella* at Ballet Club

January/February: Young man in *Ashton's Mephisto Valse* in Rambert London season

March: with Ballet Club, Pas de quatre in Ashton's *La Valse chez Madame Récamier*, Reaper in Ashton's *Lady of Shalott*, Adolphe in *Bar aux Folies-Bergère*, Bowler in Salaman's *Le Cricket*

26 March: a Stevedore in Vic-Wells premiere of Ashton's *Rio Grande*

20 May: mimed role of the King in premiere of de Valois's *The Rake's Progress* (later danced Horn Blower)

16 June: Trapezist in premiere of Susan Salaman's *Circus Wings* at the Ballet Club

10 November: A Beau in premiere of Howard's *Rape of the Lock* with Ballet Club

1936   26 January: One of the guests ('The Soldier') in premiere of Antony Tudor's *Jardin aux lilas* with Ballet Club

21 February: Nobleman in premiere of de Valois's *The Gods go a - Begging*

June: Octave in Ashton's *Valentine's Eve* and Un Abonné in Ashton' s *Foyer de Danse* during Rambert's Birmingham season

Trainer in Salaman's *Le Boxing* with Ballet Club

1937   16 February: Pas de huit in premiere of Ashton's *Les Patineurs*

February-March: Francois in *Valentine's Eve*, Mephisto in *Mephisto Valse* during Rambert's London season

27 April: Arthur in premiere of Ashton's *A Wedding Bouquet*

15-20 June: Vic-Wells season at Théatre des Champs-Elysées, Paris; Edwards and Michael Somes left in Paris for study with Pavlova's former partner Alexandre Volinine

In Rambert's Cambridge season: Scotch Rhapsody in Ashton's *Façade*, Lover in *Jardin aux lilas*, Bentley Stone's *Pavane pour une Infante defunte*

1938   January-February: last performances with Rambert, including Personage in Ashton's *Les Masques*

1939   2 February: Cavalier, etc. in Vic-Wells premiere of *The Sleeping Princess*

1940   23 January: Child of Light in premiere of Ashton's *Dante Sonata*

May: tour to Holland; narrow escape from German invasion

4 July: A Lawyer in premiere of de Valois's *The Prospect Before Us*

1941   27 January: in premiere of Ashton's *The Wanderer*
Other roles with Vic-Wells until 1941 included Ashton's *Apparitions, Baiser de la Fée, The Lord of Burleigh, Nocturne, Horoscope* (Gemini), *Wise Virgins, Façade* (Scotch Rhapsody; later Mountaineer); de Valois's *Checkmate* (Red and Black Castles), *Le Roi Nu*

1941-43   Conscripted for military service in Royal Army Ordnance Corps, later Royal Electrical and Mechanical Engineers; discharged on medical grounds when vision deteriorated

1943   7 April: Archimago in premiere of Ashton's *The Quest*

7 September: Benno in new production of *Swan Lake*

25 October: partner of 'Les Merveilleuses' in premiere of de Valois's *Promenade*

1944   Title role in *The Rake's Progress* on tour; also Ghost in Helpmann's *Hamlet*

10 October: Florestan in revival of *Carnaval,* later also Pierrot

26 October: Beggar in premiere of Robert Helpmann's *Miracle in the Gorbals* (and at all subsequent performances)

1945   January-March, tour to Belgium and France; November-December, tour to Germany

1946   20 February: reopening of Royal Opera House, Covent Garden; Cattalabutte in premiere of *The Sleeping Beauty;* also later Carabosse

10 April: The Mime (Adam's spiritual adviser) in premiere of Helpmann's *Adam Zero*

Also Wilfred and Hilarion in *Giselle,* Dr Coppelius in *Coppélia*

1946-49 tours to Austria, Belgium, Czechoslovakia, Poland, Sweden, Norway, Holland, France, Germany, Italy (and widely in Europe in later years)

12 November: La Bolero's chauffeur and partner in premiere of Ashton's *Les Sirènes*

December: Summer pas de trois in premiere of Ashton's *Fairy Queen*

1947   6 February: Policeman in SWB premiere of Massine's *The Three Cornered Hat*

27 February: American customer in SWB premiere of Massine's *La Boutique fantasque*

Red King in de Valois's *Checkmate*

26 November: Butcher in SWB premiere of Massine's *Mam 'zelle Angot*

1948   25 June: King in premiere of Massine's *Clock Symphony*

23 December: Hairdresser in premiere of Ashton's *Cinderella;* later also father

1949   October-December: first tour of US and Canada

1950   20 February: Priest in premiere of de Valois's *Don Quixote;* later title role

1951   Summer: guest teacher at Wilderness Ballet Camp, Ontario (and in subsequent years)

              12 December: King in premiere of Massine's *Donald of the Burthens*

1952   4 March: Bilby in premiere of Howard's *A Mirror for Witches*

              4 April: League of Light in premiere of John Cranko's *Bonne-Bouche*

1955   1 April: Dignitary in premiere of Ashton's *Madame Chrysantheme*

1956   1 March: Hypnotist in premiere of Kenneth MacMillan's *Noctambules*

1957   1 January: Emperor in premiere of Cranko's *Prince of the Pagodas*

              26 March: Rich Merchant in SWB premiere of *Petrushka,* later also the Charlatan

1958   27 October: Priest in premiere of Ashton's *Ondine*

1959   19 October: Oedipus in premiere of Cranko's *Antigone*

1960   28 January: Thomas in premiere of Ashton's *La Fille mal gardée*

1961   June-July: tour to Leningrad and Moscow

1962   Guest director and teacher, National Ballet and School, Washington

1963   12 March: Duke in premiere of Ashton's *Marguerite and Armand;* later played the Father and staged the ballet for itinerant performances by Fonteyn and Nureyev

1965   9 February: Escalus in premiere of MacMillan's *Romeo and Juliet*

1966   23 March: Bridegroom's Father in Royal Ballet premiere of Bronislava Nijinska's *Les Noces*

              December: Arranged fund-raising concert at Yvonne Arnaud Theatre, Guildford, including new work followed by an evening of all new works on 2 April 1967, the beginning of Royal Ballet Choreographic Group

1968   29 February: Dr Stahlbaum in Royal Ballet premiere of Rudolf Nureyev's *Nutcracker*

17 December: King in new production by Peter Wright of *The Sleeping Beauty*

1970   Summer: appointed ballet master of Royal Opera Ballet

1971   Mr Brown the Owl in Ashton's film *The Tales of Beatrix Potter*

1973   First Royal Ballet tour to South America

1975   Appointed OBE in the Queen's New Year honours
First Royal Ballet tour to South-East Asia and Japan

1978   July: assistant to Robert Helpmann for 'Stars of World Ballet' tour of Australia

1983   First Royal Ballet tour to China

1984   20 December: Captain in premiere of Wright's new Royal Ballet *Nutcracker*

1983-86   Appointed a Governor of the Royal Ballet

1987   Removed from directorship of Royal Ballet Choreographic Group

1990   Took part as Prince of Verona in gala at Covent Garden to honour Margot Fonteyn

1991   5 October: presented in Verona with award for dance in memory of Lorenzo di Medici, 'Il Magnifico'

1993   20 November: official retirement from the Royal Ballet (but returned later for a few performances)

2001   Died in London 8 February

Index